I was arrested for PEACE

Warm Fuzzy Dyke

WOMEN strike for PEACE

BRING ALL OUR MEN HOME NOW!

WOMEN'S LIBERATION CONFERENCE 1978

INTERNATIONAL WOMEN'S YEAR · AUSTRALIA

STUDENT NONVIOLENT

WE SHALL OVERCOME

COORDINATING COMMITTEE

Viva là Vulva!

ORDAIN WOMEN OR STOP BAPTIZING THEM

NOW National Organization for Women For Women's Lives

WOMEN AGAINST RAPE

MY GODDESS GAVE BIRTH TO YOUR GOD

Gay Love

it's the real thing

LESBIAN VOTE

Internationella Kvinnoåret 1975

Fredrika-Bremer-Förbundet

THE FEMINIST REVOLUTION

THE STRUGGLE FOR WOMEN'S LIBERATION 1966–1988

virago

BONNIE J. MORRIS AND D-M WITHERS
FOREWORD BY ROXANE GAY

Bonnie J. Morris
To Beth Stevens Caldwell, a feminist fighter for women's health, survival, and justice; and to many colleagues and students in the Women's and Gender Studies Program of both Georgetown University and George Washington University, whose love sustained me as I wrote.

D-M Withers
My contribution to this project is made with sincere gratitude to those who struggled to realize feminist worlds in the past, and continue to do so in the unfolding historical now and in times to come.

First published in Great Britain in 2018 by Virago Press, by arrangement with Elephant Book Company Limited, Southbank House, SB.114, Black Prince Road London, SE1 7SJ, United Kingdom.

1 3 5 7 9 10 8 6 4 2

A CIP catalogue record for this book is available from the British Library.

ISBN 978-0-349-01119-6

Created by Elephant Book Company
Editorial Director, Elephant Book Company: Will Steeds
Managing Editor and Researcher: Joanna de Vries
Book Design: Paul Palmer-Edwards, GradeDesign.com

Printed and bound in China
Papers used by Virago are from well-managed forests and other responsible sources

Virago Press
An imprint of
Little, Brown Book Group
Carmelite House
50 Victoria Embankment
London EC4Y 0DZ

An Hachette UK Company
www.hachette.co.uk

www.virago.co.uk

MIX
Paper from
responsible sources
FSC® C104723
FSC
www.fsc.org

Contents

Foreword

It has been more than forty years since the rise of feminism's second wave, and yet I often find myself dismayed when I recognize that the issues women are facing in contemporary society are much the same as they were during the feminist revolution.

Many women around the world do not have unfettered, affordable access to birth control or legal abortion. The statistics on women and sexual violence remain appalling. Sexual harassment is more the rule than the exception. Working-class women have no affordable means of childcare. The wage gap persists: according to a 2016 study done by the Institute of Women's Policy Research, while white women in the United States earn 75.3 percent of the salaries their white male counterparts earn, and Asian women 84.5 percent, black women earn only 63.3 percent and Latina women earn 54.4 percent. Transgender women are fighting for their rightful place not only in society but also within the feminist movement. Queer women continue to fight for basic civil rights such as workplace protections.

I am regularly asked, "What is feminism?" A disheartening number of people are still unclear about the definition of a movement that has existed for more than a century. Some people ask this question earnestly. They are simply unclear about feminism. Others are willfully ignorant—they don't really need feminism defined. Instead, they think of themselves as provocative, asking a question to which they already have an incorrect or incomplete answer. They would rather waste time on vocabulary than thinking about the necessary and important work of feminism. They would rather waste this time than actually do the work of feminism.

There are many people who believe feminism has an image problem. Feminists are too angry. They hate men. They are humorless. On and on the caricatures go. There are people who believe we no longer need feminism, that women have come far enough and are doing just fine. That we're still defining and defending feminism is the clearest reminder of how much is at stake. There is something threatening to the status quo about the idea of women achieving equity and equality. We must protect that idea, that hope, at all costs.

Though we have not come as far as second-wave feminists would have hoped, feminist activism is alive and well. Feminism is far more inclusive than it ever has been, due in large part to the foregrounding of intersectionality, a theory put forward by Kimberlé Crenshaw, who notes in her article "Mapping the Margins" that "intersectionality offers a way of mediating the tension between assertions of multiple identity and the ongoing necessity of group politics." Intersectionality allows for the reality that as women, we share a gender but also inhabit many other identities including race, class, sexuality, ability, and so much more. As women, we share a gender, but we are not equally affected by the ways of the world, and as feminists we need to acknowledge and accommodate these differences. The Internet is serving as a democratizing force for feminist activists to put their work into the world, in ways great and small. For every effort made to impede women's progress, there are countless feminists holding the line and resisting, voices raised.

Organizations like Black Lives Matter are fighting to bring attention to police brutality and institutionalized racism within the judicial system. We've seen Hillary Clinton become the first woman to receive a major-party nomination for president of the United States, and we've seen her win the popular vote. In the wake of Donald Trump's election, hundreds of thousands of women and men marched in hundreds of cities around the world in protest of his presidency and to take a stand for women's rights.

This is the reality of feminism—the fight is ongoing, and though it may seem slow, progress is always being made because feminists, from all walks of life, rise to the occasion time and again.

In this book, you will find some of the postwar feminist history that made today's feminism possible and images that capture this vibrant movement. As in the 1960s, we are at a watershed moment of cultural change for women. As we look forward, we must also look back.

Roxane Gay

Authors' note

This book is intended to be a celebration of the political, strategic, and cultural diversity of the women's liberation movement, as well as its creativity. We have sought to give voice to as many grassroots activists as possible, both through their own words and in the exploration of some of the lesser-known groups and activities that helped to shape and change women's lives. We have endeavored to showcase as many facets of feminism during the period of the early 1960s to the 1980s as we can in the scope of this project. The narrative of this book is told from a primarily Anglo-American, Western perspective. Given the enormous diversity of feminist movements around the world, we cannot claim to have covered the broad spectrum and nuances of the global women's movement within these pages. We have, however, attempted to place these movements in a more international, particularly European, context where possible, exploring the resonances of women's liberation as it moved across borders.

This is, therefore, but one representation of feminist movements, rather than a definitive history. Many of the histories featured in this book are buried deep in archives or in people's personal collections, or are the subject of academic research. For popular audiences, this makes it financially, practically, and discursively difficult to access many of these stories, and this collection helps to break down some of these barriers.

Women's liberation intersected with other revolutionary movements striving for racial, class, sexual and environmental justice. These struggles continue today in the face of necessity, and often converge with demands for gender freedoms and self-determination, articulated by transgender activists. Feminist activism generated, and continues to generate, unique forms of knowledge and skills that should be central to all social justice movements. We hope you will find *The Feminist Revolution* informative and inspiring in its depiction of feminist and women-centered social movements.

Terms

Given that this book encompasses a wide variety of movements in the UK, US, Europe, and beyond, terminologies do differ. We have sought to find commonality in the following ways.

The women's movements of the 1960s to the 1980s are often referred to as the period of "second-wave" feminism. Instead of this catchall term, we felt it necessary, where possible, to adopt the language activists used to describe their political identities and identifications. We do the same to differentiate among geographical locations and specific groups or campaigns within the movements.

We use the capitalized term "Women's Liberation Movement" to refer to the white-dominated women's movement in Britain and sometimes use the term "women's liberation movement" and "second-wave feminism" interchangeably to refer to the US.

We use the term "Black Women's Movement" to refer to the autonomous organization of Afro-Caribbean and South Asian women in the UK context who used the term "black" as a political identity. The phrase "black women's movement"—three active, interlocking identities—also encompasses the experiences of black women / women of color participating in and redefining American feminisms. The arc of black feminist issues in majority-white American history is both distinctive and an integral part of radical feminist change.

We use the term "women's peace movement" to refer to women whose primary concern was stopping militarism, nuclear proliferation, and violence in an international context.

We have tended to use "women's movements"—rather than "women's movement"—in the plural to emphasize that there was no single, cohesive movement, but rather a diversity of voices whose personal issues informed their specific outlooks.

"SISTERHOOD IS POWERFUL"

How the movement mobilized

Women's. Liberation. Movement.

Women's. **Who were women?** What was their history and what was their future? "The words of women have yet to be written,"[1] bellowed WOMAN, the main character in Jane Arden's 1969 play *Vagina Rex and the Gas Oven.* One of the first obstacles women's movements had to overcome was how to dispense with stereotypes—"Bird-brained—tender—intuitive—garrulous—unreliable—disloyal—weak"—and "destroy the language" of male oppression.[2] If women were not the same as men, how were their lives different?

Liberation. The women's liberation movements aimed to free women from the systems that dominated them. Across the Western world, women's liberation movements were inspired by, and part of, a wider revolutionary transformation that took place in the late 1960s—the European 1968 students' and workers' protests, the Chinese Cultural Revolution, anti-Vietnam war activism, Black Power, and other liberation struggles. Yet women's liberation invented a completely different kind of politics that claimed "the personal is political." Women's "private" and hidden experiences became the raw material from which a social movement was built.[3]

Women, newly liberated, presented explicit demands for freedom in sexuality, wage and family structure, and reproductive justice.

Movement. Change, transformation: the women's liberation movements mobilized hundreds of thousands of women and instilled in them the belief that they could change their lives and the wider world. Everything that appeared fixed before was now rigorously questioned. As they marched, sat in, sang, and wrote, feminists drew new insights from those who had called for women's rights in prior times.

Why did the women's liberation movements catapult so many "ordinary" women into political action? What made them take part in activism that fundamentally changed who they were, what they believed in, and what they did?

Transformation

During the American Revolution, eighteenth-century colonial feminist writers warned that *women* should be explicitly included and empowered in the Constitution.

> "I was so totally transformed by the [Women's Liberation Movement], sometimes I have to remember what it was like before."
>
> **Maggie Nicols,** musician and activist, interview with D-M Withers, September 2016

Far left: This popular poster by the Chicago Women's Graphic Collective from 1971 illustrated the frustration felt by many women who were daily addressed as "chick," "babe," "cupcake," and other belittling terms of endearment. The corresponding term for women in the UK was "bird." In the mid-1960s, one student review of colleges gave the ratio of "cats" to "chicks," an unfortunate positioning of predator and prey.

Left: Jane Arden's 1969 play *Vagina Rex and the Gas Oven* was performed for six weeks in front of sellout audiences at the Art Lab, London. The play was heralded for its innovative multimedia approach and its uncompromising depiction of women's existence in male-dominated society. This poster was likely the work of British graphic artist Alan Aldridge (1943–2017).

WOMEN OF THE WORLD UNITE

Page 10: "Sisterhood is blooming" was a key slogan of the burgeoning women's movements. This 1970 poster was designed by the Chicago Women's Graphic Collective, who were responsible for many iconic images of the women's movement in America.

Above: To commemorate the fiftieth anniversary of white women's suffrage (the passage of the 19th Amendment to the US Constitution in 1920), on August 26, 1970, women and a few men, too, marched along Fifth Avenue in New York City, past a banner declaring, "Women of the world unite!"

During the spring of 1776, Abigail Adams famously instructed her husband, John, "And by the way in the new Code of Laws . . . I desire you would Remember the Ladies." To her chagrin, and the disappointment of many others, the new Constitution failed to name women, Native Americans, or slaves as specific beneficiaries of equal rights. John Adams himself responded to his revolutionary-minded wife with: "As to your extraordinary Code of Laws, I cannot but laugh. . . . Depend upon it, we know better than to repeal our Masculine systems."[4]

Still lacking the opportunity to vote, testify in court, or otherwise act politically except through a husband, nineteenth-century American feminists made suffrage and the abolishment of slavery their twin goals, intent on reforming a country that owed fairness and freedom to all women. Eighty years of such campaigning resulted in property rights, the establishment of women's colleges, and the 19th Amendment granting white women suffrage in 1920; yet black women, like black men, would be intimidated from exercising the right to vote until well

into the 1960s. Women remained divided by race . . . and social class.

Similarly, women in postwar Britain grew up amid a sea of social contradictions. Numerous welfare reforms introduced by the postwar Labour government gave people unprecedented security. Throughout society, the assumption remained that men were the "breadwinners" and women would stay at home and raise the children.

Mid-twentieth-century Britain was, however, marked by a steady rise in married women's employment outside the home—26 percent in 1951, 35 percent in 1961, and 49 percent by the early 1970s.[5] This never challenged the idea that men would earn the main wage, but women did derive satisfaction and independence from earning their own money and participating within a growing consumer culture.[6]

Girls in the UK were also better educated in the postwar period. The introduction of the 1944 Education Act made education compulsory for girls and boys until the age of fifteen. This meant that women who became active in the women's liberation movements were

FEMME

et socialiste

parti socialiste 7 bis, place du palais bourbon paris 75007

generally well educated and, as a result, had higher expectations for their lives.[7] University attendance also increased, although change was slower in this area. By the mid-1970s, around 30 percent of British university students were female.[8]

Within popular culture and society, messages about women's roles were mixed. The dangers of "maternal deprivation" for children, popularized by British psychologist John Bowlby in the 1950s, were an ideological dragnet that pushed women back into the home.

In contrast, in countries with a Communist or Socialist agenda, such as the German Democratic Republic and the USSR, equality of the sexes was advocated, but in practice inequalities remained. Although women in the workplace were supported by childcare provisions and access to roles, in the end many women felt that they shouldered the burden of more menial jobs and a far higher proportion of household work than their male counterparts. Despite preaching equality, Communist male politicians were prepared to turn the other cheek to their fellow brothers' indiscretions but demanded that their female political counterparts be "untainted."[9] Equality may have been written into the party manifesto and even the constitution, but it was not always reflected in the way women felt about their place in society. A clear example of such double sexual standards was to be found in the Italian Communist Party, as demonstrated by attitudes to adultery. While a male Communist politician's indiscretions might be overlooked, a wife who was cheated on would be treated as a pariah. This was evidenced when Rita Montagnana's husband, Communist Party Secretary Palmiro Togliatti, left her after his affair with eminent female Italian politician Nilde Lotti in 1948. Montagnana's hitherto glittering career—which had seen her found *The Companion* feminist newspaper in 1922 and become leader of the women's wing of the Italian Communist Party and elected member of the constituent assembly—stalled thereafter, and she eventually left office. Togliatti, protected by his powerful position in a predominantly patriarchal system, was left virtually untouched by the scandal.

> "Thus, humanity is male and man defines woman not in relation to herself but as relative to him; she is not regarded as an autonomous being."
>
> **Simone de Beauvoir**, *The Second Sex* [1949], 1973

Opposite: Poster of the French Parti socialiste (Socialist Party), c.1970. The party naturally aligned themselves with women's liberation and the fight for equal rights.

Far right and right: Communist posters of the postwar period commonly celebrated the ideal of women (and men) contributing to an equal society, although these visualized representations did not tell the whole story of women, who were often doubly subjugated in their work and their home lives.

The Oxford conference

D-M Withers

"It was really from the Oxford conference in February 1970," Sheila Rowbotham famously stated, "that a movement could be said to exist."[10]

The first National Women's Liberation Conference in Britain took place from February 27 to March 1, 1970, at Ruskin College, Oxford. Originally planned as a women's history conference, the noticeable momentum behind women's liberation meant that the time was ripe for a political conference dedicated to women's lives.

The organizers thought "perhaps a hundred women could come. In fact more than 500 people turned up, 400 women, 60 children and 40 men, and we had to go into the Oxford Union because Ruskin was too small."[11] Famously—and radically for that time—men ran the childcare. Liberated from looking after their children, many women who had never been to a political event before dived into the cauldron of energy generated at the conference.

Discussions focused on the home and family, women's psychology, capitalism, prison, women in industry, the activism of suffragette Sylvia Pankhurst, and women in the nineteenth-century labor movement. The conference offered a platform for women to share their experiences, and those who spoke did so "with incredible passion into the microphone."[12] Some listened with wonder to women who "put into words things that made you say to yourself, 'That's what I've always thought and felt and I've never been able to put my finger on it.'"[13] Oxford is exuberantly remembered as a time when sisterhood was uncomplicated and unified. Yet not everyone shared these feelings of connection and common purpose. Gerlin Bean, active in black liberation and, later, the British Black Women's Movement, recalled her experience: "I couldn't really pick on the relevance of it, as it pertains to black women. But one woman, her name was Selma James, when she spoke, and she was down on the last day—she was a Jewish woman who was married to CLR James—she put it all in context, in the relevance, how it would affect black women and our involvement because our struggle wasn't just about women, it was an anti-imperialist struggle about black people, and women [were] just a sector within that."[14]

Selma James had been active in women's and labor activism since the 1950s. Like many other women, she felt that her "life was transformed" by being at Oxford:

"It helped launch me into the politics that I've been involved in since."[15] She was also "disturbed by the conference . . . most of the women were what you call middle or upper-middle class, and they attacked the lack of access of women to power. I always agreed, and the conference was a moment of power *for all women*."[16]

Bean and James highlight the political biases that shaped the British Women's Liberation Movement from its inception. "When we planned the Ruskin conference, I wanted working-class women to come. They didn't, really,"[17] reflected Rowbotham. Despite the strong desire to create a social movement that could liberate *all* women, from the start white middle-class women were at the center. Working-class and black women were certainly at Ruskin, but they were clearly not the dominant voices. They also had limited power to define the objectives of the movement in its emergent stages.

The first national Women's Liberation conference may not have provided all the answers or laid out an easy way forward for the movement. But one thing is certain: for those who attended, it activated an enormous amount of political energy. "We talked about Ruskin for weeks afterwards. I think it had a powerful effect. But I think we didn't really know what to say at that stage, we were still observing."[18] For women whose experiences were marginalized at the conference, this friction helped generate new perspectives on women's liberation. These would be passionately debated within the movement throughout the 1970s and beyond.

As women left Oxford, they carried forth the energy of the event and the new political perspectives they had been exposed to into their communities. In towns across the UK—Bolton, Swindon, Portsmouth, and many others—small consciousness-raising groups were formed and local campaigns instigated. The seeds that would help women's liberation spread beyond the metropolis were laid down. The British Women's Liberation Movement was born.

> "[There was] the amazing feeling of your whole being being completely opened up."
>
> **Sheila Rowbotham**, *Once a Feminist*, 1990

Above: An activist from a lobbying organization delivers an impassioned speech, while attendees at the conference—including Sheila Rowbotham, sitting behind the bottle of water—receive the message with a youthful irreverence.

Right: At the Oxford conference, male partners ran the childcare to enable women to participate fully in discussions. Cultural theorist Stuart Hall, husband of Catherine Hall (who was active in Birmingham women's liberation), is pictured on the right.

LIBERATION

THE MYTH: SEX

I AM A SEX OB-JECT

SEX SEX

OB-JECT

THE REALITY: NEUROSIS AND MISERY

Above: Visual imagery explored how objectification damaged the psychic life of women, as depicted in this illustration by Swedish painter Monica Sjöö.

The postwar era was, then, a time of simultaneous expansion and contraction for women. Old expectations about women's traditional roles were being eroded by political, economic, and social changes, yet opportunities for women to live genuinely independent lives were scarce.

In 1949, Simone de Beauvoir's *Le deuxième sexe* (*The Second Sex*) raised fundamental philosophical questions about the way in which women were viewed in society. Her exploration of women as "the Other" being central to female oppression was to later inspire feminists, not only in France but across the world.

The awakening

In the US, the early 1960s marked a watershed of cultural and social change for women. One-third of American women were in the workforce, but most languished in clerical and domestic work, limited by "help wanted" ads that separated better-paying jobs for men from the secretarial roles assigned to women. The Equal Pay Act of 1963, designed to correct an unfair structure, was passed in the same year that Betty Friedan's *The Feminine Mystique* was published. The book, which sold one million copies in the US and UK by 1970, clearly demonstrated that the specter of the immiserated housewife remained.[19]

Similarly, Hannah Gavron's *The Captive Wife*, "a study of sad, lonely mothers of the working and middle class," offered a British perspective on women confined to the home.[20] The book was published to rave reviews in 1965, months after the author—a mother with two young children—had committed suicide, poisoned by gas from a kitchen oven. The catalog of extraordinary, talented archetypal '60s women who suffered death in tragic circumstances—writer Sylvia Plath, pop artist Pauline Boty, and playwright Jane Arden—perhaps testifies most to this image of the "trapped woman." Women shared public and private testimony, voicing frustration at limits on their political and economic power and their personal agency.

The birth control pill, the participation of radical young women in left-wing groups such as Students for a Democratic Society (SDS) and the Student Nonviolent Coordinating Committee (SNCC), and demands that campus curfew laws be dismantled were signatures of a new generation of female activists, unafraid to go to jail for causes they believed in. This will to abandon feminine passivity for important causes of the day was not voiced only by young women. Elder radical folksinger Malvina

> "I think now that there was no way to be a woman and to be intelligent and articulate in the sixties."
>
> **Sally Alexander**, *Once a Feminist*, 1990

Below: Over and over, the US government's own statistics showed women earning fifty-nine cents to the male worker's dollar in wages. Women of color often earned less than white women. The focus on equal pay for equal work became a bipartisan slogan. The fair wage goal emerged as a mainstream political issue as more and more women headed families and provided for children—on an income that rarely matched what a man earned.

Reynolds declared in song, "It isn't nice to block the doorway; it isn't nice to go to jail. There are nicer ways to do it, but the nice ways always fail."

On Capitol Hill, lawmakers pushed through the Civil Rights Act of 1964, banning discrimination based on race. At the last minute, they reluctantly added Title VII, which banned sex discrimination as well. It took lawyer Pauli Murray to point out the "double jeopardy" facing black women, who still experienced legal bias based on sex in the new era of racial civil rights protections.

For black women, 1960s Britain was also a "bitter disappointment."[21] Despite the promises made by the British state, many of those who immigrated to Britain to help rebuild the "Mother Country" after World War II were faced with relentless racism and few job opportunities. One black woman recalled, "I remember getting up every morning to go to the Labour Exchange to see if there were any jobs. I was actually looking for nursing work, but they wouldn't have me . . . when I got to the hospital, the woman there offered me a cleaning job."[22]

Meanwhile in America, Congress and the *New York Times* openly jeered at the notion that sexism was a social problem; and the newly appointed director of the Equal Employment Opportunity Commission (EEOC) shared his opinion that male bosses were naturally entitled to have female secretaries. The more that women demanded to

be taken seriously as complete persons, the more American television served up prime-time shows with classic female stereotypes: *Bewitched*, *I Dream of Jeannie*, *The Flying Nun*. Could America see adult women as more than witch, sex slave, or virgin?[23]

Frustrated by the slow pace of change and the negative attitude of the EEOC despite its legal directive, Betty Friedan organized the National Organization for Women (NOW) in 1966. At the same time, women active in the anti-war Left, less interested in NOW's mainstream goals of acceptance into existing structures, turned to feminist liberation theory as they experienced belittlement and betrayal by the male leadership of radical causes. Speaking in the film *She's Beautiful When She's Angry*, activist Marilyn Webb recalled, "Why weren't we in leadership positions? I didn't expect movement men to behave that way; and I was shocked." Male revolutionaries who casually remarked that a woman's place was in bed or in the kitchen were left to contemplate their unchecked sexism as female "politicos" walked out and formed their own cells and consciousness-raising groups.

Radical men had failed to see that women, too, constituted an oppressed class under laws that treated them like children. In their famous 1965 statement, SNCC activists Casey Hayden and Mary King named the

Far right: Betty Friedan, founder and president of the National Organization for Women (NOW), talks to reporters in the lobby of the New York State Assembly in April 1967. Making sex discrimination a civil rights platform, liberalizing New York's abortion laws, and gaining greater representation for women by women in the state government were goals NOW helped to achieve.

Right: The front page of the *New York Daily News* on August 27, 1970, the day after the Women's Equality Strike demonstration in New York City.

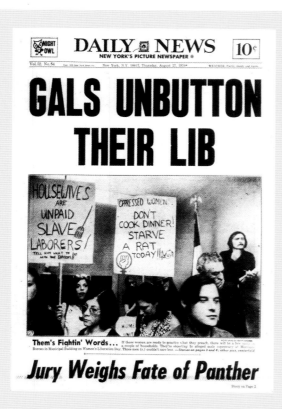

underclass treatment of women by male-led organizations as a caste position of "assumed subordination." Writers and activists Marge Piercy, Ellen Willis, and Robin Morgan each produced classic essays of disaffection with the male Left and declared that the feminist struggle was their political priority. The attraction of experienced female journalists to the women's movement gave radical feminism a literary edge, generating published broadsides and booklets throughout the 1970s and well into the '80s. These texts identified a new enemy, in addition to racism, war, and class struggle—the name of the system that had to be dismantled was *patriarchy*.

What sparked the fire of radical, "second-wave" feminism was not one lit match but rather many torches raised by women in different communities across the globe. By the early 1960s, ongoing social protest movements were converging to address concepts of liberation and self-determination. In the US, as veterans of the Civil Rights Movement, black and white women had participated in nonviolent resistance, boycotts, and street protests, gaining a more sophisticated understanding of the media's power to spread slogans. The Black Power movement saw activism and militancy combine, while those active in Women Strike for Peace leveraged their roles as mothers of sons to contest the Vietnam War and the dangers of the nuclear arms race. Older women, remembering what they had contributed to America's World War II victory as well-paid industrial workers, were fed up with postwar society's educational and workplace discriminations and began to seek change through the court system. Young women of the baby boom generation—a huge new demographic to be reckoned with—were coming of age with civil rights rhetoric and legal contraception, questioning authority on every level as their boyfriends were drafted and sent to war in Southeast Asia.

This all came to a head in 1968—a year of protest. This year of unrest had been precipitated by the killing of a student in June 1967 by police during a demonstration in West Germany. This action caused the breakdown of the Socialist German Student League (SDS), which was escalated by internal revolts, including by its female membership as the women's movement began to emerge in Germany. During February 1968, tensions between East and West Germany resulted in protests at universities throughout East Germany. Italy, too, had seen periods of unrest throughout 1967, and on March 1, 1968, fights

Below left: Women Strike for Peace was a group careful to distance itself from organized feminism, but it radicalized mothers into street action, soon overlapping with other women's political demonstrations. In this photograph by Diana Davies, a mother marching in Washington, D.C., protests against the Vietnam War with a slogan, "Mothers say: Stop the War," her prim dress, lipstick, and hat giving her what historian Gerda Lerner called, in her 1993 book *The Creation of Feminist Consciousness*, "authorization through motherhood."

Below right: Defiant young Czechs protest the Soviet-led Warsaw Pact invasion of Czechoslovakia on August 21, 1968.

between Italian students and police, dubbed the "battle of Valle Giulia," broke out, with students later shutting the University of Rome down for twelve days.[24] On March 8 and 9, thousands of Polish students campaigning for student rights were beaten and arrested, leading to twenty days of violent clashes between police and the public that were quelled only when the government shut down the universities, arrested over one thousand students, and "encouraged" Jewish Poles to flee the country through an anti-Zionist propaganda campaign. Throughout April, Spanish students protested Franco's regime, incited by a government-sanctioned mass for Adolf Hitler. In Britain, politician Enoch Powell delivered his "Birmingham" speech, now famously referred to as his "Rivers of Blood" speech, igniting anti-immigration sentiment and a political maelstrom. In Paris, students took to the streets over university reform, sparking a month-long wave of

demonstrations and strikes throughout France over virtually every issue from education to pay and working reforms. Similar protests took place later that month in Sweden, while in Czechoslovakia, the population rose up during the "Prague Spring" to champion liberal reforms in the face of Soviet repression. During that summer, the Mexico Olympics sparked a wave of anti-apartheid and civil rights demonstrations as more than forty teams threatened to boycott the games over the inclusion of segregationist South Africa among the competitors. The Rodney Riots took place that fall in Jamaica after university lecturer and Black Power activist Dr. Walter Rodney was banned from returning to his position at the University of the West Indies due to his outspoken views on civil rights and the middle classes.

Street rallies, sit-ins, and campus speakouts created visibility for every issue, from anti-war protests to free

The 1968 Miss America pageant

Bonnie J. Morris

Few images are as relentlessly recycled as the portrait of "angry feminists" burning their bras in protest of the 1968 Miss America pageant held in Atlantic City, New Jersey.

Inaccurate media publicity around that protest convinced many Americans that feminists, hostile to beauty and fashion, must be opposed in principle to attracting men—or to being attractive, period. This stereotype of feminists being deliberately unattractive and antisocial continues to haunt young women, many of whom deny any affiliation with the women's movement by stating carefully, "I'm not a feminist, but . . ."

After 1968, critics of the women's movement brought up bra-burning to mock the ideals of "women's lib," reducing feminist goals to a ban on beauty products. Bralessness also became a way of eroticizing young women, linking them to the provocative freedoms of the sexual revolution. The image of bra-burning convinced some Americans that radical women were becoming as destructive as radical men in an era when homemade bombs, the Weathermen, armed Black Panther brigades, and the slogan "Burn, baby, burn" were all combining to destabilize society. And not a few women of color and the working class puzzled over the feminist movement's derision toward nice clothing and expensive cosmetics, items many poorer women longed to afford and which symbolized upward social mobility. But the truth is that no bras were burned in Atlantic City. So, how did the myth begin?

Throughout the 1960s, protests flourished best when paired with street theater, which attracted cameras and gave causes good publicity. From young men burning their draft cards to Karla Jay's "ogle-in" (which turned the tables on harassing males near the Wall Street subway stop in New York), the public stage communicated ideas effectively in the decades before the Internet and social media. The Atlantic City protest began when members of New York Radical Women (NYRW) decided to make a statement about women being rewarded for appearance alone. Charging that real women were more than sex objects to be judged by the male viewer, NYRW decided to rally outside the popular pageant and discard symbolic items women were required to buy and wear to meet modern standards of beauty. Over two hundred women participated.

Yes, women threw girdles and curlers into a "freedom trash can." However, the historic wooden boardwalk where feminists had assembled represented a real fire hazard, and Atlantic City's anxious mayor and police requested that nothing be set aflame. Thus no bras were burned. Inside the actual Miss America event, activists unfurled a giant "Women's Liberation" banner over the audience balcony. Protest organizer Robin Morgan's comment to a New York Times reporter, "We wouldn't do anything dangerous—just a symbolic bra-burning," convinced TV viewers that bra-burning was the preferred activity of women's liberationists.

The media's relationship with feminism would remain fraught with these tensions. Mainstream broadcasts mocked feminist protests, leading women to produce and rely on their own newspapers and journals. Ironically, though it was responsible for manufacturing the stereotype of the "ugly" feminist, America's media also granted ongoing exposure to feminists who fitted conventional white beauty standards, such as Gloria Steinem, Robin Morgan, Ti-Grace Atkinson, and Germaine Greer. By the early 1970s, Gloria Steinem and other editors at Ms. magazine would critique beauty products throughout the many forms of journalism the magazine made possible, from the famous "No Comment" section of sexist ads to investigative research on the health risks of feminine hygiene sprays. Legal challenges led by minority women would also help to redefine beauty and personal hygiene as individual and multicultural expression, asking: could a black woman sport an Afro or dreadlocks and look "professional" at her place of work? Must female lawyers wear dresses or skirts to practice law? Could girls wear trousers to school? In an era where reform schools still punished young black women for daring to maintain unstraightened natural hairstyles, beauty remained a contested issue. What the Miss America protest questioned, above all, was just who profited from making women and girls conform to a look that could be achieved only inauthentically, through discomfort, expense, and artifice.

Women! Don't Miss Amerika!

BRING: MASKS, LOVE, POSTERS, ANGER SONGS, LEAFLETS, JOY, ACTIONS, GUITARS, YOURSELF

SAT. SEPT. 6, 1pm ATLANTIC CITY N.J.

DEMONSTRATE ON THE BOARD-WALK

BRING: TAMBOURINES, FURY, BANNERS, HOPE EXCITEMENT, BALLOONS, MILITANCE, YOURSELF

CHARTER BUSES: Round trip $7 Leave Sat. morning. Reservations:

PROTEST the SEXIST RACIST AUCTION-SALE PAGEANT! GUERRILLA THEATER - FILMS WORKSHOPS PICKETING

CARS: Can you take someone along? Call:

Women: Demonstrate against the Miss Amerika Pageant Sat. Sept 6, 1:00 p.m., before Convention Hall, at Atlantic City, N.J., U.S.A.

→ INFO: (212) 228-8439 (evenings) ←

Top left: Women toss items into the "Freedom Trash Can" on the Atlantic City boardwalk in protest of the 1968 Miss America pageant. This demonstration famously gave rise to the stereotype that all feminists burn their bras. Some protesters threw in hair curlers and girdles, accessories long used by both pageant contestants and ordinary women to meet otherwise unattainable standards of beauty and femininity.

Bottom left: A man studies the Miss America protest posters, which declare the contest to be nothing more than a "cattle auction."

Top right: An original flier inviting women in the New York/New Jersey area to travel to Atlantic City and protest the Miss America pageant. This poster incorrectly gives the date as September 6; it was actually held on September 7. The use of a female Venus symbol with raised fist was already popular as a rallying feminist image by the summer of 1968; the poster also draws attention to the racism of American beauty ideals and encourages participants to bring "anger" and "militance."

"On September 7th in Atlantic City, the Annual Miss America Pageant will again crown 'your ideal.' But this year, reality will liberate the contest auction-block in the guise of 'genyooine' de-plasticized, breathing women. Women's liberation groups, Black women, high-school and college women, women's peace groups, women's welfare and social-work groups, women's job-equality, pro-birth control and pro-abortion groups—women of every political persuasion—all are invited to join us. . . . We will protest the image of Miss America, an image that oppresses in every area in which it purports to represent us."

"No More Miss America," open letter, August 26, 1968, Robin Morgan papers, Duke University

speech demands. However, for the most part, women's issues remained peripheral. Even within "progressive" left-wing social movements, the persistence of sexist attitudes meant women were relegated to supportive roles, such as typing leaflets or making tea. The same attitudes were present in political groups across Europe. In Italy, women in mixed left-wing political groups were often re-entrenched in traditional gender roles such as copying documents and usually were referred to as the "angels of the mimeograph"—a new version of the Fascist stereotype of women as "angels of the hearth."[25]

Nevertheless, the "establishment" media could no longer ignore or censor social change, as journalists all over the world captured images of protest and broadcast them to a global viewing audience. There would be no turning back—women and men of all ages had taken to the streets and had spoken up, in some countries for the first time. More importantly, women had begun to learn and internalize the language of liberation.

Indeed, by fall 1968, "vague rumours of the women's movement in America and Germany reached Britain,"[26] and a new kind of revolutionary consciousness was stirring.

Between 1968 and 1969, pockets of activity started to emerge across Britain—women's liberation was in

formation. The National Joint Action Committee on Women's Equal Rights (NJACWER), formed by trade union women in the wake of the Ford Dagenham sewing machinist strike of May–July 1968, planned a demonstration for May 1969. Psychoanalyst Juliet Mitchell ran what is regarded as the first women's studies classes at London's Anti-University, and at the Revolutionary Festival at Essex University in 1969, a meeting was held about women.[27] Women's liberation groups began to meet in London, and the first publications connected to the movement—*Socialist Woman* and *Shrew*—were written, printed, and distributed, while the British leftist newspaper *Black Dwarf* declared 1969 to be the "Year of the Militant Woman."

In the late 1960s, British Prime Minister Harold Wilson's Labour government passed a "remarkable . . . wave of liberal legislation"[28] that supported women's independence. This included the 1967 Abortion Act, passed after decades of campaigning by the Abortion Law Reform Association, which made it possible for a woman to get an abortion under certain conditions.[29] Like the contraceptive pill, the introduction of the act did not mean access to abortion

> "Revolutions are about little things. . . . Little things which happen to you all the time, every day, wherever you go, all your life."
>
> **Sheila Rowbotham** quoted in *The Black Dwarf*, January 10, 1969

Far left: This poster from the Netherlands' KWJ-Emancipation Committee announcing their "emancipation weekend" of November 27–29, 1981, sums up how many women in revolutionary movements were made to feel—what does making tea have to do with emancipation?

Left: *Shrew* was the magazine of the London Women's Liberation Workshop. From 1969 to 1978, different groups in London rotated the responsibility to produce it on a monthly basis.

Above: Women sewing machinists at the Ford Motor Company plant in Dagenham, UK, took strike action on June 7, 1968, seeking parity with their male colleagues' pay grade and recognition of their skills.

was automatic. Social stigma remained and provision was patchy. Two registered doctors had to approve the procedure and women could be refused abortion on the basis of their "expert" opinion.

UK marriage laws were also relaxed in 1969. The Divorce Reform Act made it easier to leave unfulfilling or damaging marriages; the Matrimonial Proceedings and Property Act offered women a financial safety net, even if men disproportionately benefited from divorce settlements. Attitudes toward sexuality were changing, too. The Homosexual Law Reform Act, which decriminalized male homosexual acts in private between consenting adults, was passed in 1967.

Women's capacity to bear children was one of the main sources of their oppression, argued Juliet Mitchell in her 1966 essay "The Longest Revolution." Yet "once child-bearing becomes totally voluntary its significance is fundamentally different," she wrote; "it need no longer be the sole or ultimate vocation of [a] woman; it becomes one option among others."[30] The invention of the Pill in the 1960s, in this light, was nothing short of revolutionary. It introduced choice into an area of women's lives in which, throughout the whole of human history, they had had little or no control. The Pill also dislocated heterosexual sex from its reproductive function. While this sometimes fed irresponsible male sexual behavior,[31] it also created the conditions for greater female social and sexual independence.

Still, accessing contraception was not always easy. Doctors withheld information about its availability, especially if the request came from single or unmarried women. In Britain, the 1969 Family Planning Act helped change things. It gave local authorities greater freedom to advise women on birth control and contraception. In 1970, the Family Planning Association began to offer advice to anyone over sixteen, regardless of marital status.[32]

In France, women's reproductive rights were at the forefront of much campaigning, with the Neuwirth Law legalizing contraception in 1967 and the formation of the main feminist lobbying movement, the Mouvement de libération des femmes (MLF) coming the year after.

West German women had had access to the Pill since June 1, 1961, but it was not until the liberation movements of 1968 that its use became more socially acceptable. By 1972, over 30 percent of fifteen- to fifty-four-year-olds used the contraceptive.[33] The Pill was similarly introduced in Australia in 1961, but initially was made available only to married women and was subject to a 27.5 percent "luxury tax."

Other European countries, such as Sweden, had permitted contraception decades earlier, and in the Netherlands the Pill was introduced in 1964 and by 1968 was used by 40 percent of Dutch women in their twenties or early thirties.[34]

In stark contrast, despite contraception being legalized in the USSR (with the exception of Degree 770, which outlawed contraception and abortion in some parts of the Soviet Union to increase birth rates), poor availability meant that abortion remained one of the primary birth control methods through to the twenty-first century. In Italy, Fascist anti-contraception legislation was not repealed until 1971.[35]

From the 1960s through the '80s, there were many parts of the world where contraception was restricted or banned altogether (and in fact there still are). Nevertheless, the reproductive revolution of the 1960s undoubtedly energized women's liberation movements.

Coming together

From the outset, women's demonstrations were both playful and creative in attempts to subvert the patriarchy. From America's WITCH (Women's International Terrorist Conspiracy from Hell), whose members "hexed" Wall Street, to the 1968 Miss America protests, where girdles were thrown into a "freedom trash can," feminists rejected old limitations of body and mind. At the Miss World contest in November 1970, held in London's Royal Albert Hall, protesters stood outside adorned with sashes; their slogans attacked the man-made world—Mis-Fit: Refuses to Conform—Mis-Laid: Demands Free Contraception—Mis-Governed: Demands Liberation.[36]

Indeed, outside London, the women's movement in Britain grew in ways that appeared organic and accidental. Meetings were often in women's flats or

Far left: This stylized 1971 poster designed by San Francisco–based Celestial Arts, with its rather threatening undertone, is an example of how some materials associated with the movement appeared anti-male rather than pro-female.

Left: "Why Miss World?" fliers were produced for the protest against the Miss World contest in London, November 1970.

The Black Dwarf

Est 1817 Vol 13 Number 9   10th January 1969   Fortnightly 1s 6d

From *The Second Sex* to *The Feminine Mystique*

Often referred to as the inspiration for second-wave feminism, these landmark works remain the cornerstones of feminist literature today.

Simone de Beauvoir's *Le deuxième sexe* (1949) and Betty Friedan's *The Feminine Mystique* (1963) are frequently credited with sparking the rise of the women's liberation movements in the postwar era. Yet how can two books written a decade apart on different continents have resonated so strongly with an entire generation (or, indeed, generations) of women across the world?

In 1949, Simone de Beauvoir posed a fundamental philosophical question: "What is a woman?"[37] Throughout the book (first translated as *The Second Sex* in 1953), she explores the idea of woman being the "Other" entity in relation to man, who is the default definition of the human race. Women, she argued, had been relegated to a subservient position largely because of their reproductive roles. Among other themes, the book explores the upbringing of a little girl from age three or four, in contrast to a little boy. In so doing, she highlights the societal "norms" that feed into a woman's sense of her own "otherness." Beauvoir, who was herself bisexual and in a long-term non-monogamous relationship with the philosopher Jean-Paul Sartre, explores how marriage becomes a life of "service"[38] that "almost destroys a woman"[39] in her attempts to define herself as a perfect wife, mother, and social and sexual companion. Ultimately, Beauvoir's work was interpreted as a radical redefining of the terms "sex" and "gender" summed up in the famous phrase "One is not born, but rather becomes, woman."[40] For many later scholars, including the American philosopher and gender theorist Judith Butler, this was a defining moment that set out clearly how "womanhood" was not a natural state but a social construct—a construct that many liberationists sought to break free from.

The Second Sex certainly revolutionized feminist thinking, even though Beauvoir did not declare herself a feminist until 1972. The first edition of the book in the French language sold approximately twenty-two thousand copies a week on its initial release and has since been translated into nineteen languages and sold millions of copies worldwide.

It was undoubtedly a key influence upon the American author and activist Betty Friedan as she set out to explore the "myth" of the 1950s American housewife. In contrast to the mainstream media's image of a woman fulfilled entirely by matrimony and motherhood, she presented a whole swathe of women who felt caged by domesticity. She proposed that women needed to discover fulfillment, not through others, but through their own minds and bodies.

The Feminine Mystique was a startling success, not only in its sales, which exceeded one million within the first year of publication, but also in its political impact: it laid the groundwork for the Equal Pay Act and Equal Rights legislation of the 1970s.

Other important and controversial feminist tracts were to follow, notably *The Female Eunuch* (1970) by Australian-born author and academic Germaine Greer—a book that continues to receive a mixed reception to this day. Greer also argued that for too long women had been subjected to a patriarchal definition of the "female" and "feminine." Where de Beauvoir advocated economic independence and Friedan championed the importance of education, Greer proposed that women's liberation needed to be predominantly a sexual revolution of reconnecting women with their own bodies.

Importantly, it was the notion of the self-actualized woman in both Beauvoir's and Friedan's work that struck a chord with Western women who were longing for something beyond the lives lived by their mothers and grandmothers. These were the women who formed the grassroots of the women's liberation movements across Britain, Europe, and America.

> "Simone de Beauvoir kept the feminist flame alive after women won the right to vote. Betty Friedan was the pragmatic facilitator who recreated the political organisation of the suffrage movement."
>
> **Camille Paglia**, "Feminist Writers Pay Tribute," *The Guardian*, February 7, 2006

THE YEAR'S MOST CONTROVERSIAL ❧ BESTSELLER ❧

DELL 2498   75c

The Feminine Mystique

BETTY FRIEDAN

"The book we have been waiting for . . . the wisest, sanest, soundest, most understanding and compassionate treatment of contemporary American woman's greatest problem...a triumph."

—ASHLEY MONTAGU

SIMONE DE BEAUVOIR

LE DEUXIÈME SEXE

I

LES FAITS ET LES MYTHES

GALLIMARD

Above left: *The Feminine Mystique* shed light on the private lives of America's housewives and revealed the discontent of many women.

Above right: *Le deuxième sexe* undoubtedly sparked the debate over how women's views about themselves and their lives were shaped by patriarchal society.

houses, as the movement was built in informal yet productive environments. The decentralized and improvised nature of the movement empowered women to use its energy to address issues that were relevant to them. This meant that local expressions of women's liberation were varied and regionally specific.[41] To build a movement, activists developed basic communication structures, such as local newsletters, and held stalls in town centers to recruit new members and share information. Sometimes activists tapped into existing networks of women's groups—coffee-pot clubs, lunchtime groups for housebound mothers, Young Wives groups, the Women's Institute, and Ladies' Circles—to reach out to women with talks and presentations.

In France, the nascent MLF, formed from a number of women's groups and collectives, attracted national attention in 1970 when it met publicly for the first time at the Université de Vincennes wearing T-shirts emblazoned with the American feminist fist symbol. Later that year in August, ten founding members and activists from MLF, including the writers and theorists Christine Delphy and Monique Wittig, laid a wreath at the Tomb of the Unknown Soldier in Paris, making the statement "There is more unknown than the unknown soldier, [there is] his wife." Posters at the demonstration also included messages such as "One man in two is a woman." The MLF placed an emphasis on the assertion of women as a subject, not an object, in line with French feminist theoretical thinking at the time, embodied in the slogan "Our body belongs to us."[42]

Above: Women's liberation activists march from Hyde Park to Trafalgar Square, London, March 6, 1971. Over one thousand women took part in possibly the largest women's rights demonstration Britain had seen since the suffragette movement.

Below left: This 1970 poster with the logo of PAG (Pluralistische actie groep) declares, "*Vrouwen solidair.*" The open nature of this group—one of the first feminist associations in Bruges—encouraged women, whatever their political persuasion, to come together in activism across the Netherlands and to seek solidarity in the struggle for liberation.

Below right: This 1976 poster from Vienna declares, "At last we'll have a women's celebration!" as it advertises a women's cultural event, including theater, music, and literature.

Similarly, between 1969 and 1971 the first feminist collectives emerged in Italy, as women started meeting in their homes or in women's centers. The first feminist group, DEMAU (Demystification of Authority), emerged as early as 1966 when it published its manifesto denouncing patriarchal society and called for women's liberation. Although the Italian women's movement was fragmented, there was much interaction between the groups, with the first national meeting of feminist groups taking place in Milan in 1971. Among these early collectives was Rivolta femminile, which laid the basis for some of the leading theories of Italian radical feminism as they would develop throughout the 1970s and 1980s. Originally founded in Rome, Rivolta femminile gained notoriety through the declaration of its manifesto in Rome and Milan, setting out an agenda of liberation, as opposed to equality, and sexual difference: "Liberation for woman does not mean accepting the life man leads because it is unlivable; on the contrary, it means expressing her own sense of existence." Small groups soon followed in other cities, including in Milan, where art critic Carla Lonzi first introduced consciousness-raising in Italy.[43]

Whereas for some this was a period of first "coming together," for others the cracks started emerging. In the US, during the later years of the 1960s and the radical early 1970s, the split between liberal feminists and "liberationists" widened. The former continued to operate within the American political system, while women emerging from New Left collectives favored a less hierarchical format and opposed "star-tripping" leadership. The visibility of feminist writers Gloria Steinem and Germaine Greer, well-spoken and conventionally beautiful white women who became the media's go-to spokeswomen on "women's lib," prompted other groups to demand greater diversity. Any hope of a unified sisterhood was countered by obvious divisions: coalition vs. separation, men vs. women, black vs. white, straight vs. lesbian.

As women's independent groups and actions sprang up across the United States between 1969 and 1973, some (including lesbian coalitions) were investigated by the FBI as potentially violent or dangerous. However, the serious task of organizing could be found in every major American city, from the First National Women's Liberation Conference, held in Chicago in 1968, to the formation of New York Radical Women and the Redstockings. In August 1970, fifty thousand women marched through the streets of New York on the fiftieth anniversary of the 19th Amendment; that year also saw the publication of Robin

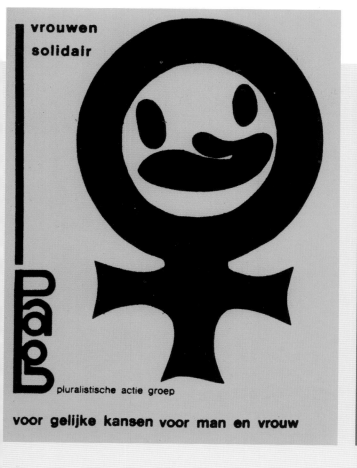

Morgan's compelling consciousness-raising anthology, *Sisterhood Is Powerful.*

Similarly, by 1971, women's liberation groups existed in towns and cities all across Britain. Birmingham, Bolton, Bradford, Brighton, Bristol, Cambridge, Canterbury, Coventry, Colchester, Exeter, Harrow, Hemel Hempstead, Hull, Keele, Leeds, Leicester, Liverpool, London, Manchester, Merseyside, Nottingham, Oxford, Sheffield, Southampton, Stafford, Warwick, Teesside, Wolverhampton, and York were just some of the places where women's liberation took hold.[44]

In the US, the 1970s would be a decade in which American women's rights were secured at least in part through two landmark pieces of legislation, Title IX of the 1972 Education Act and the 1973 *Roe v. Wade* decision legalizing abortion on demand. However, the long campaign to ratify an Equal Rights Amendment (ERA) and the burgeoning call to accept lesbian rights divided American women further throughout the '70s.

Nevertheless, the 1970s was a decade during which Western women recognized that at every level there was work to be done: from electing women to positions in government to starting rape crisis centers to changing restrictive abortion laws. Women had begun to mobilize and the movement was well and truly underway, with momentum building for legislative, social, and cultural change for women on a hitherto unseen scale.

Above: Members of the women's liberation movement parade down Fifth Avenue in New York City, summer 1970. This linked group of young women from different ethnic backgrounds carries a poster naming motherhood as a key oppressor of women, and daringly lists the contact phone number of the Anti-Motherhood League. Could pregnancy shift to a test tube and spare women's bodies? Many feminists theorized about the likely political changes in birth control, abortion rights, and day care if men were the ones to get pregnant.

Right: The imagery of this poster for a feminist art exhibition (year unknown) in Brixton, London, spoke to an awakening sense of female power. This was embodied during the early 1970s in women taking to the streets to demonstrate, protest, and celebrate a newfound sense of liberation and independence.

2

"THE PERSONAL IS POLITICAL"

The struggle for liberation

The late 1960s witnessed an army of women fighting for legislation to regain control of all aspects of their lives and their bodies.

On a global scale, the movements for women's liberation were incredibly diverse, reflecting the social, cultural, ethnic, and political makeup of each nation's womanhood. Still, there were commonalities of approach across the transatlantic divide and further afield. In many countries, consciousness-raising groups were established, large-scale protests were held, conferences and teach-ins were organized, and political lobbying to change or defend existing laws was underway. Women were also creating, as well as campaigning—setting up rape crisis centers, women's centers, and supplementary schools; performing agitprop (political propaganda) street theater; playing music with other women; foregrounding the female experience in art; and writing, publishing and printing pamphlets, books, and magazines. Elsewhere more "radical" action ranged from breaking into squats, fire-bombing porn shops, and defacing sexist advertising. Liberation also meant openness to personal transformation, whether that was learning how to do a vaginal self-examination, experimenting with lesbian sexuality, or living apart from men.

These are just some of the ways women in the movement expressed their politics, but there were many others. Actions were inventive and multifaceted, and ranged from the spectacular to the mundane. All areas of life were politicized as women began to question every aspect of their existence.

In battling to make women full participants in society, feminists with varying styles and strategies for leadership negotiated the question left unresolved by their nineteenth-century forerunners: should women argue that they are the same as men in the eyes of the law or different? In demanding equal access to education, jobs, and public roles that were available to men, women declared that all citizens were entitled to the same opportunities. But feminists also spoke from the platform of difference, identifying what would soon be called "women's issues": birth control and abortion rights, childcare for working mothers, public breastfeeding without shame, gynecological healthcare for incarcerated women, and accountability to women's history in the classroom.

Bringing the private realm of the body into greater public discussion, the feminists of the 1960s debated issues that shocked many of their listeners unused to hearing about sexual harassment, incest, marital rape,

Page 34: "Beauty is in the street," declares this French poster designed for the May 1968 protests.

Below left: Women's Liberation Movement rally in Trafalgar Square, London, March 6, 1971. The importance of childcare in liberating working women is clearly demonstrated by the protester in the center with her poster calling for "Free 24 Hour Nurseries."

Below right: The activist Flo Kennedy (left) on October 31, 1974, accompanied by an unknown protester, advocating the Year of the Woman, which was declared in 1975. This photograph was taken by Bettye Lane, who amassed one of America's most important collections of images of the feminist movement.

Opposite: Poster rallying women to attend the London Women's Day March on March 8, 1975.

SOLIDARITY WITH WOMENS STRUGGLES ALL OVER THE WORLD

WOMEN UNITE

WOMENS DAY MARCH

1·30 ASSEMBLE AT   ⊖ ALDGATE EAST
ST. MARYS CHURCHYARD WHITECHAPEL HIGH ST. E.1
2·30 MARCH TO
VICTORIA PARK HACKNEY E.9
contact: WOMENS LIBERATION WORKSHOP, 38 EARLHAM ST. W.C.2.

MARCH 8th 1975

SEE RED WOMENS WORKSHOP

or a woman's right to orgasm. Hence a rallying cry in the US during the 1970s was "the personal is political." This political reframing of laws to expand women's personal agency rapidly brought about stunning reforms in America, Britain, Europe, and beyond.

From mobilizing to meeting

While the reforms women lobbied for in the US would grant them more legal control over personal decisions, they still left women dependent upon a government overwhelmingly run by men. It was, therefore, vital that women began to organize themselves as they sought to take on the patriarchy.

American groups such as Redstockings and New York Radical Women were committed to naming women as an oppressed class; separating from men in order to study the nature of that oppression; and demanding that radical men study their own sexism in word and deed. Consciousness-raising or CR groups facilitated much of the dialogue for women awakening to their own personal/political location, and a variety of representative essays came together in Robin Morgan's anthology *Sisterhood Is Powerful*, which included provocative works such as Anne Koedt's "The Myth of the Vaginal Orgasm." Women who believed in the power, even the superiority, of female difference began to create and support a feminist alternative counterculture, choosing to patronize woman-owned

businesses, to divert their political dollars to feminist causes, and to name and disrupt patriarchal norms.

In Britain, the focus was on mobilizing women on a national and local scale like never before. After the first national Women's Liberation Movement conference in Oxford in 1970, a Women's National Coordinating Committee (WNCC) was established to coordinate the activities of groups around the country. However, the WNCC was disbanded at the 1971 Women's Liberation Conference, held in Skegness, due to sectarian squabbles as women from the trade union and socialist movements sought to exert control over the organization. This "left a great deal of hostility amongst feminists towards socialist women and a deep distrust of structures and methods of organising which were associated with the male left."[1] In its place, the Women's Liberation Movement adopted a decentralized organizational structure led by local and regional groups.

How the movement was organized in the UK became an important political question in itself. If women's liberation was to be effective, it could not mimic a "male way" of doing things. There could be no leaders, stars, or gurus. Power could not be concentrated in a central location and delegated outward. Throughout the 1970s and '80s, the movement remained decentralized and "leaderless." The main coordination came from the Women's Information, Referral and Enquiry Service (WIRES), which was established in 1975 to provide "contact addresses of all local, special interest and

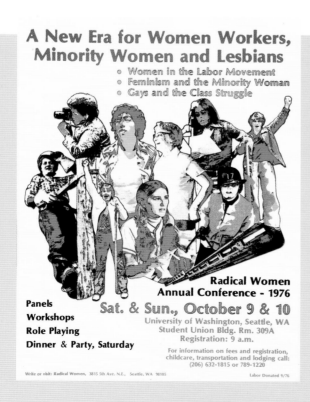

A New Era for Women Workers, Minority Women and Lesbians
- Women in the Labor Movement
- Feminism and the Minority Woman
- Gays and the Class Struggle

Radical Women Annual Conference - 1976
Sat. & Sun., October 9 & 10
University of Washington, Seattle, WA
Student Union Bldg. Rm. 309A
Registration: 9 a.m.

Panels
Workshops
Role Playing
Dinner & Party, Saturday

For information on fees and registration, childcare, transportation and lodging call:
(206) 632-1815 or 789-1220

Write or visit: Radical Women, 3815 5th Ave. N.E., Seattle, WA 98105   Labor Donated 9/76

Consciousness-raising

D-M Withers

Consciousness-raising (CR) is probably the most widely known idea to emerge from the women's liberation movements, but what was it?

CR was "a creative inheritance from a wider political rebellion in more than one country,"[2] with roots in the liberation struggles of Black Power, student movements in the US, the Algerian war for independence, and the Paris student protests of 1968.

In the hands of women's liberationists, CR became a tool that enabled women to unlock knowledge that had been historically overlooked by male-dominated politics and culture. Within CR groups, personal experience and so-called private issues such as motherhood and sexuality became *public* political problems.

In the early days, CR groups were the basic organizing unit of the movement. Women met in small groups in order to study their personal experiences. Through gaining insight or "consciousness" of *how* they were oppressed, women acquired courage to transform their lives. Soon they realized that other women shared similar grievances, and such insights became the basis for *collective* political action as new groups were established in the 1980s and beyond.

Women's liberation, in its early manifestations, was built upon women's shared private experiences of social isolation, whether that was through sexual abuse, boredom, menstruation, abortion, or childbirth. In this way, the movements provided a social context where connections were made between oppression by the state, law, and economy and the keen frustrations women felt in the home. The personal became political.

"Study groups" were the most common manifestation of CR within the British Black Women's Movement. Focused on specific issues, such as anti-imperial history, study groups helped situate the political consciousness of the Black Women's Movement within internationalist, decolonial struggles. In the early 1970s, Gerlin Bean remembers, black activists "were working together in organisations like the Panthers, the Black Liberation Front. Within that we would have a little woman's caucus where we sit or we read or we study together."[3] When the Organisation for Women of Asian and African Descent (OWAAD) was established in 1979, they had a Study Committee whose aim was "to study and discuss issues relevant to black women; to make their findings available, organise study days, teach ins, discussion."[4]

Women's liberation movements in Europe adapted CR to their own cultural contexts. For example, the Italian women's movement developed such approaches into a new departure—the practice referred to as *autocoscienza*, which translates as "self-consciousness." Practicing *autocoscienza* in small groups enabled women to understand how patriarchal ideology affected them. The small group also provided a context where women could articulate their own ideas and knowledge. *Affidamento*, translated as "entrustment," is, as historian Alex Martinis Roe describes it, "a term used by the Milan Women's Bookstore cooperative to describe a particular kind of political relationship between two women, which was developed as a political practice out of *autocoscienza*, and which involves a commitment to supporting each other's political desires. By referring to one another, each woman gives the other authority in her spheres of political practice and the alliance of their differences makes their respective social endeavors more effective. These specific and committed relations among women starting from their differences became a way to enrich and harness the liberating relational politics of *autocoscienza* in feminist political projects outside of the women's group." The cooperative advocated that "the social relationship of entrustment between women is both a content and an instrument of this most basic struggle [for women's liberation]."[5]

Creating social spaces where trust and solidarity could be built between women was therefore a vital function of the CR group. Within Britain in the late 1960s and early '70s, there were very few public spaces where women could meet and form independent political and social relationships. Early accounts of CR groups revealed it was challenging for women to spend time with other women, due to feelings of intuitive distrust or dislike.[6] "Rivalry for men is the great factor which divides us and mutilates our relationship with each other."[7]

Participating in CR did not always lead to immediate or obvious change. It could be hard to trust the group and the process, as this participant wrote: "Occasionally, I've almost despaired of getting anywhere at all. But slowly

Opposite top: A Native American consciousness-raising group at the Native American Women's Rights Conference, February 25, 1975.

Opposite, bottom: The AUF-Frauenzentrum collective meet to discuss issues in Vienna, 1976.

> ## "Consciousness-raising cannot be outgrown: it must remain the basis of all our theory and practice."

Jessica York et al., "We Are the Feminists That Women Have Warned Us About: Introductory Paper," 1979

things got better, we concentrate on ourselves, and each other. We share feelings, ideas and experiences more and more—gradually the barriers between us are lowered, we support each other."[8]

As a form of political activism, CR is often misunderstood. Compared to more obvious forms of activism, it may appear self-indulgent or even apolitical. Yet without the existence of CR groups, key ideas in women's liberation would never have emerged; neither would the social relationships that sustained the movement have been created. CR groups supported women to question every aspect of their lives. They gave women confidence to study, learn, think, and act. In an environment that nurtured collective solidarity among women, CR groups helped invent a new kind of politics.

Above: A group of women discuss issues at what would be the final National Women's Liberation Conference, Birmingham, April 1978.

campaign groups, and women's centres." Different regional groups ran the service, yet it was never based in London to avoid the perception that the capital was the "powerhouse of the movement."[9]

Despite this move toward decentralization, large national conferences were held in Britain throughout the 1970s, organized by groups in Bristol, Manchester, London, Newcastle, Edinburgh, and Birmingham. Movement policy and strategy were debated, as activists from different parts of the country met to report on their activities. The policy and strategy originally flowed from a set of "demands" agreed upon at conferences. Demands were framed as a starting point for discussion and action, and some viewed them as reformist, "represent[ing] only a partial statement of what we mean by liberation."[10] Initially the movement organized around four demands: Free 24-Hour Childcare; Equal Pay Now; Equal Education and Job Opportunity; and Free Contraception and Abortion on Demand.

Further demands were added as the political focus of the British movement evolved throughout the 1970s. The fifth demand—Legal and Financial Independence for All Women—and the sixth—An End to Discrimination against Lesbians and The Right to a Self-Defined

Sexuality—were passed at the 1974 national conference in Edinburgh. The final and seventh demand, passed at the 1978 Birmingham conference, focused on ending violence against women.

By the 1980s, the original seven demands came to be seen by some activists as "a disparate collection of aims passed by national conferences between 1970 and 1978"[11] and were viewed as irrelevant. Yet they endure today as a compelling reminder that the feminist revolution imagined by women's liberationists— a political project that involved economic, legal, structural, and personal change throughout all levels of society—has not yet been realized.

National conferences could be heated and intense affairs. In a practical sense, it was often difficult to make decisions, due to the large number of women present. Sometimes fierce disagreements arose between the diverse political "tendencies" in the Women's Liberation Movement;[12] on other occasions, differences of class, race, ethnicity, and sexuality generated painful conflict. National conferences created the pragmatic conditions for activists to connect

> "The new feminists had no respect for established procedures or structures. They wanted to create the kind of power that would grow organically, rather than seize the citadels that men had already constructed."
>
> **Anna Coote and Polly Pattullo**, *Power and Prejudice: Women and Politics*, 1990

with each other and helped ignite new conversations and political ideas, as one attendee, Takumba Ria Lawal, explains: "I remember the big women's liberation conferences. There is nowhere, even today, where you'd have 3,000 women all staying with women—not even the unions had that—then after the big women's liberation conferences you'd get break offs. 'Well actually, I'd like to talk about lesbianism, or another issue.'"[13]

National conferences also had political and social importance for the movement. "I have this memory of conferences and things in other bits of the country ending with people singing,"[14] one participant remarked. In reflections from the Acton conference, held in 1972, one attendee welcomed the inclusion of more creative forms of feminist expression, such as theater and women's bands. Perhaps this was a way "to include sisters who do not yet consider themselves 'creative' or 'intellectual.'"[15]

Alongside national conferences, other events were organized that covered diverse topics such as feminism and nonviolence, images of women in the media, women and fascism, women and Ireland, women and mental health, women in manual trades, and revolutionary/radical feminism. These regional, political, and interest-based conferences continued into the 1980s, after the large national conferences ceased to operate.

Alongside the formal conferences of the Women's Liberation Movement, a number of early campaigns denoted the concerns of the burgeoning British women's movement. "Contraceptive advice and its availability is something that must affect us all," wrote the Contraception & Abortion campaign group in Wandsworth, London, in 1971, "and we felt an investigation of the facilities and attitudes in our area would be of value to us and to other women in the community."[16] Such an approach was mirrored by many regional women's liberation groups throughout the UK, whose early campaigns began by collecting information about issues that affected women in their locality. The group compiled a questionnaire that was sent to Family Planning Association clinics, and later wrote to social services and the press. These actions created a body of modest feminist research that was used in campaigns or to negotiate for better service provision through local government.

Campaigns similarly focused on local issues, such as hospital closures, lack of accessible childcare, poor

> "One purpose of the national conference is just to be together. Another is to build an autonomous mass movement which will be an impetus—I think—*the* impetus—to change our lives."
>
> Gillian, "Thoughts on the Acton Conference," 1972

Far right: The original demands of the British Women's Liberation Movement created a strong public statement that communicated the movement's political intent.

Right: The Women's Information, Referral and Enquiry Service (WIRES) coordinated information produced within the British Women's Liberation Movement from 1975 onward.

Below: This badge is from the final national conference of the British Women's Liberation Movement, held in Birmingham in April 1978. It was here that the seventh demand was agreed upon.

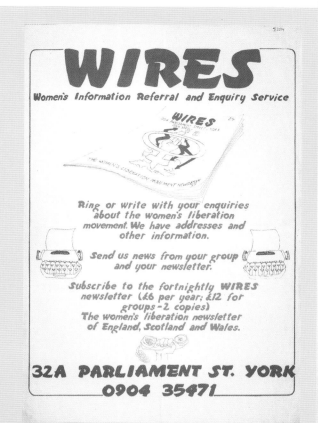

WIRES
Women's Information Referral and Enquiry Service

Ring or write with your enquiries about the women's liberation movement. We have addresses and other information.

Send us news from your group and your newsletter.

Subscribe to the fortnightly WIRES newsletter (£6 per year; £12 for groups—2 copies) The women's liberation newsletter of England, Scotland and Wales.

32A PARLIAMENT ST. YORK
0904 35471

EQUAL PAY NOW

EQUAL EDUCATION & JOB OPPORTUNITY

FREE TWENTY FOUR HOUR CHILD CARE

FREE CONTRACEPTION & ABORTION ON DEMAND

LEGAL & FINANCIAL INDEPENDENCE FOR ALL WOMEN

AN END TO DISCRIMINATION AGAINST LESBIANS & THE RIGHT OF WOMEN TO A SELF DEFINED SEXUALITY

Left: Much of the energy of British women's activism in the late 1970s was spent protecting legislation passed in the late 1960s, most notably in relation to abortion. Successive Conservative politicians sought to modify the 1967 Abortion Act, with activists crossing out the names of their opponents on this poster by the National Abortion Campaign.

> "[Over] the past couple of years many women's centres have been started round the country. By meeting in one another's houses small groups of women have gained the confidence to start centres where they can talk to other women, share their common problems, support one another, and begin to change their world."
>
> **Anon**, "Women's Centres and Women's Aid," *Spare Rib*, 1974

education facilities, equal pay disputes, abortion restrictions, and domestic abuse. Sometimes they converged with larger, national campaigns such as the National Abortion Campaign (NAC), which defended women's access to safe and legal abortion. Even though abortion was made legal in Britain in 1967, Conservative MPs proposed several Abortion Amendment Bills in the 1970s. For example, the James White Abortion Amendment Bill aimed to restrict the circumstances in which a woman could get an abortion and change which doctors could perform one. In response, the NAC organized a large demonstration in 1975, attended by twenty thousand people.[17]

Other significant campaigns included the Women's Abortion and Contraception Campaign (WACC), the Working Women's Charter, and the Family Allowances Campaign. Family Allowances were introduced in the UK in 1945 as part of wider postwar welfare forms. Paid directly to the mother, they were often the only money women had access to. When the Conservative government proposed abolishing the maternal benefit and paying it to the husband in the early 1970s, it was viewed as a threat to women's social and economic independence. Child Benefit eventually replaced the Family Allowance in 1975, which provided a benefit for each child, paid to mothers. The Campaign for Legal and Financial Independence or "YBA Wife" (the "YBA" stood for "Your Best Acronym" and was a campaign aimed at highlighting women's subjugation in marriage) similarly battled against state policies that structurally curtailed women's economic independence.[18]

Creating independent cultural spaces run by and for women was vital for the development of the British women's movement. Women's centers became spaces where women could meet and discuss their ideas, hold events, build networks, and seek support.

In 1974, there were women's centers across Britain in London, Bristol, Cardiff, Lancaster, and Edinburgh. Women's centers made the Women's Liberation Movement a visible and well-established activist presence in towns and cities and were a point of contact for women who were not involved in the movement. "Women are constantly 'dropping-in' for a chat or a cup of tea, for a rest with their kids while shopping, to breast-feed, or to look at the jumble or bookshop."[19]

Some women's centers were squatted; others were rented from private landlords or the local council.

Far right and right: While national women's liberation conferences in Britain ceased to happen in 1978, conferences dedicated to particular ideas or campaigns continued through the 1980s. Often they were more informal group gatherings taking in a broad range of women's issues, although sometimes they took the formal approach of covering a specific topic, such as women and Ireland.

Title IX and women's sports

Bonnie J. Morris

With the passing of Title IX into US law, sports became one area worldwide where women sought to level the playing field.

Feminist history includes many athletic triumphs, but few were as revolutionary as tennis player Billie Jean King's victory over male challenger Bobby Riggs in what was dubbed the Battle of the Sexes. With the eyes of so many hopeful women and little girls upon her, King defeated her opponent (and the oddsmakers) in three straight sets, a match broadcast live from the Houston Astrodome on September 20, 1973. Through television, ninety million viewers saw that a female athlete could beat a male contender. King had already taken on the world of tennis by contesting obvious discrimination in the prize money given to male vs. female players, and, after her 1973 victory, she continued to advocate tirelessly for female athletes to be given greater opportunities and visibility. Her fight for female athletes' rights would prove to be the toughest game of all.

Sports participation had been a battleground for female athletes throughout the twentieth century, whether those athletes identified as feminists or just wanted to play. For nonwhite sportswomen, challenges to opportunity and access were compounded further by entrenched racial segregation in facilities ranging from top country club memberships to local public pools and tennis courts. From the postwar 1940s through to the 1970s, many black women in America found support and coaching at historically black colleges and universities, which produced outstanding athletes like the Tiger Belles track team at Tennessee State; white women's college programs were less likely to support track and often banned physical education majors from competing off-campus. All American women were banned from the Boston Marathon, from Little League, and from Olympic events ranging from marathon to pole vault to ski jump and ice hockey. Those women who made Olympic teams were subjected to humiliating "femininity tests," which presumed that athletic achievement in any woman meant excess masculinity or an abnormal gene. The No Girls Allowed climate affected adult congresswomen as well; they were banned from using the "members only" gym that congressmen enjoyed.

But soon, female students and the emerging female athletes of the 1972, 1976, and 1984 Olympics (the US boycotted the 1980 games held in Moscow) found federal support for women's sports programs through a law called Title IX. Easily one of the most misunderstood statutes in education history, Title IX—which was never intended to be about sports—ushered in a quarter-century of dynamic advancement for women in college athletics and academia.

What was Title IX? Signed into law by President Nixon on June 23, 1972, this one section of the Education Amendments declared that no one should be discriminated against on the grounds of their gender. The initial impetus for such a law was the sad state of sex bias in American schools and colleges. In 1972, some top universities still did not accept women (Princeton was the final holdout), while Harvard, Yale, Cornell, and others maintained an admissions quota of two women for every three men. Beyond official exclusion, qualified women in higher education were routinely turned away from graduate programs, medical school, and law school, with questions such as "Why should we admit you when you're just going to get married and pregnant?" or "Don't you know you're taking a place that could go to a man?" Even at age twenty-one, and despite the sexual revolution, female students at most colleges were governed by *in loco parentis* regulations with mandatory curfews, chaperones, and restricted housing. Bright high school girls were denied admission to magnet schools for the gifted, such as Bronx Science, and vocational public schools. Women were also usually forbidden to take shop or auto mechanics, which might result in higher-salaried trade skills. Instead, girls were funneled into commercial typing, cooking, or beautician courses.

With so much sex discrimination and inequality at schools receiving federal or public funds, women protested that their own tax dollars were used to limit their goals and their daughters' future success. Research and activism led by US Representatives Edith Green and Patsy Mink, scholar Bernice Sandler and Congressman Birch Bayh helped shape Title IX as a legal remedy for academic sexism. Mink had already broken ground in her own way as the first nonwhite woman elected to Congress.

> "No person in the United States shall, on the basis of sex, be excluded from participation in, be denied the benefits of, or be subjected to discrimination under any education program or activity receiving federal financial assistance."

Title IX, Education Amendment, 1972

Opposite: Signed into law by otherwise conservative President Richard Nixon on June 23, 1972, Title IX banned sex discrimination in any US educational program receiving federal funding. This portion of the Education Amendments greatly increased opportunities for girls and women to enter college, graduate school, law school, and medical school, as well as directing funds to women's athletic programs; yet, as this button proclaims, few women knew what their rights were—unless directly taught about Title IX's provisions.

Far right: Martina Navratilova was the greatest female tennis player in the world in the years 1965 to 2005 (*Tennis Magazine*, 2005), yet sexism, homophobia, and distrust of her Czech socialist upbringing kept her from the mainstream acclaim and publicity she deserved. She was World No. 1 for a total of 332 weeks in singles and a record 237 weeks in doubles, making her the only player in history to have held the top spot in both singles and doubles for over 200 weeks.

Right: *Daily News* front page, September 21, 1973. Billie Jean King gives contender Bobby Riggs a comforting pat on the back after beating him 6-4, 6-3, 6-3 in the "Battle of the Sexes" at the Houston Astrodome. Thirty thousand fans watched King defeat Riggs—and his claims of masculine superiority—in two hours and five minutes. Throughout the 1970s, "lib" continued to be shorthand slang for the women's liberation movement. In this case, it was athletic prowess that gave Billie Jean King her victory, but feminist supporters and fans certainly played a role.

BILLIE JEAN KING OUTLIBS THE LIP
Wallops Riggs in Straight Sets

6-4, 6-3, 6-3, And No Love For Bobby . . .

Billie Jean King gives former superman Bobby Riggs comforting pat on back after she beat him, 6-4, 6-3, 6-3, in their "Battle of the Sexes" at Houston Astrodome, last night. Billie, 29, took more two hours and five minutes to destroy 55-year-old hustler's myth of masculine superiority before an exuberant crowd of 30,000 fans.

Stories on page 3

MARTINA NAVRATILOVA
the best & most successful tennis player to date...

Title IX did not change attitudes overnight. But at a moment when the Equal Rights Amendment (ERA), too, was gaining ratification state by state, women now felt nationally encouraged to challenge their exclusion from architecture and engineering programs, and they demanded access to federally funded military academies (gaining entry to West Point in 1976). Others read Title IX's ban on discrimination in "any program or activity" as an invitation to look at sports. Athletic programs—divided by gender at most colleges, with a larger men's gym and an inferior women's gym, and two differently paid male and female athletic directors—offered the most glaring examples of bias in any educational activity. When Title IX was first introduced, 99 percent of college sports budgets went to men's athletics.

The push to see women as fully fundable athletes deserving of a fair chance met with stiff resistance—from football programs in particular. Few schools were fined for remaining noncompliant with Title IX, and a 1984 Supreme Court decision, *Grove City College v. Bell*, put Title IX on hold for four years until that decision was reversed by the Civil Rights Restoration Act of 1987 (implemented in March 1988). Even with support lagging, the gradual impact of Title IX on female achievement could be seen in the early 1970s. The first year that

women's basketball became an official Olympic event, at the 1976 games in Montreal, American women brought home a silver medal. Their team included two of the first women to go to college on basketball scholarships, Ann Meyers and Nancy Lieberman.

The next generation of American women, granted better access to training and play, would win gold in the once male-only Olympic events of distance running, ice hockey, and basketball, and eventually American women would win the World Cup victory in soccer. The year that Title IX became law, 1972, American women won forty-six Olympic medals; by 1984, that number had increased to 144. By 1996, American women were bringing home more medals than American men. In 2012, for the first time, the US sent more female athletes than males to the Olympic Games. On the fortieth anniversary of Title IX, Arthur Bryant wrote in the *Christian Science Monitor*, "From 1972 to 2011, the number of girls and women participating in high school sports grew from 294,015 (7 percent of all interscholastic athletes) to three million (44 percent.) In colleges, it grew from 29,977 (15 percent of all inter-collegiate athletes) to 193,232 (43 percent). . . . Here's the problem: 43 percent is not equality—especially when 57 percent of the undergraduates are women."

They could be situated in shop premises or in sympathetic venues, such as art centers. These ventures aimed to "provide the space and physical focus [for women] to expand in a personal and political way." As independent, women-run spaces, this sometimes necessitated learning traditionally "male" skills, such as plumbing and electricity.[20]

For those outside and even for those inside the movement, the organization of the British Women's Liberation Movement could have appeared "shambolic at times, but by god we got things done."[21] Like other social movements, the bulk of the organizing often fell upon the shoulders of a few committed individuals, which could lead to frustration and desperation. The movement nonetheless provided women with a unique context to act on their own authority and reinvent their lives.

The same balance of national and localized activism was found in feminist movements throughout Europe and in the US. For example, in Sweden, the Stockholm-based Group 8 was founded in 1968 and championed issues of the workplace—such as pay and childcare—and lobbied against pornography. Their work was recognized at a national level through major exhibitions such as *Women in the Modern Museum*, and also through the work of women across the country to promote access to work, childcare, and education. In France, groups emerged from the Mouvement de libération des femmes (MLF) to focus on specific issues at both a regional and a national level, while in Italy various groups originated in different regional contexts throughout the early 1970s, some of which became part of wider (inter)national networks such as the Wages for Housework campaign.[22] In West Germany, the feminist movement was fragmented as it sprang from the student lobby and formed a loose coalition under the umbrella Deutsche Frauenrat (German Women's Council), with frictions developing between it and other factions in the movement, from the Berlin Women's Center to the Lesbian Action Center.

Despite having strong central lobbying bodies such as NOW and feminist "stars"—including Gloria Steinem, Bella Abzug, and Betty Friedan—the US women's movement throughout the 1970s spawned a number of state and regional groups that worked at the grassroots to empower women and change lives. From the East Coast to the West

Above: The Mouvement de libération des femmes (MLF) brought French women together to protest a range of issues from work-related rights to reproductive healthcare. These MLF activists are showing solidarity with International Women's Day on March 8, 1981.

Above left: This 1979 Danish poster urges "women to know their own being." A key goal of women's groups and centers was to create a women-only space where women could explore intimate or personal issues safely.

Above right: This German SPD poster invites women to come to discuss women's liberation. The Socialist Party in Germany (and, indeed, socialist movements in other countries) provided an initial platform for women to come together politically.

Opposite: The Liberation School for Women was run by the Chicago Women's Graphic Collective, which designed this poster in 1972. 348-2011 was the number to ring with any inquiries. The school offered "three sessions each year to help [women] learn, develop skills, and work together."

Below: Members of the Union County NOW chapter march on the Atlantic City boardwalk in September 1974, holding their national convention while the Miss America pageant was once again staged at the same location. This photo is a reminder that men served as important members and supporters of NOW.

Coast, women formed day centers and childcare cooperatives and offered advice on issues from abortion to the workplace. Many of these groups sprang up spontaneously in reaction to the momentum of the movement or specific local events. They were often independent from any form of national infrastructure and would reach out to other local organizations to create their own alliances, whereas others were "chapters" of NOW in towns from Columbus to San Francisco. These chapters were encouraged to embrace what "your NOW" meant by focusing on local issues, although in many cases these would then inform the lobbying platform at a national level.

From lobbying to legislation

In the US, by 1966, feminists were using the court system to push for equality on every front from job opportunity to birth control. Their campaigning wrought some notable successes. In 1965, the US Supreme Court, in *Griswold v. Connecticut*, ruled that a state law banning contraceptives violated a woman's right to privacy. Connecticut's law had been unusually severe, prohibiting a private physician from prescribing the oral birth control pill to a married couple. This set the stage for reforming abortion rights under the "right to privacy." In 1966, a federal court decision, in *White v. Crook*, found that the exclusion of women from juries violated the 14th Amendment, which supposedly granted women equal rights protections—Alabama had been one of the last US states to ban women from jury duty. In *Reed v. Reed* (1971), a case argued in part by future justice Ruth Bader Ginsburg (then a young lawyer for ACLU), the Supreme Court overturned an Idaho law that automatically made men the executors of estates. This was just one of many legal changes slowly giving women greater authority over their own money—whether as workers, inheritors, or consumers. But 1971 also saw a spectacular loss for American women, as President Nixon vetoed the Comprehensive Child Care Act. Twelve million working

International Women's Year

The first International Women's Year was declared in 1975.

The first National Women's Day was celebrated in America on February 28, 1909. The following year, a conference of over a hundred women from seventeen different countries approved the concept of International Women's Day (IWD). After these early beginnings, IWD, now observed on March 8, was adopted across the world. In December 1972, the United Nations General Assembly declared that 1975 would be International Women's Year and that the decade following through to 1985 would be the United Nations' Decade for Women. As part of International Women's Year, the first UN Conference on Women was held in Mexico City, and countries across the world issued stamps, posters, badges, and declarations of support. Leading on from the conference, the United Nations Development Fund for Women (UNIFEM) was established, the World Congress of Women was held in East Berlin the same year, and in 1976, the International Tribunal on Crimes against Women took place in Brussels. These events proved a powerful force in bringing together networks of women from across the globe to lobby for real change in women's status and their everyday lives.

ዓለም አቀፍ የሴቶች ዓመት ፲፱፻፸፯—፲ክ

Development

ኢትዮጵያ

International Women's Year 1975

ETHIOPIA 50c

ABIYE MEKONNEN

10c INTERNATIONAL WOMEN'S YEAR 1975

SINGAPORE EQUALITY

1975

WHY NOT!

INTERNATIONAL WOMEN'S YEAR

Opposite page and this page: Countries throughout the world produced stamps and badges in celebration of International Women's Year, often with artwork demonstrating the role women played in their national heritage or in present-day society.

4c Swaziland

International Women's Year National Symbol

In Swaziland, "Phezu kwemkhono-on we go"

3·20

1975

JUGOSLAVIJA

A. MILENKOVIĆ   HARRISON & SONS LTD

1975

НРБЪЛГАРИЯ-ПОЩА

МЕЖДУНАРОДНА ГОДИНА НА ЖЕНАТА

cm 13

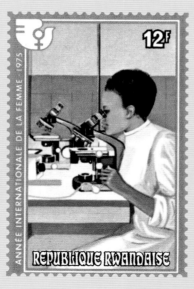

12F

ANNÉE INTERNATIONALE DE LA FEMME 1975

REPUBLIQUE RWANDAISE

8F

ANNÉE INTERNATIONALE DE LA FEMME 1975

REPUBLIQUE RWANDAISE

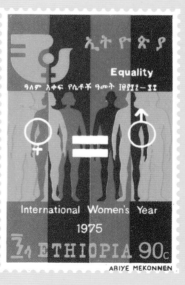

ኢትዮጵያ

Equality

ዓለም አቀፍ የሴቶች ዓመት ፲፱፻፸፯—፲ክ

International Women's Year 1975

♀ = ♂

ETHIOPIA 90c

ABIYE MEKONNEN

日本郵便 NIPPON

20 1975 国際婦人年

IWY 5c

QUEEN LABOTSIBENI-GRANDMOTHER OF HIS MAJESTY KING SOBHUZA II

SWAZILAND

LANDSKVINDER TIL ♀-KONFERENCE NAIROBI

1985

DEUTSCHE BUNDESPOST ANNETTE KOLB 1875–1967

30

DEUTSCHE BUNDESPOST ELSE LASKER-SCHÜLER 1869–1945

50

DEUTSCHE BUNDESPOST GERTRUD VON LE FORT 1876–1971

70

DEUTSCHE BUNDESPOST RICARDA HUCH 1864–1947

40

mothers saw a bill that would have funded day care for preschoolers go down in defeat; but Nixon's staunch anti-Communism informed his insistence that day care was a socialist practice and, therefore, un-American. Nevertheless, legislative reform carried on, and 1972 saw the passage of Title IX of the Education Amendments, banning sex discrimination in federally funded educational institutions, and the extension of the 1963 Equal Pay Act. Then, momentously, in 1973, *Roe v. Wade* granted women the right to a legal abortion. Also that year, a bill submitted by Congresswoman Bella Abzug became Public Law 93-392, officially making August 26 "Women's Equality Day." Abzug had led the battle to ban discrimination in credit on the basis of sex or marital status, as up to that point, married women could not receive or use a credit card in their own name.

Arguably, in the US the culmination of all this reform was the idea for one central piece of legislation. Feminists began to ask, considering the slow law-by-law approach to legal reform and the limits of falling back on the 14th Amendment or Title IX: Why not ratify one giant constitutional amendment guaranteeing women equal rights? Where their sister-ancestors had thrown their energy behind suffrage, hoping that women could gain political power and equality through the vote, millions of twentieth-century American feminists put their faith and activism behind ratifying the Equal Rights Amendment (ERA) to the US Constitution. First introduced to Congress by National Woman's Party leader Alice Paul in December 1923, the ERA initially stated that "men and women shall have equal rights throughout the United States and every place subject to its jurisdiction." This bill languished in Congress for almost half a century, passed by the Senate but not by the House of Representatives (it was the Republican Party that first endorsed the ERA in 1940, followed by the Democrats in 1944 and a presidential endorsement from Truman in 1945). Then, after reintroduction in 1970 and 1972, Congress passed the newly worded amendment, which now read, "Equality of rights under the law shall not be denied or abridged by the United States or by any state on account of

Far left: A march for the passage of the Equal Rights Amendment, held on International Women's Day in 1977. Frustrated that the US Constitution still had no guarantee of women's equal rights under the law, and that states were slow in ratifying an amendment first introduced by suffragist Alice Paul in 1923, this protester reminds onlookers that women's progress was not as promising as the glib ad slogan ("You've Come a Long Way, Baby") from Virginia Slims cigarettes.

Left: Few conservative opponents of the Equal Rights Amendment were as tirelessly active as STOP ERA's Phyllis Schlafly. Here she addresses a rally at the Illinois State Capitol rotunda in 1978. Illinois was one of a handful of states feminists hoped would add up to the thirty-eight-state/three-fifths majority necessary to ratify the ERA. The ERA died after only gaining ratification by thirty-five states, despite an impressive fasting sit-in at the Illinois capitol led by ex-Mormon feminist Sonia Johnson.

sex." Representatives from six states ratified the ERA within the next two days (Hawaii was first), with a total of thirty-one states passing the legislation by late 1973. But only thirty-five of a necessary thirty-eight states (the mandated three-fifths majority) would ratify by the 1978 deadline. In the last years of the 1970s, when anti-ERA rallies proliferated, feminists fumed, protested, canvassed, boycotted non-ratifying states, and managed to extend the deadline for a thirty-eighth state ratification to 1982. They pinned their hopes on the three final states most likely to ratify: Florida, Illinois, and North Carolina.

> "From the moment I realized that I was going too fast, I knew it would be wildly misunderstood. . . . It was being undertaken by women, after all, and everything women do partakes of our low status. All our acts are devalued simply because we do them; all our strengths are automatically turned into weaknesses. . . . And though women have for centuries been programmed to be courageous in defense of men's happiness, to bear anything for men, we have been taught to look upon such courage on our own behalf as selfish, immature, and—especially—as ridiculous."
>
> **Sonia Johnson**, *Going Out of Our Minds*, 1987

Their hopes were buoyed by enthusiastic bipartisan support. President Ford signed legislature declaring 1975 to be International Women's Year, with a first UN World Conference on Women held in Mexico City (followed by another in Copenhagen in 1980 and a third in Nairobi, Kenya, in 1985). White House support for the passage of the ERA also came from past and present First Ladies Betty Ford, Lady Bird Johnson, and Rosalynn Carter, advocates who not only talked the talk but walked the walk by attending the Houston National Women's Conference of 1977, which drew over twenty thousand participants.

But American feminists had a powerful foe in Phyllis Schlafly, a conservative housewife turned activist lawyer whose STOP ERA campaign was underwritten by her well-funded Eagle Forum. Schlafly ironically benefited from feminism in her enshrinement as a counterpoint figure, popular on talk shows and at conservative women's conferences; her supporters emerged as powerful anti-feminists, replicating in some ways the suffragists who once debated opponents known as "antis." Schlafly's arguments mobilized millions of conservative women and men to fret that the ERA would draft women, force shared bathrooms, and vacate any legal protections or privileges based on sex difference, such as support for widows and pregnant women. Calling the ERA a Communist plot, both Schlafly and the right-wing John Birch Society began opposing the amendment in 1974, challenging the extension of the deadline and pressuring the Republican Party to drop its support for the ERA altogether. It did so in 1980. Along with another conservative writer, Marabel Morgan, whose books *Total Woman* and *Total Joy* urged wives to submit to their husbands, Schlafly referred to feminists as "femlib fanatics" in her book *The Power of the Positive Woman*. Their critiques portrayed feminists as selfish and self-interested rather than being available to husbands and children. Cultural references to the 1970s as the "Me Decade" further stigmatized women's quest for political and personal liberation as a self-centered crusade.

The role of American churches in condemning the ERA led to actual excommunication of the law's supporters by leaders in the (Mormon) Church of Latter-Day Saints. Former Mormon housewife Sonia Johnson, excommunicated in 1979 for her support of the ERA, later led a thirty-seven-day fast for state ratification in the Illinois state house. In her memoir *Going Out of Our Minds*, she recalls that while many politicians admired *male* dissidents who were fasting for freedom under Communism, like Anatoly Shcharansky, they jeered at American women fasting for equality.

The ERA failed to gain ratification, and Schlafly's supporters joined with religious lobby groups that gained enormous latitude after the 1980 election of Ronald Reagan. Although many traditional conservatives believed in limited government, the Moral Majority, founded by Reverend Jerry Falwell, sought to halt feminist gains via legislation that would install "traditional family values." The Family Protection Act, the Human Life Amendment, and other proposed bills sought to limit abortion rights, gay and lesbian rights, and other personal/private choices for women (and men). And in an era that saw the rise of women's studies programs at many universities, conservative husband and wife team Mel and Norma Gabler established the nonprofit Educational Research Analysts, investigating "secular humanism" in textbooks, gaining public support, and influencing the Texas textbook-approval process by lobbying for limits on feminist content (up to and including images of women working outside the home or any nontraditional families).

Televangelists and radio hosts were able to spread ugly stereotypes about feminists to millions of listeners; Pat Robertson, the popular TV preacher who presided over religious talk show *The 700 Club*, famously warned families that "the feminist agenda is not about equal rights for women. It is about a socialist, anti-family political movement that encourages women to leave their husbands, kill their children, practice witchcraft, destroy capitalism, and become lesbians." Equality, opponents of feminism warned, was not godly. The rising tide of conservative power throughout the 1980s eventually inspired feminist writer Susan Faludi to publish a best-selling book simply entitled *Backlash* in 1991.

Legislative reform was certainly not restricted to America, and women lobbied on a variety of platforms on an international scale. In France, the Bobigny trial saw legislation surrounding rape and abortion enter the realm of public discussion and laid the groundwork for the abortion legislation of 1975. In Italy, family law reform saw divorce legalized in the early 1970s and changes to maternity law in 1971.[23] Iceland passed its Equal Pay Act in 1961, granted women a nationwide "day off" on October 24, 1975, and established the Gender Equality Act and Gender Equality Council in 1976. Denmark passed legislation prohibiting workplace sex discrimination with the Equal Pay Act in 1976, followed by the Equal Treatment Act in 1978; other Scandinavian countries followed suit shortly afterward.

The 1960s and '70s also saw women being granted suffrage, albeit with restrictions. Women in Iran gained the right to vote in 1963, Jordan gave women the vote in 1973, and Nigerian women got the vote in 1977.

From the 1960s through to the 1980s, the world witnessed a movement of women organizing for the clear purpose of liberating themselves from a society that they felt didn't understand their personal and political aims—that in some, indeed many, cases didn't speak for them or even recognize them as individuals. Women's structure and strategy, political agenda and approach differed widely, even wildly, but the motivation was equally passionate across the globe. It was this burning determination to be seen and heard that would give rise to a new culture, seeking to reclaim and reinvent the portrayal of women in all spheres of life and work.

Below left: This quirky French poster proudly proclaims that now, in 1965, "Women are equal to men" because they can open a line of credit with a bank.

Below right: International Women's Day inspired numerous posters in celebration of women's global solidarity. This one was designed by the Chicago Women's Graphic Collective in 1972.

Right: International Women's Day on March 8 is often celebrated visually, with designers and artists championing the cultural diversity of women across the world. This poster was reprinted by the Chicago Women's Graphic Collective from a Cuban artwork.

MARZO 8   MARCH 8th   MARZO 8   MARCH 8th

DIA INTERNACIONAL DE LA MUJER
INTERNATIONAL WOMEN'S DAY

Reprint from a Cuban poster, Women's Graphics Collective, Chicago Womens Liberation Union, www.cwluherstory.org

BLACK SISTERHOOD

Civil rights and liberation

3

In the 1970s, women of color began to define a feminist voice
that spoke for their individual experiences and concerns.

For many women of color identifying as African American, Afro-Caribbean, Latina, Asian, Native American, Third World, or First Nations in the US, there seemed little point or liberation in joining a feminist sisterhood that did not address racism as a structure of oppression.

Those who worked as domestic servants in white women's homes, whose ancestors had been owned by white women, and who had never enjoyed the privileges or expectations of white femininity were far more likely to identify with the men and the issues of their own ethnic communities. Moreover, some white feminist theorists were outspoken in their criticism of the family and religion—two institutions that had sustained black women as community support networks and in which they had visibility, agency, and influence.[1]

There were other, more specific points of cultural alienation at the time. For example, in the US some middle-class white feminists preferred wearing denim farm overalls, which many black women from the South associated with oppressive legacies of sharecropping poverty. Elsewhere, white feminist critique of beauty products and parlors seemed strange to some black women, who had long found camaraderie and identity through neighborhood beauty salons, partly because white stylists often refused to cut black hair. White department stores also often blocked black customers from trying on new fashions or experimenting with the latest makeup or fragrances. Perhaps the greatest discordance between white and black feminist politics was the different framing of the beauty contest. While white feminists in America and

Page 58: This image is taken from the "Black Woman's Manifesto," which was published in 1970 (see page 67).

Opposite: A women's liberation contingent marching in support of the Black Panther Party, New Haven, Connecticut, November 1969. Another reminder of intersectionality in the women's movement of the late 1960s, this banner also was carried by black feminists through the streets of a very racially divided Connecticut— a state notorious for "restrictive covenants" in home ownership and memberships in towns like Darien, effectively preventing both black and Jewish residency. Connecticut's real estate racism was later explored in the book *Sundown Towns* by James Loewen.

Right: This 1971 Monica Sjöö poster proclaims the rallying cry "Sisterhood Is Powerful!"

SISTERHOOD IS POWERFUL!

ANGELA DAVIS

Above left: The Third World Women's Alliance at the Women's Equality Day demonstration in New York City, August 26, 1970. This revolutionary organization of women of color, formed in 1970, joined together Puerto Rican women activists and members of the Black Women's Alliance.

Above right: Today's Black Lives Matter movement, protesting police violence toward African Americans, draws upon decades of frustration and activism. In this 1976 demonstration, black women made clear that ending police brutality was already a top community concern.

Britain denounced such events as demeaning to women, in the early 1960s, Claudia Jones, the Trinidad-born journalist and activist deported from the US to Britain in the 1950s for being a Communist, organized all-black beauty pageants in London to "show black people that they were beautiful and, more importantly, were 'allowed' to be beautiful."[2] Hair was a particular point of cultural dissonance: some schools in the US required black women to straighten their hair, forcing a white-assimilationist femininity that writer Alice Walker mocked in her 1976 novel *Meridian* (describing undergraduate life at the historically black liberal arts Spelman College in Atlanta, Georgia). Some national hotel and service chains that did employ women of color forbade cornrowed hair and dreadlocks. For all of these reasons, Angela Davis, with her iconic Afro, became a symbol of radical resistance to white standards. And although many white women had worked side by side with black women in the civil rights struggle, shared street activism was not equivalent to growing up breaking bread together in homes, churches, and school cafeterias. The legacy of social segregation in American history meant that black and white women were far more likely to encounter one another through the unequal roles of the service worker and the served. And, finally, white feminists' seemingly progressive rhetoric about rights for *women and minorities* disappeared and divided those who occupied both identities. For these and many other reasons, black women's specific experiences and struggles were often not visible in the 1960s, '70s, and '80s, as the media only grudgingly featured even those events specific to black male power or white feminist imagery.

In America, black feminists walked a fine line between supporting their black brothers and also calling men out for unacceptably sexist practices. In autonomous groups,

The first OWAAD conference

D-M Withers

In March 1979, the Black Women's Movement in Britain came together in an incredible demonstration of solidarity.

"Today is a historical day, the first time, as black women we come together to sit and discuss things that oppress us as women, to exchange ideas, and to contribute our experiences."[3] These were the introductory remarks spoken at the first conference organized by the originally titled Organisation for Women of Africa and African Descent (OWAAD) on Sunday, March 18, 1979, at the Abeng Centre in Brixton, London. (The group's name went on to become the Organisation for Women of Asian and African Descent.)

The conference energized, organized, and connected the Black Women's Movement in Britain on an unprecedented scale. "Nearly 300 black women got together from places as far afield as Birmingham, Brighton, Leeds, Coventry, Manchester, Sheffield, Bristol and London to discuss some of the many issues which concern us because we are black, female, working class or all three."[4] Women involved in Zimbabwe's national liberation movements also attended, locating black women's activism in internationalist struggles.

The first OWAAD conference was held in the shadow of ongoing debates about British citizenship. During the late 1970s, new citizenship and nationality laws were proposed that would further tighten immigration control. The 1981 Immigration and Nationality Act redrew the rights of residency for many passport holders from the former British colonies who had previously been welcomed to Britain to bolster labor shortages in the aftermath of World War II. Devising strategies to resist increasingly restrictive immigration laws was therefore a priority at the conference.

It was also an occasion to share information and political theory about specific issues, such as the relationship between imperialism and capitalism. These perspectives grounded the British Black Women's Movement in a wider historical struggle, a struggle in which "we are militant. We have been militant and we will continue to be militant. This potential, and militancy,

didn't develop with our immigration to Britain, but is part and parcel of our historical experience of resistance under slavery, under colonialism and under neo-colonialism."[5]

Other papers discussed specific campaigns within the black community, such as resistance to police brutality in the form of "Stop and Search" (SUS) laws that disproportionately targeted young black men. Health was another key area, from the sterilization of black women in Britain and the Third World to the lack of adequate National Health Service (NHS) healthcare for black communities.

In the 1970s, black children were routinely labeled "educationally sub-normal" by Britain's racist education system and placed in disruptive units as a form of punishment and social control. "The only way forward is for black women to become totally involved in our children's education," one activist proposed, "not just our individual child, but the education of all black children."[6] Many activists established supplementary schools to ensure their children were properly educated, or championed black studies to ensure a more balanced education.

Alongside political papers, performance poetry was met with rapturous laughter and applause. There was food and childcare, facilitated by male allies, while "Black Woman" by Judy Mowatt played constantly in the background.

An important legacy of the conference was the publication of *FOWAAD!*, the OWAAD newsletter, which aspired to become "the genuine mouthpiece of black women in Britain."[7]

In the letters section, attendees offered their feelings about the conference: "[I] really felt high after the conference, and after attending the London call-back meeting, I decided to join the Newsletter committee, in order to be able to voice a few of my views as regards our appearance as Black women."[8]

> **"I don't think until then we realised our own strength, our own pulling power."**
> **Stella Dadzie**, "The Heart of the Race Oral Histories," Black Cultural Archives, 2008

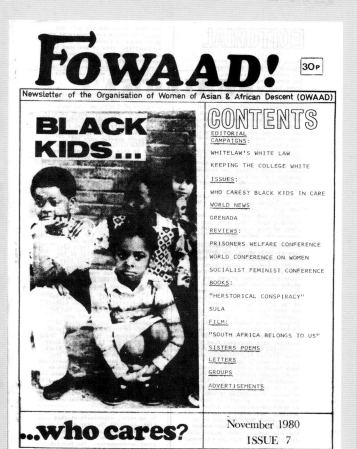

Above left: *FOWAAD!* was the newsletter produced by OWAAD in order to facilitate the growth of the Black Women's Movement in Britain. It featured articles, campaign news, letters, and poetry.

Above right: OWAAD held four national conferences between 1979 and 1982. This poster promotes the second conference in 1980, which carried the theme "Black Women Fighting Back!"

Other women offered feedback on how the conference was organized: "I just felt frustrated that there was no time for the most important items—the workshops and discussions for further action. I think people only learn through discussion."[9]

The first OWAAD conference was a catalytic event that inspired many new black women's groups to form, such as the East London Black Women's Organisation and the North Paddington Black Women's Group.

For those who attended, the significance of the conference was enduring, as OWAAD founder Stella Dadzie elaborates:

For us it was such a high to see so many black women under one roof, none of us had seen that before. In our own groups there must [have] been 10, maximum fifteen people at any one time, if that. But to see what must have been over 100 women converge from all over the country, some of whom were completely gobsmacked, some of them were like the only black woman in their village, it was just a real high and an achievement, it was a very empowering experience.[10]

collectives, publications, and protests, activists developed the main points for defining black women's liberation:

- women would never unite as a group unless all feminists acknowledged and worked to overcome systemic racism and classism;
- black women had always worked outside the home and were not impressed by a movement that equated wage work with liberation;
- as family providers who also were expected to lend political and intimate support to frustrated male partners in struggle, black women continued to be attacked and stereotyped as strident matriarchs by both white and black men;
- while false accusations of black-on-white rape had historically driven the lynching of black males, neither white nor black male sexual violence against black women had seen serious consideration in the US courts of justice, and black women in the prison system continued to be raped by white guards;
- while constantly defending their black brothers, black women nonetheless experienced patriarchy in their own communities and church rhetoric, yet were expected to remain silent rather than expressing criticism of their own men where whites might see and hear it.

Similarly, an independent Black Women's Movement emerged in Britain in the early 1970s, parallel to and distinct from the white-dominated Women's Liberation Movement.[11] Women-only caucuses met within the Black Power movement and, from early on, activists used a socialist-influenced intersectional analysis to understand their experiences.

In the words of the Brixton Black Women's Group, black women needed to create independent groups because "there was rampant racism in the Women's Liberation Movement and no space in which to discuss it. And there was rampant sexism and marginalization of women's issues in the Black Liberation Movement."[12]

In Britain, Asian women from the Indian subcontinent and Afro-Caribbean women largely organized under the moniker "black." Separate groups, such as Awaz and Southall Black Sisters, were, however, established in order to address issues that specifically affected Asian women. Jewish feminists had been active in the women's liberation movements in Britain since the 1970s but became increasingly visible in the wake of debates about the 1982 Israel-Lebanon war. Among Left movements in

Britain there had been widespread condemnation of Israel's decision to invade Lebanon, but this was expressed in ways Jewish feminists and their allies perceived to be anti-Semitic. *Spare Rib*'s controversial article "Women to Speak Out against Zionism" ignited fractious exchanges about Zionism, anti-Zionism, Jewish identity, and feminist politics that would stretch into the 1990s.[13]

In the 1970s, many radical black men and women perceived feminism as a movement for white middle-class women dominated by man-haters, irrelevant to black women and the political interests of revolutionary black struggle.

The sexism of black men was, however, challenged in Michele Wallace's 1976 book *Black Macho and the Myth of the Superwoman*, which daringly explored oppressive practices within the black community. Wallace later recalled, "I had indiscreetly blurted out that sexism and misogyny were near epidemic in the community and that black feminism had the cure. I went from obscurity to celebrity to notoriety overnight. At twenty-six I had written the book from hell."[14]

The interests of Asian, Latina, and Native American women also rarely were given space in the anti-colonialist writings of radical men, other than to merit praise as mothers of revolutionary sons. Latina feminists, whose cultural roots as immigrants, Chicanas, Tejanas, Afro-Cuban exiles, or Puerto Ricans differed widely, contended with a strong Catholic culture in which birth control, abortion, and homosexuality were strongly condemned.

In the US, Native American women had often experienced sterilization without consent or adoption of their babies by whites during their interactions with white social services, an extension of far-too-familiar genocide in their communities. And where Asian women were present in the media of the 1970s, the roles offered to them in television and film were often limited to servant, war victim, or sexual slave. These tropes were evident in otherwise "progressive" American programs such as *The Courtship of Eddie's Father* and *M*A*S*H* (years later, comedian Margaret Cho would complain that she hadn't studied theater for twelve years just to look terrified and shout, "Rambo! No!"). The passivity ascribed to Asian and Native American women, shown submitting to occupation and colonization in televised roles, was a contrast to the armed, threatening "superbad chick" image of Pam Grier and other black actresses in 1970s films such as *Foxy*

"Black women suffer in three ways!
1. We are poor.
2. We are Black.
3. We are women."
Black Women's Action Committee, 1970

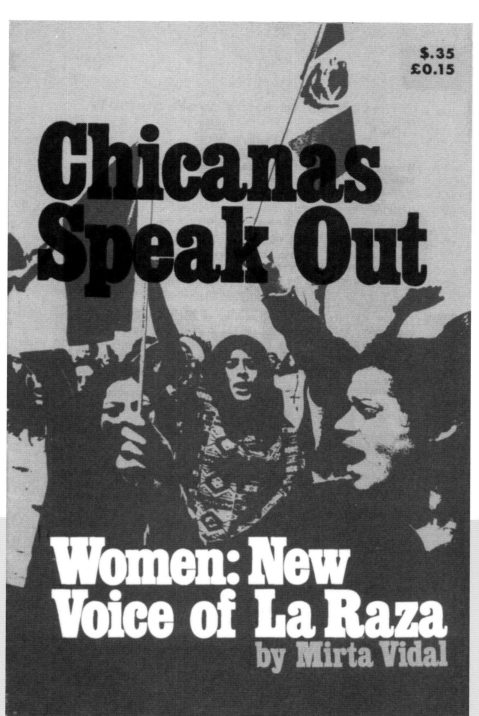

Above: Chicana or Mexican American women had concerns both separate from and overlapping with the issues highlighted by black and white feminists. The term *La Raza*, or The Race, emphasized identification as an ethnic minority population having roots both in the US and in Mexico. This book was first published in 1971.

Top right: The "Black Woman's Manifesto" pamphlet was distributed by the Third World Women's Alliance in 1970 and cosigned by Frances Beale, Linda La Rue, Gayle Lynch, Eleanor Holmes Norton (who became Washington, D.C.'s nonvoting congresswoman), and Maxine Williams. The manifesto addressed specific oppressions against black women.

Bottom right: This 1971 first issue of the Third World Women's Alliance publication *Triple Jeopardy* shows women enacting the armed militancy advocated by men in the Black Power and Young Lords (Puerto Rican) movements. Particularly unique is the assault rifle held by the familiar raised fist of the women's symbol in the upper right corner—a departure from pacifist feminism.

"Yes, I was there & I'm still moving": womanist/feminist writers of color

Bonnie J. Morris

The first thing you do is to forget that i'm Black.
Second, you must never forget that i'm black.[15]

Pat Parker, "For the white person who wants to know how to be my friend"

In poetry and prose, plays, and open mic speakouts, black and brown women of all backgrounds constructed a visibility of their own during second-wave feminism. Their writings and words spoke to how both race and gender (and often class, too) shaped the realities of their lives and the women they knew in struggle. Couched in language specific to lived experiences, often tender in self-love as well as shocking in its revelations, this new literature drew on established traditions that white critics had long neglected: writings by Zora Neale Hurston in the 1930s, Gwendolyn Brooks in the 1940s, playwright Lorraine Hansberry in the 1950s, and the lyrics of freedom songwriters like Odetta and Bernice Johnson Reagon in the 1960s. By the early 1970s, a new wave of writing by black women novelists and theorists could be found in feminist bookstores and, eventually, in mainstream literary criticism.

Some of the most influential writers and titles of the 1970s and '80s included Maya Angelou (*I Know Why the Caged Bird Sings*), Angela Davis (*Women, Race, and Class*), bell hooks, who preferred her name to appear in lower case (*Ain't I a Woman: Black Women and Feminism*), Audre Lorde (*Zami, Sister Outsider*), Toni Morrison (*Beloved, The Bluest Eye*), Ntozake Shange (*For Colored Girls Who Have Considered Suicide / When the Rainbow Is Enuf*), Alice Walker (*Meridian, The Color Purple, In Search of Our Mothers' Gardens*), and the poets Cheryl Clarke, Nikki Giovanni, June Jordan, and Pat Parker. By the early 1980s, required reading in many women's studies courses included Walker's novel *The Color Purple* and two groundbreaking anthologies: *All the Women Are White, All the Blacks Are Men, but Some of Us Are Brave: Black Women's Studies*, edited by Gloria T. Hull, Patricia Bell Scott, and Barbara Smith; and *This Bridge Called My Back: Writings by Radical Women of Color*, edited by Cherríe Moraga and Gloria Anzaldúa.

Alice Walker, who became an editor at *Ms.*, expressed concern that the label "feminist" too often suggested a white middle-class woman whose issues and perspective were informed by a different set of experiences. In her own anthology *In Search of Our Mothers' Gardens*, Walker suggested that the word "womanist" more accurately defined black women who put their sisters' concerns at the center. She was not unique in this: Fran Beall suggested that "*feminism* just seemed to be dealing with the female aspect of your being."[16]

Walker's insistence on making female identities and priorities visible led to a later essay entitled "Becoming What We're Called," in which she gently scolded women who accepted or employed "you guys" as an all-inclusive term. Audre Lorde's essays "Poetry Is Not a Luxury," "The Master's Tools," and "The Uses of the Erotic" electrified readers who, in the 1980s, were newly discovering the range of lesbian expression in print.[17] And the appearance of *SAGE: A Scholarly Journal for Black Women* (1983) ushered in a new era of scholarship as universities (not always happily) debated the place of diverse voices in the academic canon.

Ranging from scholarly treatises to performance art, black feminist works constituted a diverse platform of their own, but for women of color to occupy equal time at radical feminist events, white women had to learn when and how to sit down and listen—as well as how to share structural power as organizers. Individual black artists and authors were often frustrated by their tokenism in white feminist spaces such as women's studies classrooms, bookstore readings, academic conferences, and women's music festivals. Alice Walker, Audre Lorde, and Pat Parker were sought after as headliners for conferences otherwise dominated by white feminists, but black women were not always included/invited to be part of the planning for such events. As one reviewer described a feminist

> "It is necessary to remember that it is first the potential oppressor within that we must resist—the potential victim within that we must rescue—otherwise we cannot hope for an end to domination, for liberation."
>
> **bell hooks**, *Talking Back: Thinking Feminist, Thinking Black*, 1989

"**Womanist. 1.** From *womanish*. (Opp. of 'girlish,' i.e., frivolous, irresponsible, not serious.) A black feminist or feminist of color. From the black folk expression of mothers to female children, 'You acting womanish,' i.e., like a woman. . . .
2. *Also*: A woman who loves other women, sexually and/or nonsexually. Appreciates and prefers women's culture. . . . Traditionally capable, as in: 'Mama, I'm walking to Canada and I'm taking you and a bunch of other slaves with me.' Reply: 'It wouldn't be the first time.'"

Alice Walker, "Womanist," 1983

Above left: Writer Maya Angelou (*I Know Why the Caged Bird Sings*) with Gloria Steinem, marching together in Washingon, D.C., for Women's Equality Day, 1983.

Above right: Audre Lorde, Caribbean American writer, poet, and activist, teaching students at the Atlantic Center for the Arts in New Myrna Beach, Florida, 1983. Out as a lesbian, with her "biomythography" memoir *Zami: A New Spelling of My Name* selling in women's bookstores throughout the US, Lorde was also Master Artist in Residence in central Florida's arts center that year.

conference on race and ethnicity that met on a majority-white college campus in the late 1980s, "Many women speaking during the open-mike [sic] session harshly criticized the conference for the lack of women of color attending and presenting papers; for its academic, intellectual approach to racism; for the absence of action-planning or coalition-building sessions, and for its showcasing of well-known feminists of color for the benefit of white women." In this case the well-known feminist of color who gave a key address was Audre Lorde; soon afterward, plans began for a conference centered on Lorde's writing that would admit white women only by application. Called "I Am Your Sister," the Audre Lorde conference was unique in requiring interested white participants to submit a résumé detailing proven activism in

coalition with nonwhite women. Here the argument was that more affluent white women had the ability to register for conferences and performances as soon as they were announced, usually leading to tickets being sold out before working-class women of color were able to fundraise for their own travel, housing, and participation. Confrontation, as well as coalition-building, would continue into the 1990s and beyond. From the outset, feminist bookstores were also conscious of the imperative to offer a diverse range of writers and poets in order to ensure that all voices within the wide range of women's movements were heard. It was Pat Parker who contributed the phrase "Your silence will not protect you," a slogan that became visible throughout the burgeoning LGBT movement.

SELF-PROTECTION

* Do not accept rides from strangers.

* Do not get into unlicensed cab services or cabs with 2 people in the driver's seat.

* Lock your car doors at all times. Check back seat before entering.

* Lock your house door at all times, make sure all windows are locked.

* Vary your route to and from home. Stay on well-lighted main streets. Avoid side streets and alleys.

* Travel in pairs or groups.

* Learn some simple self-defense like how to get out of a hold or how to use available objects as weapons: comb, keys, hair brush, lighted cigarette, edge of books, whistles, salt, red/black pepper.

* Always have your keys ready in your hand as you enter your house.

* Let someone know where you are at all times and your planned route. Phone ahead to your destination.

* Get to know your neighbors on your street. Keep an eye out for each other. Make an effort.

* If you hear someone in distress, don't ignore it. If you can't safely investigate, call 911.

* Call your local hotline number at 445-1111 if you need to talk or if you have information.

* If you feel like you are being followed... check first—change directions, then REACT. Stay calm, change your pace, cross street, walk next to curb or in middle of street against the traffic...DO NOT GO HOME, the attacker will follow...run to the nearest lighted place.

* Yell FIRE! if someone is attacking you, people are more likely to come to your aid, than if you call "Help".

* Encourage your friends to take these precautions.

[handwritten] Wear shoes and clothes you can easily run in.

This pamphlet can be reproduced without permission.

RESOURCES

Weekly neighborhood meetings organizing against the recent murders.

CRISIS
HARRIET TUBMAN HOUSE
7:00 TUESDAY EVENING
566 Columbus Ave.
Boston (South End)
536-8610

ASWALOS HOUSE
7:00 WEDNESDAY EVENING
246 Seaver St.
Roxbury
442-9645 or 442-9646

COOPER COMMUNITY CENT.
7:00 THURSDAY EVENING
1891 Washington St.
Lower Roxbury
445-1813

Community organizations providing services in connection with the recent violence.

WOMEN INC. 442-6166
(Forming a network & information clearing house for all the groups working on the recent murders.)

COMMUNITY PROGRAMS AGAINST SEXUAL ASSAULT (C.P.A.S.A.) 442-9603
(Services for preventing rape, support for women who have been assaulted.)

DORCHESTER GREENLIGHT PROGRAM 427-4910
(Building a safe-house network where women can go to designated houses in danger on the streets.)

BLACKSTONE COMMUNITY SCHOOL 262-2190
(Classes in self-defense.)

HOTLINE: ROXBURY MULTI-SERVICE CTR. 445-1111

[handwritten] Jamaica Plain Phone Chain and Greenlight Program 522-8644

Other organizations working against & providing services for violence against women.

CASA MYRNA VAZQUEZ 262-9581
(Temporary shelter for women and their children in crisis.)

TRANSITION HOUSE 661-7203 24 hour#
(Temporary shelter for battered women and their children.)

ELIZABETH STONE HOUSE 522-3417
(Temporary refuge for women in emotional crisis.)

[handwritten] Domestic Violence and Technical Assistance Project 266-43055 (South End) (Provides information concerning domestic violence and violence against women)

TAKE BACK THE NIGHT 492-0120
(Organizers of August 26, 1978 march against violence against women. Another march is in the planning stages.)

AASC: ALLIANCE AGAINST SEXUAL COERCION 482-0329
(Information and services for women who are sexually harassed at the workplace.)

JAMAICA PLAIN BATTERED WOMEN'S TASK FORCE 524-9206 9AM to 1PM Monday Thru Friday
(Assistance for battered women.)

WOMEN INC 442-6166
(Residential drug program for women and their children.)

BOSTON AREA RAPE CRISIS CENTER 492-RAPE
(Information, counselling, support services.)

WAVAW: WOMEN AGAINST VIOLENCE AGAINST WOMEN H/O The Cambridge Women's Center 354-8807
(Organizing against pornography, violence in the media.)

EMERGE 267-7690
(Amen's counseling service on domestic violence.)

ELEVEN ~~SIX~~ BLACK WOMEN

8 ~~7~~ WHY DID THEY DIE?

—This pamphlet was prepared by the Combahee River Collective, a Boston Black Feminist Organization (c/o AASC, P.O. Box 1, Cambridge, MA. 02139). It was created for Third World women. If you are not a Third World woman, please read it and share it with Third World Women.

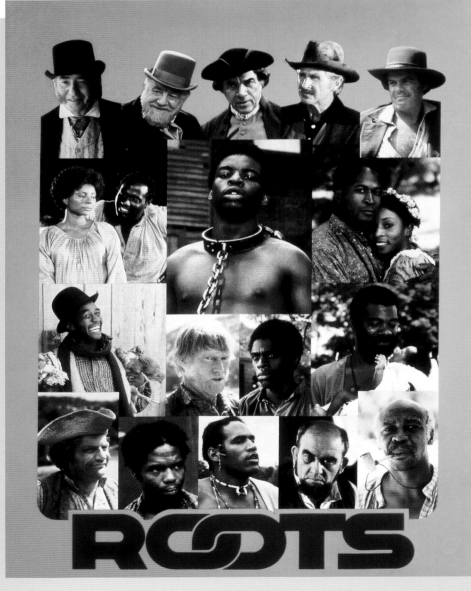

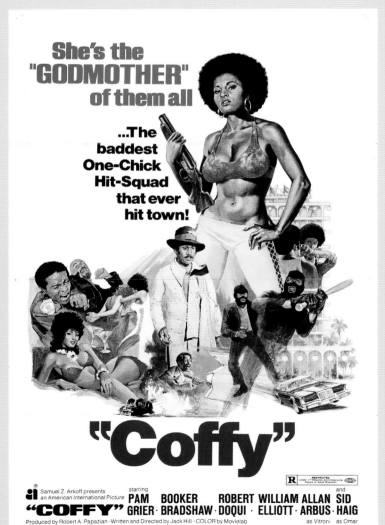

Opposite, top: The Combahee River Collective was a powerful voice in raising awareness of issues affecting black women. This pamphlet on self-protection against violence offers contacts for resources to support victims.

Opposite, bottom left: In the 1970s, Alex Haley's award-winning television miniseries *Roots* compelled millions of black and white Americans to confront the legacy of slavery in the US. Yet, as this poster suggests, the focus lay primarily on the black male experience; the specifically sexual slavery endured by black women was not at the core of the production.

Opposite, bottom right: *Coffy*, an example of what critics called the "blaxploitation" film genre of the early 1970s, made a star out of actress Pam Grier—but relied on the sexualized and violent images portrayed in this popular marquee poster.

Brown and *Coffy*. It was therefore a relief to both black and white feminists when new film works aimed at a mainstream audience offered authentic roles exploring black women's lives from slavery to civil rights, in projects such as *The Autobiography of Miss Jane Pittman* and the popular US miniseries *Roots*. Despite these cultural depictions coming into popular media, whether through schoolbooks or television, in the real world, few Americans saw images of groundbreaking black women like US Representative Patsy Mink (Hawaii), the first congresswoman of color, or Dolores Huerta, vice president of the United Farm Workers.

In the pages of new feminist writing, a constant debate was whether racism or sexism was most responsible for women's oppression, and where leaders invested in coalition-building should direct energy and resources. These conversations, whether onstage at conferences or in print, were some of feminism's most important debates. In her introduction to the best-selling 1970 anthology *Sisterhood Is Powerful*, editor Robin Morgan had this to say:

Black women, who are obviously doubly oppressed, have, for the most part, chosen to fight beside their black brothers, fighting racism as a priority oppression. But male chauvinism is rampant in the Black Liberation Movement. . . . *How*, we are asked, *can you talk about the comparatively insignificant oppression of women when set beside the issues of racism and imperialism?* This is a male-supremacist question. Not only because of its arrogance, but because of its ignorance. First, it dares to weigh and compute human suffering, and it places oppressed groups in competition with each other (an old, and very capitalistic, trick: divide and conquer). . . . It also seems obvious that half of all oppressed peoples, black, brown, and otherwise, are *women*, and that I, as a non-starving white American woman . . . must fight for those sisters to *survive* before we can even talk together as oppressed women.[18]

In response to this ongoing debate surrounding issues of racism and liberation were the narratives emerging from black feminist collectives, activists, radical theorists, and artists who were already a vital part of the women's movement, offering a new politics of identity while challenging white feminists to move beyond mere self-interest and sexual freedom. Articles ranged from Toni Morrison's August 1971 piece in the *New York Times Magazine*, "What the Black Woman Thinks about

Women's Lib," to the Combahee River Collective's famous statement offering one of the first clear definitions of intersectionality. The statement also offered a radical message of lesbian solidarity while rejecting white lesbian separatism as a solution or cultural practice:

We are actively committed to struggling against racial, sexual, heterosexual, and class oppression, and see as our particular task the development of integrated analysis and practice based upon the fact that the major systems of oppression are interlocking. . . . As Black women we see Black feminism as the logical political movement to combat the manifold and simultaneous oppressions that all women of color face. . . . Although we are feminists and Lesbians, we feel solidarity with progressive Black men and do not advocate the fractionalization that white women who are separatists demand. Our situation as Black people necessitates that we have solidarity around the fact of race, which white women of course do not need to have with white men. . . . We have a great deal of criticism and loathing for what men have been socialized to be in this society. . . . But we do not have the misguided notion that it is their maleness, *per se*—i.e., their biological maleness—that makes them what they are. As Black women, we find any type of biological determinism a particularly dangerous and reactionary basis upon which to build a politic.[19]

Building solidarity

In Britain, black women's groups were initially concentrated in large cities such as London, Manchester, Birmingham, and Liverpool, with later groups established in Cambridge, Sheffield, Edinburgh, and Wolverhampton. Organizing was grounded in local issues but often placed in an internationalist, anti-imperialist perspective, with activists inspired by national liberation struggles in Vietnam, South Africa, and Guinea-Bissau, within which black women took strong leadership roles. Concerns such as everyday survival, health, housing, education, and police mistreatment of black youth informed activism in the Black Women's Movement.

Liverpool Black Sisters, established in 1973, addressed lack of childcare provision and inadequate mental health services for black women. The Manchester Black Women's Cooperative, also set up in 1973, helped run educational training for young mothers in Moss Side, an economically deprived area of the city. In 1979, the

Manchester Black Women's Cooperative became the Abasindi Black Women's Cooperative, their name taken from a Zulu word meaning "survivors." For Diana Watt, active in Abasindi for decades, Abasindi "reflects a continuation of black women's activism, as in the work of Claudia Jones, the founder of Britain's first black newspaper, the *West Indian Gazette*." The Abasindi center "provided a sanctuary for women and children faced with deportation and space for women to begin to determine and redefine their conditions."[20] Abasindi tackled educational under-achievement and ran the Abasindi Saturday Supplementary School, which taught classes in English, science, math, and black history. They had a strong focus on women's issues, but like many black women's groups, worked with men to challenge the institutional and everyday racism they faced. Abasindi celebrated the cultures of the African diaspora and

hosted activities such as music, dancing, theater, and sewing.[21] Their activism helped "give the black woman a new 'self-image'"[22] untainted by harmful white supremacist and sexist stereotypes. Such activities were mirrored in other black women's centers set up during the 1980s in Brixton, Haringey, Peckham, and Southall in London, and in other parts of the UK such as Liverpool. These centers offered practical support that responded to the specific problems faced by black women and provided childcare, playgroups, and craft activities.[23]

In 1972, two black women ran for president of the US, Flo Kennedy on the Feminist Party ticket and, more seriously, Congresswoman Shirley Chisholm as a Democratic Party contender. Chisholm was the first black woman in Congress;

> "The pre-condition for the black woman generally fighting on a general women's platform is a commitment by white women, in both word and deed, to struggle for the freedom of the black woman from racism."
>
> Black Women's Action Committee (UK), 1972

Opposite: Backed by minority women at Houston's Civic Center, Coretta Scott King addresses the National Women's Conference of 1977. Here she promoted a minority resolution later adopted by the feminist conference: a declaration that minority women suffer discrimination based on both race and sex. The Houston conference was unique in having bipartisan support and was attended by both Democratic and Republican First Ladies.

Clockwise from top right: The Abasindi Black Women's Cooperative was based in Moss Side, Manchester, from the late 1970s.

This art exhibition was held in London's Brixton Art Gallery in June and July 1985. The Brixton Black Women's Group was very active in bringing together black women of the area in both activism and a range of cultural activities.

Liverpool Black Sisters were one of the first black women's organizations established in Britain.

Shirley Chisholm stunned American voters by running for the highest office in the land in the 1972 presidential election.

ABASINDI CO-OPERATIVE

'SI ZALELWE UKUSINDA'
We Were Born to Survive

BRING U.S. TOGETHER

VOTE CHISHOLM 1972
UNBOUGHT AND UNBOSSED

N.G. SLATER CORP. 220 W 19 St—NYC–10011

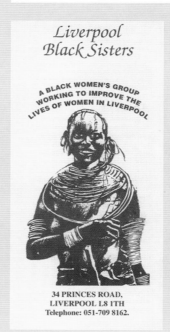

Liverpool Black Sisters

A BLACK WOMEN'S GROUP WORKING TO IMPROVE THE LIVES OF WOMEN IN LIVERPOOL

34 PRINCES ROAD, LIVERPOOL L8 1TH
Telephone: 051-709 8162.

MIXED MEDIA ART by
Acting
Mime
Poetry
Dance
Music
Video
Workshops
Food
Creche
june 18–july 6 (contact .... d.......)

WHY A BLACK SHOW?
It is an opportunity for black people to exhibit– a challenge to racism.

WHY A WOMEN'S SHOW?
It is an opportunity for women to exhibit– a challenge to sexism.

WHY A BLACK WOMEN'S ONLY?
To exhibit the diversity within the concept black women and challenge people's expectations, perpetuated by stereotypes.

WHY THE TITLE "MIRROR REFLECTING DARKLY"?
To exhibit the differing perspectives expressed through our art and to challenge the way we have been encouraged to associate black and its derivative with the negative/darkness.

This exhibition of black women's art at Brixton Gallery is a celebration of our creativity and until such time that we are able to come together with real sexual and racial equality, it will be important to have these points of exhibiting to assert our visibility in all areas.

Angela and Olive

Angela Davis and Olive Morris remain pioneers of the black women's liberation movements.

During the 1970s, Angela Yvonne Davis became the poster girl for the black women's liberation movement in America as her fight against segregation during her time in prison came to symbolize the racism inherent in the US political and public system.

Angela Davis's journey from philosophy professor to, in President Nixon's words, "dangerous terrorist," was an extraordinary one. Davis was implicated in the siege of a Californian courtroom by African American teenager John Jackson, resulting in the death of a judge, Jackson, and the two inmates he had attempted to free. The firearms used in the incident were traced back to Davis, who had also been publicly backing the defendants; a warrant was issued for her arrest, and an FBI hunt was launched within days as she was placed on the FBI's Most Wanted list. Despite protesting her innocence, Davis was remanded in a women's detention center and segregated from her fellow, white prisoners on the grounds of her race (as was often the case for black people entering the prison system at the time).

Her campaign against such segregation and her fight for freedom caught the public imagination. Soon civil rights and women's liberation protests across America would include banners bearing the slogan "Hands Off Angela," while artists from across the world dedicated songs to her, including the Rolling Stones, John Lennon and Yoko Ono, and Todd Cochrane.

After being acquitted, Davis set off on a speaking tour of Communist countries, including Cuba, Russia, and East Germany.

She continues to advocate for social justice, ecological issues, racial, and gender equality, participating both in grassroots activism and academia to this day.

In many ways, the controversy surrounding Davis's imprisonment has overshadowed her extraordinary intellectual and humanitarian contributions to the civil rights and women's liberation movements.

In contrast, the pioneering work of Olive Morris did not see her reach such worldwide acclaim or fame. Nevertheless, Morris was a similarly fearless campaigner for social justice.

Olive Elaine Morris was born in Jamaica in 1952 and arrived in Britain when she was nine years old. Although

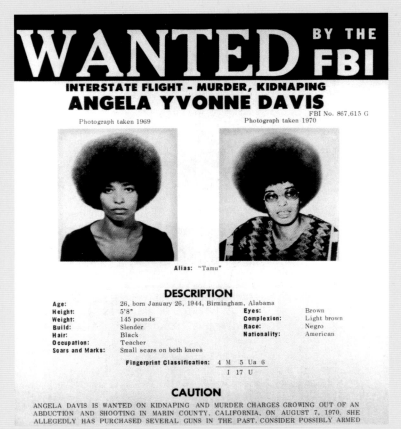

she left school with no qualifications, she went on to complete a degree in social sciences at Manchester University and became an extraordinary agitator for social change. As a founding member of the Brixton Black Women's Group and Manchester Black Women's Cooperative, Olive Morris was an important figure in the British Black Women's Movement. She had originally laid the groundwork for a greater movement, yet Morris never lived to see that movement blossom. Olive Morris died from leukemia in 1979 at the age of twenty-seven, shortly before OWAAD's first national conference.[24] The many tributes to her memory paint a picture of a remarkable and committed activist, and her legacy "leaves with us the inspiration to resist. OLIVE LIVES AND THE STRUGGLE CONTINUES!"[25]

It is hard not to wonder, when viewing these two women, what Olive Morris might also have achieved if she had lived longer.

Above: FBI Wanted poster for Angela Davis, 1971. This image was to become a rallying symbol for her supporters, both in the women's and in the black liberation movements.

Above left: Olive Morris protests against housing discrimination in London.

Above right: Morris was a committed internationalist. This image was taken on a visit she made to China in 1977.

"It is reasonable to expect that Olive Morris's heroism will be immortalised alongside such black luminaries like Marcus Garvey, Malcolm X and many others who were proud to be black."

Anonymous, Nigerian student on the death of Olive Morris, 1979, in Lizzie Cocker, "Olive Morris: Forgotten Activist Hero," *Morning Star Online*, 2009

"I think the importance of doing activist work is precisely because it allows you to give back and to consider yourself not as a single individual who may have achieved whatever but to be a part of an ongoing historical movement."

Angela Davis, interview with PBS, *The Two Black Nations of America*, 1997

representing constituents from one of New York's majority-black inner-city districts, she refused to serve on the House Agricultural Committee and insisted in her electrifying speeches that she was "unbought . . . and unbossed." Although she lost her bid for president (the Democratic Party nominated Senator George McGovern), Chisholm won the support of both black and feminist voters. Such political firsts paved the way for the formation of the National Black Feminist Organization in 1973.

In Britain, women of color also broke into government. In 1983, Merle Amory became the first black council leader of Brent, a borough of London, with Linda Bellos becoming the second in 1985, before serving as leader of Lambeth London Borough Council between 1986 and 1988. In 1987, Diane Abbott became the first black woman to hold a seat in the House of Commons.

Like lesbians (of all colors) in the same era, black and Latina women in America simultaneously organized their own events and publications while participating in (and demanding better representation at) national and local feminist conferences. In *The Feminist Memoir Project*, writer Barbara Omolade shared her own activist diary from the years 1978–82. Her notes from a March 1979 conference titled "The Black Woman: Her Past, Present, and Future," organized by Darlene Clark Hine and Patricia Hill Collins at Purdue University, Indiana, reveal that for Omolade, this conference was the "first time I heard a black woman, Bettye Thomas, call herself a feminist."[26]

By 1976 there was an American National Alliance of Black Feminists, and, through the women's music collective Olivia Records, the "Varied Voices of Black Women" concert tour featured poetry and music with a woman-loving sensibility. However, the roles black women played as entertainers or celebrity authors at white feminist events would soon raise still more questions about tokenism, appropriation, and long-term coalition.

The Black Women's Movement in Britain began to mobilize on a national scale at the end of the 1970s. Its genesis was a meeting in Coventry in 1977, when several women's groups came together to discuss plans for an organization that would oversee the development of the movement in Britain. OWAAD was soon established, its acronym originally standing for Organisation for Women of Africa and African descent.

> "We had to work out the practicalities of the operation of [Afro-Asian] unity. We had to extract what that was, what we could come together to work on, along with creating a space for things unique to African women to develop and for things unique to Asian women to develop separately."
>
> Brixton Black Women's Group and Alice Henry, "Black Politics = Black Feminism," 1984

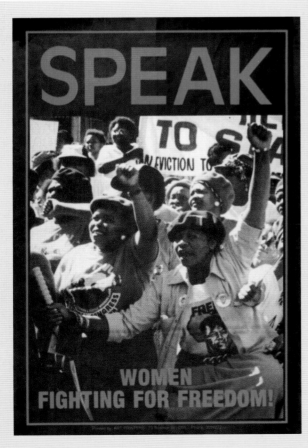

Far left: *SPEAK* magazine was launched in 1982 to provide a platform for black women to lobby against apartheid and issues affecting the black community around the world, including deportations and evictions.

Left: This black women-only campaign organized in Leeds was ultimately successful in stopping the deportation of Halimat Babamba in 1983.

Above: In this photograph by Diana Davies, the Third World Women's Alliance demonstrates at the Women's House of Detention in New York City, December 1970. Through the 1970s, immigrant women and lesbians continued to be poorly treated in this well-known jail, centrally located in Greenwich Village. Women charged with possession, distribution, or warehousing of weapons used in political conflict (such as Angela Davis) were often viewed by police as more dangerous than male offenders, having abandoned traditional "ladylike" roles.

Many who attended were students from African countries such as Zimbabwe and Eritrea, and they wanted to focus on liberation struggles in their countries of origin. As plans for OWAAD developed, the organization's focus shifted from international to domestic issues. Women of Afro-Caribbean, Asian, and African descent living in Britain shared a history of colonial violence and contemporary experience of demonization within Britain. From 1978 onward, OWAAD formalized its objective to represent women of Asian and African descent (its name also changed to Organisation for Women of Asian and African Descent), and "black" was used to symbolize a political project located in Afro-Asian unity.

OWAAD facilitated networks, conducted research, distributed information, and organized conferences; its ambitious coordinating activities helped the Black Women's Movement in Britain to grow. Nevertheless, there were problems. There was very little consensus over contentious issues such as the legitimacy of feminism—due to its association with white women—or the status of lesbianism.

Establishing Afro-Asian unity was not straightforward either, and activists struggled to solidify connections across differences of class and ethnicity.

OWAAD held four conferences between 1978 and 1982. While the first conference culminated in euphoria, connection, and hope, attendees remember the final conference as a "debacle."[27] OWAAD folded due to the aforementioned pressures, but it did so at a time when black women's activism was thriving, partly from the necessity to resist persisting oppression, but also from a newfound collective spirit among black women. Groups such as the Birmingham Black Sisters sustained campaigns, while new projects, such as *Zami*—a bimonthly black lesbian newsletter—were launched. Conferences such as 1984's "We Are Here: Black Feminists in Britain" demonstrated that "feminist" was no longer such a controversial identity for black women. Resisting state-sanctioned violence remained a key issue for the Black Women's Movement in the early 1980s, as Britain's diverse ethnic communities adjusted to new immigration and surveillance regimes introduced by the Conservative government.

The British Nationality Act 1981 came into force in January 1983 and placed further restrictions on who could live and work in the UK. It also "formalised the surveillance and harassment which had been going on on an ad hoc basis," with information on immigration status "now demanded by almost every sector of the welfare state, not only the NHS, but schools, colleges, housing departments, DHSS, etc."[28]

Similarly, the Police and Criminal Evidence Act 1984 made immigrant communities vulnerable to the new forms of legal authority available to the police. Under the act, the police had a mandate to conduct strip and intimate body searches, forcibly fingerprint and detain suspects, enter their properties, and extend their powers of arrest. In the wake of both pieces of legislation, activism to stop deportations intensified.

Groups such as the Sari Squad—South Asian female activists who battled against racial injustice—ran high-profile campaigns that raged against the UK's immigration laws. Their focus fell on the recently bereaved Afia Begum and her daughter, in a campaign that highlighted the acute precariousness of immigrant women and children. Afia had been living in Britain for two years, yet after her husband's death, immigration officials told her that "circumstances had changed" and she would have to leave.

Many migrant women were in a similar position to Afia, with immigration status dependent on their marital status. If relationships broke down through agreement, or because women wanted to flee a violent situation, or even ended in more tragic circumstances as with Afia, deportation was likely. Immigrant women in these situations had very few rights. They could not claim benefits, be housed as homeless, or work because they did not have a work permit. Due to the UK's immigration policies, many women like Afia were forced into destitution.[29]

When Afia and her daughter went into hiding in May 1984, five members of the Sari Squad chained themselves to railings outside the house of Home Secretary Leon Brittan, demanding that Afia and her daughter be allowed to stay in Britain. They were arrested for this action and allegedly received abusive treatment from male officers while in police custody.[30]

The Sari Squad used feminist media to amplify their message and organized a UK-wide speaking tour that visited Manchester, Birmingham, Coventry, Exeter, Bradford, Brighton, and Bristol, "addressing public gatherings, increasing public awareness of racism and deportations."[31] In May 1984, the Sari Squad "hit Europe." Fifty women visited groups in Paris, Amsterdam, and Bonn before reaching their final destination—the European parliament in Strasbourg. Here they presented a petition on behalf of Afia Begum that demanded she be allowed to stay in Britain. These activities were, however, in vain. Grassroots feminist newspaper *Outwrite* reported that Afia's hiding place was uncovered on May 3, 1984. She was subsequently detained at Harmondsworth detention prison and deported two days later.

The Sari Squad's campaign to keep Afia in Britain is an example of many anti-deportation campaigns organized throughout the 1980s, which continue to this day. While other campaigns were successful, the abrupt ejection of Afia and her daughter from the UK underlines how clinical and unforgiving immigration policy became in Margaret Thatcher's Britain.

Throughout the 1970s and '80s, the British Black Women's Movement evolved alongside and independently of the Women's Liberation Movement, with increased convergence in the 1980s.

Black and women of color movements were incredibly diverse; some women may never have seen themselves as part of a coherent "black women's movement," while others shied away from hard-line political identifications. Some would never identify as feminist, due to the term's associations with white feminism, while others embraced the word. The common thread that ran through the American National Alliance of Black Feminists, the Black Women's Action Group, Abasindi Black Women's Cooperative, OWAAD, Sari Squad, and similar groups was their determination to create practical, lived conditions in which women of color, their children, and communities could "define for themselves a course of action" and exercise greater control over their lives.[32] Their activisms created alternative contexts and knowledge that enabled women of color to survive and thrive, embodying the "powerful forces of change that are determined to prevent the dying cultures of racism, hetero-patriarchy from rising again."[33]

POUR UNE MAISON
DES FEMMES NOIRES

GALA AU BATACLAN
1er et 2 Mai 18 heures

LA TROUPE SANGANA Présente :
ODJIBI ou la patience a des limites
Conte poétique chanté et dansé

ET
Nyama Macalou   Charles Ewanjé
Les Brimstone   Dybie Ayké
                     Mango Vert
Mango Vert   Ovo

Guy Conquet et le groupe Ka

Kofi Koko

Places disponibles à :
Carabosses
Dambala
Bataclan
Présence Africaine
Harmattan

ENTRÉE 40 F

MAISON
DES
FEMMES
NOIRES

INTERNATIONAL WOMEN'S PARTY TO CELEBRATE

NAMIBIAN WOMEN'S DAY ♀♀♀

WITH

SISTAHS IN SONG
SISTA CULTCHA DJ

FOOD DRINK EXHIBITIONS CRECHE

8pm WEDS 17th DEC
AFRICA CENTRE
KINGS STREET, COVENT GARDEN.

£3/£2/£1

SOLIDARITY
WITH
SWAPO

ALL WOMEN WELCOME

ORGANISED BY TOWER HAMLETS INTERNATIONAL SOLIDARITY, WISER LINKS, INTERNATIONAL WORKING GROUP ON WOMEN

WOMEN UNITE AGAINST APARTHEID

MEDU ART ENSEMBLE

Top left: This French poster invites black women to a celebration of black culture at Paris's Bataclan theater.

Bottom left: SWAPO, the South West Africa People's Organisation, championed black people's rights and raised funds for African causes at benefits such as the one advertised on this poster.

Above right: This c. 1981 poster by the Medu Art Ensemble shows how black women consciously aligned themselves with the anti-apartheid movement and campaigned not only for their own rights, but also for those of disenfranchised African men and women.

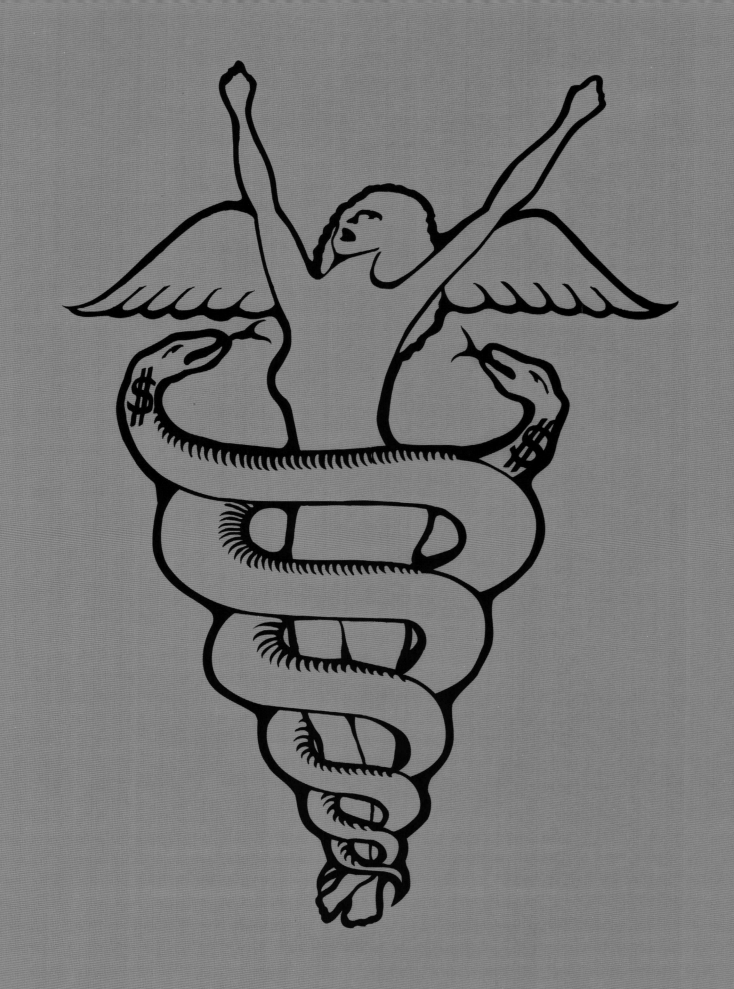

BATTLEGROUND OF THE BODY

Reclaiming the physical and mental treatment of women

The women's liberation and black women's movements transformed
the female body into a public site of resistance, power, and refusal.

For the first time in history, activists publicly named damaging "private" male behavior—such as "wife battering," psychological intimidation, and rape—as violence. The home was revealed to be a potentially dangerous place for women, and the idea that a man had the "right" to do what he wanted with a woman because she was his "property" was fundamentally challenged.

Women's liberationists' arguments moved beyond victimhood to new ideals of empowerment, self-esteem, and sexual freedom. Challenges to sex discrimination in education also meant that more women were enrolling in medical and law schools, so that feminists brought professional credentials as well as self-taught knowledge to public issues of women's health and safety.

Emphasizing the right of every woman and girl to control her own body meant teaching others to see the female citizen as an individual with the right to say *no*: no to unwanted touching, to unwanted pregnancy, to sexual harassment in the street or the workplace, to forced intercourse within marriage, to intimate violence and incest in the supposedly safe space of the home.

In Western democracies, these rights and protections were slowly inscribed in law, reversing many centuries of religious and social custom, and introducing new values in the judicial system. In many countries, courts and juries were directed to stop questioning any victim of sexual violence about her sexual history and to stop excusing rape based on what the victim had been wearing. In the US, young women forced to wear skirts as part of a school uniform—an athletically limiting regulation in itself—demanded the right to wear trousers, contesting that longer-legged girls were unfairly punished for their teenage growth spurts when their skirts were judged too short by authorities. Feminists of all ages rejected fashion that left women's bodies uncomfortable, injured, unwell, and unable to run from danger. And lesbians, by defining pride in female sexuality on their own terms, asserting different stances on femininity, and demanding healthcare based on their sex practices, were making history.

But women's increasingly outspoken pursuit of sexual freedom and pleasure, regardless of marital status, shocked society, and politicians remained ambivalent

Page 80: This illustration is taken from a 1975 poster by the Chicago Women's Graphic Collective. The image was originally accompanied by the slogan "Healthcare is for people, not for profit" to highlight the issues many women had accessing free and safe healthcare.

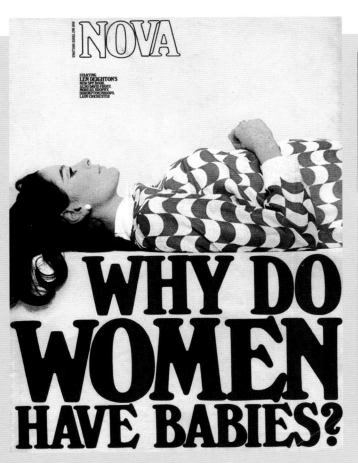

Far left: *Nova* magazine was established in 1965 and described itself as "the new kind of magazine for a new kind of woman." The magazine became known for its strong cover visuals and its readiness to explore issues such as reproduction, as in this May 1967 issue, which "traditional" women's magazines had hitherto shied away from.

Left: The Eve cigarette came and went, but it capitalized on the seductive myth of the willful and disobedient woman—in this case, a woman flouting health advisories in order to smoke. This ad campaign competed with the Virginia Slims "You've Come a Long Way, Baby" slogan; both companies used the feminist revolution of the 1970s as a platform to sell cigarettes. In the US, some colleges banned smoking for women yet permitted male students to smoke.

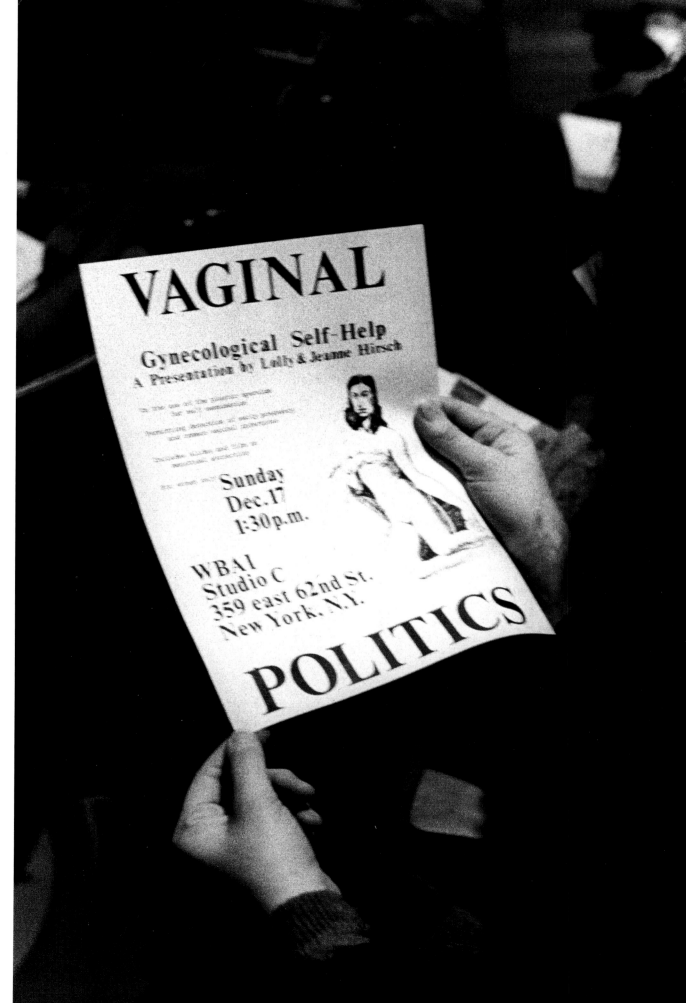

Right: *Vaginal Politics* was the title of a best-selling 1972 book by author Ellen Frankfort; here, women attending the December 1972 Sexism in the Schools conference in New York are encouraged to attend a presentation on gynecological self-help. Few women were comfortable challenging the authority of the male medical establishment, and fewer still had access to clear and direct health information about their own reproductive systems.

about supporting feminist demands for reliable, legal, and affordable birth control and abortion. The female body, though admired, remained legally suspect well into the 1980s.

In the US, women could be arrested for going topless on a beach or attempting to breastfeed an infant on a park bench, and just entering a primarily male bar or trying to rent a group house off campus marked female students as potential prostitutes. In tackling the full range of these issues, feminists discovered they were also deeply divided over issues such as pornography, non-monogamy, lesbian rights, and indeed prostitution itself—or sex work, as many feminists reconceptualized it. By the 1980s, the "sex wars" had feminists squaring off against one another over issues of censorship, erotica, and sex work—pitting anti-pornography activists such as Andrea Dworkin and Catherine MacKinnon against advocates for sex workers' rights such as Margo St. James, founder of COYOTE: Cast Off Your Old Tired Ethics.

These conflicting demands for recognition of female sexual agency informed the feminist agenda for the next forty years. From literature to law, from film to pharmacy shelf, societies throughout America, Britain, Europe, Australia, and beyond were engaged in radical discussions about the female body: an increasing openness that many men welcomed, too. However, as political and legal demands for access to contraception and abortion were recast as "women's issues," some traditionally conservative women chose to distance themselves from the feminist movement.

Birth control and abortion

The 1960s began with the marketing of the Pill, after it had been tested on a small selection of Puerto Rican women. Some of these women later claimed they had been coerced into being test subjects as a condition for retaining their medical school scholarships.[1] In a pamphlet distributed by the Third World Women's Alliance, the plight of Puerto Rican women was addressed.

The commercial release of the Pill, which introduced new sexual freedoms but exposed women to complicated side effects, was both celebrated and

Above: The Dutch feminist group Dolle Mina marches for free access to the contraceptive pill in Amsterdam on October 10, 1970.

questioned by feminist investigators: which birth control methods were safe? Why was there no effort to create a male birth control pill?

In the US, state by state, laws differed wildly in terms of unmarried women's access to contraception and abortion; protest marches emphasized the right to choose and the typical lack of female representation on committees "studying" abortion laws.

Similarly, in Britain contraceptive drugs remained within the hands of an often sexist, racist, and classist medical establishment. Due to this, the potential for these drugs to truly support women's social and political independence was undermined. The use of the contraceptive injection Depo-Provera is a powerful example of how women's bodies remained a site of medical, political, and institutional control, despite these medical advances.

Depo-Provera was introduced in 1963 and began to be used widely in 1972. It was also first tested on women in Third World countries, who were essentially guinea pigs for the drug. Following these tests, it became clear in the early development of Depo-Provera that birth defects, menstrual disruption, and cancer were possible side effects. The drug was also used as a form of population control administered by "developed" nations in the context of postwar US imperialism.

In Britain, Depo-Provera was disproportionately given to black and working-class women, in some cases without their knowledge or consent. The Campaign against Depo-Provera reported that in one East London clinic, two-thirds of the women given Depo-Provera were Asian. West Indian teenage girls were also given the drug, often after having abortions. Among white women, inhabitants of Women's Aid shelters were targeted. "It seems very probable," the Campaign against Depo-Provera advised, "that doctors are deciding that women such as these are 'problem' women, who will give birth to 'problem' children."[2] The belief that certain groups of women should not be allowed to have children was evidence of "doctors' highly trained contempt for women and women's bodies."[3] Through the Campaign against Depo-Provera, activists in the British Black Women's Movement connected local and international struggles and highlighted the need for a wider politics of reproductive freedom beyond the third demand of the British Women's Liberation Movement: "Free Contraception and Abortion on Demand."

Meanwhile, in the US negative publicity around illegal abortion gradually moved Congress to act, while organizations such as the underground "Jane" movement in Chicago trained women to help other women secure abortions outside the law. In 1973, the Supreme Court upheld a woman's right to choose with the landmark *Roe v. Wade* decision, which to this day is both protested and defended in America.

Far right: At this 1975 demonstration for abortion rights, women of color demand authority over their bodies. A key issue in black feminist dialogue was the sterilization of black and Native American women, typically without their consent during other medical procedures; Latina women also experienced involuntary sterilization, but in their majority Catholic communities were more likely to get care at Catholic hospitals, where tubal ligations—as well as birth control and abortion—were strictly forbidden.

Right: This member of French group MLF holds a poster supporting the right to free contraception for everyone and legalized abortion at a rally in 1972.

Women's Aid in Britain

D-M Withers

In the early 1970s, domestic abuse, or "wife battering," as it was called then, was often viewed as a normal part of the relations between husband and wife. Behind closed doors, it was far more common than assumed for men to beat, control, torture, violate, and terrorize their female partners.

Women in Britain received very little support from the police, who often refused to intervene in domestic issues. Inequality in the workplace and lack of access to state benefits meant it was not easy for women to be financially independent. If a woman was trying to leave a violent partner, there was little housing provision available for her. The only option was the shelter of family and friends, or temporary housing. This situation effectively trapped a lot of poorer women in violent relationships.

As the Women's Liberation Movement began to grow, it established women's centers in towns and cities throughout Britain. Although women's centers were not specifically set up as shelters (or refuges) for "battered women," they quickly became so. Women who literally had nowhere else to go were referred by social services and charities to these ad hoc shelters, which became the first manifestation of the Women's Aid movement.

Improvised responses offered by women's centers soon became more organized. In 1974, the National Women's Aid Federation (NWAF) was established. NWAF coordinated the growing movement of activists setting up shelters, safe houses, and support for women who experienced physical or mental abuse. During the late 1970s, "refuges sprang into being on an almost weekly basis"[4] in towns and cities across Britain.

At the heart of Women's Aid was a desire to "encourage women to determine their own futures and to help them effect their decisions whether this involves returning home or starting a new life elsewhere."[5] Shelters accepted any woman who needed refuge. "She was not asked to prove she is battered—or battered 'badly enough' or without 'cause.'"[6]

Shelters created new opportunities for women's independence, as activist Gill Hague explains:

No one before had thought it possible—more or less—that you could leave your marriage and go and live in a house full of women and children. It was just like, "what?!" And the women just flocked. Every single time a refuge opened it was full almost instantly. So where were those women and children before?[7]

Shelters were not, of course, utopias. They were often overcrowded due to demand, and precariously set up in temporary, short-term housing. Women also came to shelters at an uncertain time in their lives. Women's Aid nevertheless provided a lifeline for many thousands of women and children.

'Twas after a very bad beating
whilst my eyes and body were black,
and I lay sobbing in the dark,
that I felt I'd had enough . . .

The next thing I remember . . .
A warm hand came on my shoulder,
a voice said "worry no more,"
you can stay at our refuge,
where no husband passes the door.[8]

As time went on, Women's Aid directly engaged with local authorities and the state. Toward the end of the 1970s, NWAF helped lobby for changes that offered women greater legal protection, such as the first Domestic Violence and Matrimonial Proceedings Bill (1976) and the Housing (Homeless Persons) Act (1977), which recognized battered women as homeless, and therefore a priority for rehousing. These activities continued throughout the 1980s as activists lobbied for domestic violence to be seen as a criminal and civic matter.

Women's Aid groups also provided support to women who killed their abusive husbands. Edinburgh and Lothian Women's Aid launched the "Free June Greig" campaign in 1979. June had suffered years of extreme abuse, which she described as a "life of hell." She was still sentenced to six years in prison—a sentence that many felt was unduly harsh in order to show that the judicial system would not be pressurised by the Women's Aid organisation.[9] Campaigns for

Above: Edinburgh and Lothian Women's Aid poster displayed in an Edinburgh bus station advertising services for women, c. 1977.

Far right: Illustration of living in a shelter from "You Can't Beat a Woman: Women and Children in Refuges," published by Women's Aid c. 1976.

Right: Scottish Women's Aid banner being carried in the Five Specific Funds protest, which demanded dedicated funding for Women's Aid, Edinburgh, October 1999.

other convicted women continued jointly with organizations such as Justice for Women. The message from supporters was defiant: "Battered women have served enough time."[10]

Various groups, such as Southall Black Sisters, campaigned to ensure husbands and partners were convicted of criminal offenses. Following the murder of Balwant Kaur by her husband in 1985, they wrote: "We demand that domestic violence is recognized as a crime, and that men who assault women are not allowed to get away with spurious arrangements about their 'provocation' and their 'passion.'"[11]

Research collected, campaigns run, and services provided by Women's Aid have changed society's perceptions of domestic violence. Nevertheless, the problem has not been eradicated, and the struggle to end violence against women continues across the world.

Most feminists defined their stance as pro-choice, not pro-abortion, asserting that ending a pregnancy was a traumatic personal decision that should be shielded from government intervention and public scolding. Women and men with religious objections to abortion often supported exceptions in the case of rape, incest, and risks to the mother's life, introducing fresh discussion about the prevalence of incest within families. However, in the wake of Pope Paul VI's publication of *Humanae vitae* (*On Human Life*) in 1968, the powerful Vatican and the US Conference of Catholic Bishops pressured American courts to limit contraception as well as abortion. *On Human Life* instructed faithful Catholics that all forms of birth control, sterilization, abortion, and sex outside of procreative marriage were absolutely forbidden. The few theologians who dared to question these directives were sanctioned and silenced, but many Catholics simply ignored the specific Church teachings on birth control. For example, in 1973 activist Frances Kissling organized the political group Catholics for a Free Choice.

For many worldwide women's liberation movements, access to birth control and abortion was key to their campaigning agenda. In France, a historically Catholic country, unprecedented action was taken with the publication in 1971 of "Le Manifeste des 343 salopes" ("The Manifesto of the 343 Sluts"). The manifesto publicly acknowledged both well-known French female personalities and anonymous women who secretly had had an abortion and called for free access to abortion and contraception. The manifesto challenged the authorities to take action against the women for these illegal abortions by stating that if one was prosecuted, then they would all have to be. One of the signatories was feminist lawyer Gisèle Halimi, a founding member

Mrs. Peters had no choice in 1968.

Now she does.

ABORTION ON DEMAND

A Woman's Right to Choose

ACTION GUIDE

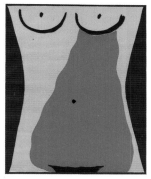

HELP FIGHT THE ABORTION AMENDMENT BILL

ABORTION LAW REFORM ASSOCIATION
186 KINGS CROSS ROAD   LONDON WC1X 9DE

15p.

Clockwise from top left: "Voters for choice" became a clarion call in the US, as demonstrated by this pin from the 1980s.

A terrifying reminder of the many women who, desperate with an unplanned pregnancy, turned to self-induced abortions using any materials on hand in the home. Knitting needles, coat hangers, and other implements had deadly consequences, but in 1968 most states in the US offered no access to abortion beyond hospital intervention to save a mother's life. This comment on the importance of safe, legal abortion reintroduced the rhetoric of "choice," language that soon defined the "pro-choice" movement for abortion rights.

The National Abortion Campaign in Britain advocated strongly for free access to safe, legal abortions.

This Italian poster by V. Vecchi questions who has control over a woman's womb.

This 1982 Dutch poster demonstrates the urgency of women's need for access to free and safe contraception.

WIJ VROUWEN EISEN:
DE PIL UIT HET ZIEKENFONDS...
NEE!
ABORTUS IN HET ZIEKENFONDS...
JA!!

LANDELIJK COMITÉ WIJ VROUWEN EISEN, POSTBUS 1147, LEIDEN.

DI CHI È LA PANCIA DI QUESTA DONNA?

DELLA CHIESA? DELLO STATO? DEI MEDICI? DEI PADRONI?

NO, È SUA!

VOGLIAMO L'ABORTO LIBERO, GRATUITO, CON ASSISTENZA MEDICA
PERCHÉ 3'000'000 DI DONNE ALL'ANNO, SOLO IN ITALIA, SONO COSTRETTE AD ABORTIRE E 20'000 LO PAGANO CON LA MORTE.
SOPRATTUTTO NON VOGLIAMO PIÚ ESSERE COSTRETTE AD ABORTIRE
VOGLIAMO IL CONTROLLO SUL NOSTRO CORPO. FARE FIGLI SE E QUANDO LI VOGLIAMO. ANTICONCEZIONALI SICURI, NON NOCIVI PER LA SALUTE E GRATUITI, CONSULTORI SOTTO IL NOSTRO CONTROLLO.
CONTROLLO DEL NOSTRO CORPO VUOLE DIRE ANCHE VIVERE LIBERAMENTE LA NOSTRA SESSUALITÀ E VIVERE SENZA ESSERE DISTRUTTE DALLA ESTENUANTE FATICA DEL LAVORO IN CASA E FUORI.
MOVIMENTO FEMMINISTA

of Choisir la cause des femmes (often referred to as Choisir). One of Choisir's stated aims was to offer free defense to any woman prosecuted for an abortion. This soon turned into a reality when Halimi took on what became known as the Bobigny trial in 1972. The trial centered around a sixteen-year-old girl from a high-rise estate in the suburbs of Paris, who after being raped had become pregnant. The girl, Marie-Claire, wanted to terminate the pregnancy, given her experience of the hardships that her mother, as an unmarried woman, had had to suffer. Both the abortion practitioner and Marie-Claire's mother were found guilty under the 1920 act of procuring an illegal abortion and given suspended sentences. The case sparked outrage that boiled over into a major national debate in France surrounding abortion laws.

France's response to the issue of abortion certainly presented a landmark in Europe, but it was not unique. On June 6, 1971, the front cover of the West German magazine *Stern* was emblazoned with the banner "Wir haben abgetrieben" ("We have had abortions"). Similarly to the French manifesto, 374 women (including a number of prominent figures, such as the actress Romy Schneider) publicly admitted in the magazine that they had had illegal abortions in contravention of Paragraph 218 of German criminal law, restricting abortion solely to medical reasons.

In Italy, the Pierobon trial sparked debate in the way that the Bobigny case had in France. The trial was centered around twenty-three-year-old Paduan resident Gigliola Pierobon, who had admitted having an illegal abortion when she was seventeen in 1967. As abortion at the time was illegal—termed "an attack on the integrity of lineage" under Article 546 of the Italian Criminal Code—she opened herself up to prosecution and a potential prison sentence. Pierobon's plight mobilized feminist groups and collectives, particularly Lotta femminista (Feminist Battle) in Padua, with women publicly declaring that they, too, had had abortions. Pierobon was eventually found guilty but pardoned. Similarly, the case paved the way for Italian legislative reform in 1978.[12]

Other countries saw abortion made legal (with restrictions varying by nation) throughout the 1970s and '80s, including East Germany in 1972; Austria in 1974; Iceland in 1975; Norway in 1978; Greece in 1984; and Czechoslovakia in 1986.

Still, there were numerous challenges to overcome, with abortion proving a divisive and legally thorny issue for many governments right up to the present day. For example, Belgium did not legalize abortion until 1990, being one of the last European countries to do so. In Canada, from the 1960s to the 1980s many attempts were made to increase access to safe, free abortions, but they were contested through to the twenty-first century.

Below left: *Le nouvel observateur* published what would become known as the "Manifesto of the 343 Sluts" in 1971. The headline reads: "The list of the 343 French women who have the courage to sign the manifesto 'I have had an abortion.'" The effect of the publication was profound and ignited national debate.

Below middle: In one of many popular "Take Back the Night" demonstrations, the National Organization for Women's rape commission targets City Hall in New York, August 28, 1974. These demonstrators point out that six women had been raped and murdered in the past week alone, leaving other women afraid to go out while male perpetrators walked free.

Below right: This highly provocative poster by an unknown feminist lobbying group, c. 1980s, satirizes the bias of the British judicial system against rape victims of the day. Activist groups such as Women against Rape fought hard to eliminate this bias, which, sadly, was not restricted to British courts.

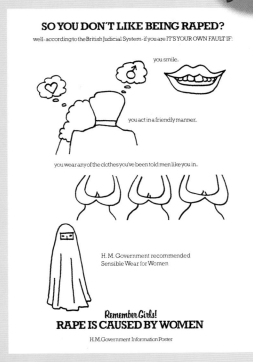

Above: Lawyer Gisèle Halimi talks to the press about her defense of sixteen-year-old Marie-Claire, her mother, and "accomplices" during the Bobigny trial in 1972.

In Ireland, at the time of writing, abortion remains illegal except in cases of fetal abnormalities, rape, and incest. Similarly, abortion remains illegal (with some exceptions) in countries throughout Africa, South America, and the Middle East, as well as in some Asia-Pacific countries.

Reclaim the Night

Alongside the abortion campaign, women's movements urged a wider debate on violence against women. As it became less taboo to talk about the impact of rape and domestic violence on women of every age group, race, and class, feminists took up self-defense and offered compassionate counseling and legal aid services through battered women's shelters and rape crisis centers.

In the US, the first centers opened were Bay Area Women against Rape in 1971 and Women's Advocates in St. Paul,

Minnesota, in 1973. No state offered women legal orders of protection against an abusive husband or partner until 1976 (Pennsylvania), and marital rape remained legal in forty-four states as late as 1980, so shelters were often the only alternative for women escaping abusive relationships. Whether they were well-identified urban sites or discreet call-in centers staffed by volunteers, safe spaces for women and their children grew into a network of over seven hundred shelters in the US by 1983.

In Britain, the Rape in Marriage Campaign, instigated in the early 1980s, aimed to make marital rape a criminal offense. Following intensive lobbying, rape in marriage became illegal in 1991. Similarly, in Italy it took until 1981 for the legal status of rape to change under Article 544 of the 1931 Rocco Penal Code; prior to that, the law allowed for "reparatory marriage," or *matrimonio*

Choisir

A woman's right to choose became one of the most central arguments of the women's liberation movements.

For many feminist thinkers, including Simone de Beauvoir, self-determination was vital to liberation and reproductive choice was one of the pathways to women being able to choose their own destiny.

For many women's liberationists, these reproductive rights included the right to free contraception and the legalization of abortion. However, these rights sat at odds with many religious teachings, including those of the Catholic Church. Nevertheless, women in predominantly Catholic countries such as France began to speak up against the years of reproductive injustice, in part empowered by advances in oral contraceptives, such as the Pill.

One of the foremost organizations in France lobbying for women's rights was Choisir la cause des femmes, founded in July 1971 by Simone de Beauvoir, lawyer Gisèle Halimi, author Christiane Rochefort, and two men—biologist Jean Rostand and Nobel Prize winner Jacques Monod. The group was bound by their belief that both societally and medically, the legalization of contraception and abortion would improve the lives of women.

Choisir's (as it was often known) original aims were to

- repeal the repressive statute of 1920, which prohibited abortion;
- provide free defense for women sued for illegal abortion;
- ensure the legal and free provision of contraceptives.[13]

The organization came to wider public prominence through Halimi's defense of sixteen-year-old Marie-Claire, who had procured an illegal abortion, in the Bobigny trial of 1972. During the trial many prominent figures lent their voices to the call for the legalization of abortion, and scores of French women took to the streets to protest in solidarity with the cause. The wave of public opinion and the lobbying by Choisir eventually led to the overturning of the 1920 statute and the passing of a new law legalizing abortion on January 17, 1975, known as the Veil Law after the French Minister for Health, Simone Veil, who championed its passage.

Choisir la cause des femmes was (and is) not a single-issue group, and since 1974, their objectives have widened to encompass

- struggle against rape, physical, and moral violence and cultural sexist schemes;
- struggle for equal professional rights;
- struggle for a better representation in public life.[14]

As they continue to be headed by president Gisèle Halimi, the group lobbies for women's rights both on a national and an international scale. In 2010, Choisir presented the case for "The Clause of the Most Favored Women"—the adoption of best practices in gender equality across the European Union's member states to achieve harmonization of legislation relating to reproductive rights, gender violence, representation of women in politics, workplace discrimination, and family law. Having compared laws across the European countries, they identified fourteen countries whose laws in a given area could be upheld as the "gold standard" of progressive legislation that all member states should adopt:

- procreation and sexual education, *Denmark*;
- birth control, *the Netherlands*;
- termination of pregnancy, *Sweden*;
- labor, *France*;
- domestic violence, *Spain*;
- rape, *France*;
- prostitution, *Sweden*;
- sexual harassment, *Lithuania*;
- homosexual unions and divorce, *Spain*;
- civil unions, *Belgium*;
- weddings, *Austria*;
- parental authority, *Estonia*;
- parental leave, *Sweden*;
- political representation, *Belgium*.

The clause has yet to be written into European law, but it has gained the support of many member states and is testament to the vision of Choisir la cause des femmes, which reaches far beyond the borders of France.

C'EST TOUT DE MÊME PLUS CHOUETTE DE VIVRE QUAND ON EST DÉSIRÉ

AVORTEMENT ET CONTRACEPTION

LIBRES ET GRATUITS

MLAC

Mouvement pour la Liberté de l'Avortement et de la Contraception
34 rue Vieille du Temple 75004 PARIS

Opposite: French badge, c. 1970, proclaiming that women should decide about abortion, contraception, and sterilization.

Above: French women march on November 20, 1971, for access to free and safe abortion. The large poster reads, "Do not let the Pope, do not let the politicians, do not let other men decide for us. Our body belongs to us."

Right: French poster, c. 1970, supporting free contraception and abortion: "It's much better to live when one is wanted."

Reclaim the Night

Women Demand an end to male violence + the right to walk alone without fear. Join us - all women welcome Friday 20th July 9.30 pm Kingsmead Square bring lights + noise

BATH

This page and opposite: Reclaim the Night / Take Back the Night inspired activists across the world to demand women's access to public space at any time of the day or night. Reclaim the Night coincided with an increasingly militant and, at times, separatist approach within the movement that sought accountability from men for their role in perpetuating violence against women.

riparatore (enabling the crime of rape to be "absolved" through marriage). The idea of "reparatory marriage" was largely built on the notion that rape was a crime against morality rather than a violent attack on an individual. Rape-marriage laws remained (and still remain) in force in some parts of the world, particularly the Middle East, in the twenty-first century.[15]

One of the most iconic protests to emerge from the women's liberation movements is Reclaim the Night or Take Back the Night (as it is known in the US). The inspiration for Reclaim the Night originated from the International Tribunal on Crimes against Women in Brussels in 1976. Attended by over two thousand delegates from forty countries, the conference was an opportunity for activists to share information about male violence against women internationally.[16] Participants were enraged and saddened by what they heard, and at the end of the conference they spontaneously held a candlelit procession through the streets of Brussels. This visible and defiant reclamation of public space at night—a space often deemed too dangerous and therefore "off limits" to women—sparked the imaginations of activists. Similar marches began to crop up in countries across Europe, often in direct response to the rape or murder of local women, as with a 1976 march in Rome that was part of a massive feminist uprising in response to the Circeo massacre of 1975, in which two women had been raped and tortured by three men. One of the women died, while the other survived by pretending to be dead. The Circeo massacre and trial, which was followed by millions on television, was a landmark moment in feminist mobilization against sexual violence.[17]

The first "official" Reclaim the Night march happened in Berlin on March 1, 1977. A month later, several orchestrated marches took place throughout West Germany, as more and more activists were inspired by the demonstrations.

Reclaim the Night hit Britain in a wave of synchronized marches on November 12, 1977. Leeds, Lancaster,

> **"Why must we women restrict our lives when it's men who are to blame? Many women work at night: they can't stay at home. Anyway, home may not be safe for many of us. A quarter of all the crimes of violence reported is wife battering. And we're expected to take this without defending ourselves."**
>
> "Women, Angry at Male Violence, Say 'Resist the Curfew!,'" *Leeds Other Paper*, November 28, 1980

Manchester, Brighton, London, Bristol, Bradford, Guildford, Salisbury, York, and Newcastle all took part. The action was coordinated by the Leeds Revolutionary Feminist Group in response to the murder of several women by Peter Sutcliffe, aka "The Yorkshire Ripper," in the Leeds and Bradford area. Amid the attacks, the West Yorkshire police advised women to stay indoors for their safety. In response, the Leeds Revolutionary Feminist Group encouraged feminists to "Resist the Curfew!"

Reclaim the Night marches became a collective expression of self-defense that enabled women to refuse victimization or blame for Sutcliffe's brutal violence. Women walked defiantly "down to town from Woodhouse, where rapists lurk on the moor, or Chapeltown, Ripper '77 territory. Strong, knowing our sisters all over Britain are marching tonight, too."[18]

In the US, women also took up self-defense, carried pepper spray, and organized a series of Take Back the Night marches through city streets and college campuses, demanding the right to go out after dark without fear of assault. The retitling of the march was inspired by a memorial read by NOW activist Anne Pride at an anti-violence rally in Pittsburgh in 1977. The first official march took place in San Francisco in 1978. Prior to that, marches raising awareness of sexual violence had taken place in New York, Philadelphia, Pittsburgh, and other locations, often—as in Europe and the UK— in response to a local tragedy or event.

The Canadian Fly-by-Night Collective also organized a 1978 march in Vancouver, and marches continued in the country throughout the early 1980s at the instigation of Vancouver Rape Relief, the first rape crisis center in Canada.

Reclaim the Night / Take Back the Night was part of an increasingly combative feminist politics that emerged at the end of the 1970s. The aim was to tackle violence against women in every form, from the state to the media, the street to the bedroom. The name of the British group Women against Rape (WAR) captures the sense

Above: Ongoing campaigns against pornography divided feminists, some of whom feared that their own erotica and new lesbian literature might become banned as well. But at this 1979 rally, photographed by Freda Leinwand, marchers firmly defined pornography as "anti-female propaganda" and asserted, "Pornography is not art—it's violence."

of battle and total conflict. Yet the battle against male violence was of a completely different kind to the wars waged by men throughout history. It rallied against images, myths, behavior, and institutions, and sought to protect the territory of women's bodies, rather than land or material resources. Women took practical measures in order to fight back against the perceived and actual threat of male violence. Activists challenged violence embedded in everyday personal relationships and in laws.

The British Black Women's Movement resisted invasive state-sanctioned violence experienced by some black and Asian immigrant women. In February 1979, the Asian women's group AWAZ organized a protest at Britain's Heathrow airport after the media revealed immigration officers were giving vaginal examinations or so-called virginity tests to Asian women entering the UK. "The Immigration Act gives the police and immigration officers amazing powers," an AWAZ activist reported in feminist publication *Spare Rib*. "They can act in an extremely racist way and still be within the law."[19] "Virginity tests" were meant to determine whether women were telling the truth about being married to a UK resident and relied on stereotypes of the "submissive, meek and tradition-bound Asian woman."[20] As well as invasive medical examinations, women could be intensely questioned about their personal and sexual lives.

At the heart of all this activism were the key questions: What were the root causes of intimate gender violence? How might women protect themselves? These questions both united and fractured feminists into countless groups, theories, and coalitions. Some blamed the easy availability of brutal pornography as a cause of men's aggression toward women and called for the removal of billboards featuring near-naked models. Ads seeming to celebrate female physical humiliation drew their share of graffiti activists; feminists weren't shy about transforming a hateful image with creative spray paint. Others took public defacement a step further and destroyed pornographic magazines. But there was no consensus on the efficacy of these actions. The American Feminist Anti-Censorship Task Force and Women against Pornography had opposing views on how to limit women-hating in pop culture, each group asserting that their stance was the better feminist response.

Popular culture could and did begin to reflect a feminist sensibility on issues such as sexual harassment at work. By 1980 the hit US film *Nine to Five* exposed working women's trifecta of low wages, lack of access to promotion, and harassment on the job. As a reprisal for second-wave feminists' street-ogling of powerful Wall Street men—a guerrilla action originally organized by Karla Jay and captured in Mary Dore's recent

Far right: Lt. Mary Keefe of the Sex Crimes Analysis Unit talks to women about rape prevention. In 1974, few women occupied leadership roles in police units, and female victims of rape and abuse were often frustrated by the police's responses (or lack thereof) to their reports. By the twenty-first century, American television program *Law and Order: SVU* entirely focused on victims of sex crimes and featured women in empowered roles as detectives, prosecutors, and pathologists.

Right: PIVAW (Porn Is Violence against Women) coordinated a fortnight of action to protest pornography, which culminated in a demonstration on May 28, 1983, attended by around one thousand women in Soho, London.

documentary *She's Beautiful When She's Angry—Nine to Five* included three office workers' fantasies about turning the tables on a groping boss.

Throughout the 1980s issues of sexual and domestic violence were addressed regularly on Western prime-time television—in talk shows, in movies like *The Burning Bed*, and on evening news. Police teams and hospitals initiated new protocols for assisting victims who reported rape, and universities began to include mandatory workshops for students to understand the definition of date rape. Nevertheless, the legal system remained unfriendly and often prohibitively hostile to women who sought justice.

Reclaiming the body

Even in the 1970s, medical knowledge about women's health lagged behind other issues; women's bodies were generally considered a problem to be cured or a mystery to be ignored. To challenge this, women's liberation activists gathered research and provided advice to women that was not available through official medical channels.

Women's health centers were established throughout the 1970s and into the 1980s, particularly in the US, to help offer practical healthcare and also disseminate information, regardless of race, class, sexual orientation, and (in the US, in some cases) insurance coverage. In 1970, the Boston Women's Health Collective published "Women and Their Bodies: A Course," which was the forerunner to the groundbreaking work *Our Bodies, Ourselves*, which urged women to take full ownership and responsibility for their bodies, and which has sold millions of copies worldwide since its first publication. This publication and the work of health centers, such as that in Boston, inspired feminists further afield in Europe, including Italy, where neighborhood women's collectives established women's health centers in several cities and spearheaded the institutionalization of women's health throughout the country by the mid-1970s.[21]

Alongside the British adaptation of *Our Bodies, Ourselves* published in 1978,[22] smaller-scale publications provided women with information about health in their local area. The *Bolton Women's Guide to Medical Issues*, produced by the Bolton Women's Liberation Group, included advice about menstruation, menopause, pregnancy, abortion, and contraception. It demystified

Copyright © 1972 by Women's Graphics Collective, Chicago Women's Liberation Union, www.cwluherstory.org

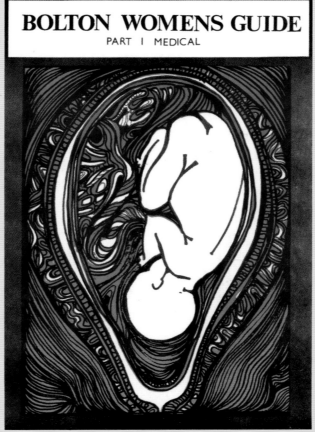

Far left: Signaling a return to midwifery and female control of birthing practices, this poster extended the natural childbirth movement of the 1960s and '70s to include home birth options. The bilingual outreach to Spanish-speaking women in the greater Chicago area acknowledged Latina mothers' poor experiences with local hospital care.

Left: The *Bolton Women's Guide* was an example of a smaller-scale and locally focused health pamphlet that provided women with information about medical issues that specifically affected them.

ik ben een gewenst kind

dit kan op het:

CENTRUM VOOR SEXUELE VOORLICHTING

OPENINGSUREN:

recepties
ma., di., do., vr.: 9u/12u 13u30/17u
woensdag: 9u/12u 19u/20u
zaterdag: 10u/12u

dokterskonsultaties
18u/20u
12u/14u

c.g.s.o./gent willem tellstraat 13
tel: 091/25 06 52

TANDEM   5s

I ACCUSE !

METTE EJLERSEN exposes the travesty of women's sexual lives, created by men and endured by women

The Scandinavian bestseller that strips away the misconceptions surrounding feminine sexual experience. with an afterword by ___ and Sten Hegeler authors of *The ABZ of Love*

DOWN THERE

AN ILLUSTRATED GUIDE TO SELF ~ EXAM

by Sophie Laws

Top left: Poster for a sexual health clinic in Ghent, c. 1976.

Bottom left: The Swedish book *I Accuse!*, first published in 1969, became a global sensation with its forthright exploration of the female sexual experience.

Above: *Down There* (1981) by Sophie Laws was a no-nonsense guide to the "self-examination," a process that empowered women to gain knowledge about and explore their bodies in new ways.

Paths to feminist health information

Bonnie J. Morris

The women's liberation movements sought to reclaim the female body for women, and one pathway to this was encouraging women to explore their own bodies.

A platform for feminist revolution was every woman's right to control her own body. Yet in the movements' new publications, in media interviews, and in the truth-telling space of consciousness-raising groups, many women admitted they barely knew their bodies. Few had been encouraged to explore or understand their own reproductive organs, whether for health concerns or pleasure. The female body was too often a source of shame: exploited for male desire and commercial benefit, ruled by the state or burdened with the complications of pregnancy and motherhood, it seemed to belong to everyone but the woman herself. Girls coming of age encountered degrading euphemisms and slang for *vagina*, *menstruation*, *loss of virginity*, and *pregnancy* that encouraged a culture of shame.

Few women had been raised to speak openly about bodily functions or to use their *correct* names. In Western cultures, even the scientifically correct names for female anatomy derived from medical Latin or were named for male research scientists. The so-called Fallopian tubes were named for sixteenth-century Italian anatomist Gabriele Fallopio. Women who delivered a baby surgically had a "Caesarean," their birth forever associated with a Roman emperor. And Greek terms had long defined the womb and vagina in terms of deficiency or male dominance: female emotional *hysteria* was supposedly caused by a woman's unstable womb, a condition that could be cured only by a radical *hysterectomy*; and *vagina* meant the sheath for a sword in ancient Greek. In the US, sex education, limited and contested throughout the twentieth century, might introduce the term *vagina* but never mention *clitoris*, the location of female pleasure. Even early twentieth-century nicknames for the clitoris were male-identified: "the boy in the boat,"[23] "the little man in the boat." A lesbian was defined in male terms through nicknames such as "bull dyke" and "bulldagger."

Simply learning about oneself was not possible when human sexuality textbooks on library shelves were limited to readers eighteen and older. Pornography also did the average woman an additional disservice by presenting unrealistically touched-up photos, designed to excite males, as the ideal womanly body type.

Feminists demanded change. They also learned from one another that even women who had developed the confidence to fend off male street harassment were not necessarily proactive in the doctor's office. Socialized to see the male physician as an authority whom patients should not challenge, women now had to learn to assert themselves during both routine and crisis medical appointments. After generations spent passively accepting prescriptions and long subject to a healthcare system riddled with race, class, and sex bias, women turned to feminist health sources for self-diagnosis and empowerment. Feminists began offering informed critiques of medical and cosmetic products that actually hurt women's health, such as feminine hygiene sprays, the miscarriage prevention drug DES, and flawed birth control methods such as the Dalkon shield (an intrauterine device, or IUD, that was found in the 1980s to induce pelvic inflammatory disease).

Who gave women the information they needed for informed self-care? One source in the US was Planned Parenthood. But in 1971, the publication of a groundbreaking guidebook called *Our Bodies, Ourselves*, compiled by the Boston Women's Health Collective, finally put open information into American women's hands.

The book's first printing (on newsprint) sold 240,000 copies; its chapters carefully followed women's physical functions, life cycles, sexual identities, and experiences with contraception, pregnancy, sex, exercise, and aging. Most controversial in the eyes of would-be censors, educators, and some librarians was the section on self-exploration: "If you have never masturbated, we invite you to try."[24] These chapters were eye-opening for men as well.

Both humor and distress accompanied the wave of new feminist articles and discussions on female sexual pleasure.

> "There is no record of a woman with an absolutely regular menstrual cycle. . . . Myths have endowed menstruating women with everything from supernatural healing powers to supernatural destructive powers. Too bad they aren't true."
>
> Boston Women's Health Collective, *Our Bodies, Ourselves*, 1979

OUR BODIES, OURSELVES

WOMEN UNITE

A BOOK BY AND FOR WOMEN

REVISED AND EXPANDED

BY THE BOSTON WOMEN'S HEALTH BOOK COLLECTIVE

Above: The cover of the Boston Women's Health Collective best-selling self-help volume. The book's first printing—on newsprint, in 1971—sold 240,000 copies; chapters drew from personal experience and allowed diverse women's narratives to show their frustration with the sexist healthcare system.

Texts prompted a range of questions, such as: if women were not dependent on male penetration for fulfillment (as Freud had argued), and were able to climax alone, with a sex toy, or with one another in lesbian partnerships, were men even necessary any more? However, for most women, the goal was not to move away from men or male practitioners, but to establish more effective and honest communication.

The right to self-care was not granted freely. Feminist self-help groups teaching women to care for their own vaginas were regarded as practicing medicine without a license. These self-examination sessions were first held in 1971 at Every Woman's Bookstore, led by activist Carol

Downer, who together with Lorraine Rothman founded the Los Angeles Feminist Women's Health Center (FWHC). During one self-help clinic in 1972, the FWHC was raided by the police. Downer had been active in demonstrating how any woman might view her own cervix in a mirror by inserting a plastic speculum, and along with Colleen Wilson was arrested while showing how the application of yogurt in lieu of a then costlier drug prescription might cure a common yeast infection. During the police raid, a lunch yogurt was mistakenly seized as evidence. Angry (if humorous) protests followed, including one feminist's complaint, "What man would be put under police surveillance for six months for looking at his penis? What man would have to spend $20,000 and two months in court for looking at the penis of his brother?"[25] Male feminists, in the struggle to educate women about their options, were also persecuted; Bill Baird, a tireless activist for safe and legal birth control, was charged with "crimes against chastity" and "impersonating a pharmacist" after handing a can of contraceptive foam to a female student attending his Boston University lecture in 1967.

Feminist health activists also made a positive self-image part of resistance to the exploitation of women's bodies. An important element of this was to raise awareness of eating disorders in young women due, in part, to issues surrounding body image. The harmful influence of advertising, which turned women (or just body parts) into sexual objects, became a regular theme in *Ms.* magazine's back page "No Comment" gallery. By the 1980s, author and speaker Jean Kilbourne began touring campuses and conferences with her slide show "Killing Us Softly," addressing the impact of photographic retouching and subliminal messages on women's self-image. She demonstrated how models appeared flawless through new computerized retouching. This introduction to media literacy allowed women and their daughters to remain vigilant in evaluating those products targeting female guilt, shame, and self-worth.

what happens during childbirth, the impact of drugs, epidurals, and the effects of postnatal depression.

Learning how to carry out a self-examination became a key moment of personal transformation in the new politics of health and sexuality that emerged from the women's movement. "Having a good hard look at our external and internal genitals is a very good way to face up to and start to change the fear and hatred of our female bodies which this male-dominated culture has taught us,"[26] wrote health worker and researcher Sophie Laws in the introduction to *Down There: An Illustrated Guide to Self-Exam*, published by Onlywomen Press in 1981. Pregnancy testing regularly took place within women's centers across Britain well into the 1980s. Ellen Malos, an activist involved in the Bristol Women's Liberation Movement, explained how although "you could get a pregnancy test from your GP, a lot of women didn't want to for various reasons—he was unsympathetic, they didn't feel comfortable, they may not have wanted to be pregnant . . . and it took a long time for the results to come back, about a week. With our little thing, we could do it and tell them immediately. Women used to come and queue up into the street sometimes by the time it opened at 9 am on Saturdays."[27]

By the 1980s, women's health concerns were overshadowed by the scourge of AIDS. Feminists who willingly gave time and energy to gay men in crisis found that little research or education went into issues of women living with AIDS, or to the transmission of the HIV virus from mother to infant. But another long-hushed global health issue soon emerged as a factor in HIV transmission—female ritual circumcision. In the 1970s, feminists all over the world began confronting the risks associated with female circumcision, a centuries-old practice in parts of Africa and the Middle East designed to limit young girls' sexuality until marriage. Too often it led to sterility, incontinence, infection, and even death. It also increased susceptibility to HIV transmission due to the tearing of unhealed wounds (created by the circumcision) during intercourse. Nevertheless, millions of women and girls the world over were reluctant to challenge a custom that defined them as chaste, pure, and marriageable in the eyes of their community elders. Nor did local educators appreciate the intervention of critical Western feminists, who had renamed the ritual circumcision FGM (female genital mutilation), thus criminalizing parents and midwives. This created tension between Western feminists shocked by FGM and African women activists for whom water rights, famine, and education were more important issues—a conflict of priorities that gained attention at the UN Women's World Conference in Nairobi in 1985.

Elsewhere, within the women's movements, groups such as the UK-based Sisters against Disablement (SAD)

Below left: Betty Dodson was the author of *Liberating Masturbation* and a vocal advocate for women's self-pleasure. Here she demonstrates a vibrator at a 1973 sexuality conference. Female self-exploration shocked conservative religious authorities and threatened some men, who feared women would no longer need them as sexual partners; but sex toy stores marketing to adult couples proliferated in the 1970s, although they were banned in states like Texas.

Below right: An unidentified woman attends a 1988 rally for homeless and mentally ill women. In the feminist movement, as was true across cultures throughout history, disability rights lagged behind other causes—until the success of the US Disabilities Act. However, disability access and, in particular, sign language interpretation became vital hallmarks of the women's music movement, which offered "differently abled" workshops and seating at concerts and festivals.

MAKING IT

A Woman's Guide to Sex
in the Age of AIDS

by Cindy Patton and Janis Kelly

Spanish Translation by Papusa Molina
Illustrations by Alison Bechdel

Revised and Updated

Long-term AIDS journalists and activists Cindy Patton and Janis Kelly have addressed one of the critical questions: How can women—heterosexual, lesbian, bisexual—enjoy full sexual lives *and* protect themselves from this deadly disease?

Firebrand Sparks Pamphlet #2

Firebrand
Books
Ithaca, New York

$4.95   ISBN 0-932379-32-X

HACIÉNDOLO

Guía Sexual para Mujeres en
la Era del SIDA

por Cindy Patton y Janis Kelly

Traduccion al Español de Papusa Molina
Ilustraciones de Alison Bechdel

Revisada y puesta al Día

Cindy Patton y Janis Kelly, quienes por largo tiempo han sido periodistas y activistas en asuntos del SIDA, han confrontado una pregunta muy crítica: ¿Como pueden las mujeres—eterosexuales, lesbianas, bisexuales—disfrutar plenamente su vida sexual y protegerse *al mismo tiempo* de esta enfermedad mortal?

Un Panfleto de la Serie Chispas de Firebrand #2

Firebrand
Books
Ithaca, New York

$4.95   ISBN 0-932379-32-X

Above: This guide by Cindy Patton and Janis Kelly, illustrated by Alison Bechdel, was published by Firebrand Books in 1987. It was translated into Spanish and sold worldwide. It addressed the often overlooked issue of women and sex during the AIDS epidemic.

challenged discrimination against disabled women. They produced the "SAD Access Code," a checklist to ensure events were accessible for *all* women, which included information about parking at the venue, public transport, entrance, door and premises dimensions, toilet facilities, type of floor surface, lighting and heating quality, and how activities were to be structured. The SAD access code can be found in publicity for numerous activist events in the 1980s. Nevertheless, women's liberation events would sometimes be organized in "partially accessible" venues, and this was a source of obvious and immense frustration for disabled activists. Partially accessible venues limited "which workshops we go to"

and prevented women "from socialising over meals with other participators," wrote SAD in an open letter to the 1983 Lesbian Sex and Sexual Practice Conference. It also dictated "the amount of time some lesbians with disabilities can stay at the conference because of the lack of an accessible toilet."[28]

Through politicizing the female body, the women's movement constructed new political and territorial boundaries. Activists invented new ways to understand the intimate violence done to women's bodies by the state or partners, and discovered how medical knowledge, when placed in the hands of women, could provide a pathway to liberation.

ONLY IN SOLIDARITY ARE WOMEN STRONG

WE UNDERSTAND OPPRESSION AND STEREOTYPE SEXISM BECAUSE WE ARE WOMEN

STRAIGHT SISTERS AND DYKES EVERYWHERE LESBIAN LIBERATION CONCERNS YOU

"THERE'S NO PENIS BETWEEN US!"

Sexuality and lesbian feminism

Is there more to life than being a wedlocked woman or an undesirable spinster? Is heterosexuality natural or is it a social construction? Do women have the right to sexual pleasure, just as their husbands do? Is romance an ideological mirage? Is it possible to love and have sex with other women? Is non-monogamy politically progressive?

For women who became active in the women's liberation movements, confronting such questions was an inevitable part of personal and political transformation. In the confines of consciousness-raising groups or through reading "detonating"[1] feminist texts, women began to deconstruct the "traditional" views of women's roles in sex and female sexuality that had been handed to them; women's liberation helped open up other ways.

Living politics through the intensity of personal life was never easy. It involved big changes—psychological, economic, and sexual—as well as personal bravery to defy social taboos and transgress received morality. For some women, the challenge to become sexually liberated was too disruptive, and they left the movement. It was, according to British writer and activist Beatrix Campbell, "very clear that they just couldn't stand it, and it was going to destroy their marriages, and of course it was."[2]

Lesbians and the women's movement

During the feminist revolution of the 1970s, the lesbian community emerged as a newly visible, politically energized group, determined to speak and to be heard as women who loved women. Critics jeered that "feminist" was just a code word for "lesbian" and, indeed, some separatists would later produce pins declaring, "Feminism is the theory: lesbianism is the practice." But not every feminist was a lesbian, or comfortable with gay culture; and certainly, not all lesbians were feminists, or comfortable in the academic and political settings of feminist liberation.

In the twenty-four years between World War II's "tolerance" of lesbians in wartime roles and the fight for public acceptance of America's gays and lesbians during the Stonewall Riots of 1969, America had retreated to the homophobia embodied by Senator Joseph McCarthy's

> "The subject of lesbianism is very ordinary. It's the question of male domination that makes everybody angry."
>
> **Judy Grahn**, *A History of Lesbianism*, 1971

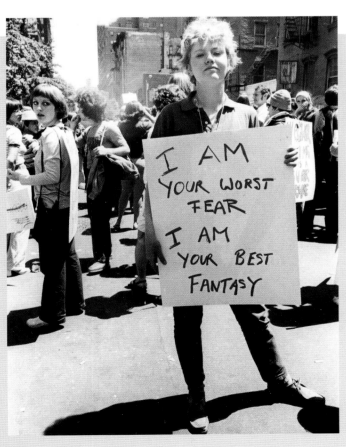

Page 104: This c. 1975 British poster offers a message of unity for the women's liberation movements, regardless of sexual orientation.

Far left: In this photograph by Diana Davies, activist Donna Gottschalk attends the Christopher Street Gay Liberation Day parade in New York, 1970, with a poster that reads, "I am your worst fear, I am your best fantasy." The sentiment acknowledges the contradictory ways in which contemporary men viewed lesbians, whether as objects of desire in porn movies or as threats to "traditional" male-female relationships.

Left: This 1982 Red Women's Workshop poster demonstrates how women's movements created new social contexts where lesbians could publicly express their identities.

geen diskriminatie
van de
homofiele vrouw
doet
de vrouw

diskriminatie=
onderdrukking   art.372 bis

zie stand homofiele vrouwen

I ♥ WOMEN

Opposite, top right: Gay rights pin from 1974, evoking the famous branding of Coca-Cola.

Above: Lesbian women protest discrimination against homosexuals in society and within the women's movement itself at the national women's day in Hasselt, Belgium, on November 11, 1975.

Below: Women-loving badge from the late 1980s.

purges of suspected homosexuals in government jobs. The work of activists Del Martin and Phyllis Lyon in administering America's first lesbian-positive organization, the Daughters of Bilitis (with a national newsletter, *The Ladder*, first published in 1956), stood out in the late 1950s and early 1960s, when most lesbians found reflections of their lives only in bar culture and sensationalist paperback books. Even lesbian bars were typically male-owned, with state laws actually forbidding women from employment as bartenders; moreover, much of bar culture reflected the ills and biases of society at large, with lesbians of color asked to show several forms of identification, and military women at risk of being "outed" by undercover police.[3] Desperate to find others like them, expelled by their own families, and even at risk of involuntary commitment to mental institutions, lesbians in the US flocked to bohemian sites such as New York's Greenwich Village, Berkeley, and San Francisco, hoping to find tolerance and love.

By 1970, lesbians were ready to come out of the shadows as political constituents within feminism, attracted to a movement that placed women at the center and openly critiqued male chauvinism. But many of feminism's critics already assumed that a feminist was simply a man-hating "lesbo," and during the 1960s–80s that stereotype haunted leaders of feminism who wanted to gain political credibility or serve in government alongside men.

In the US, NOW founder Betty Friedan's famous remark that lesbian rights were a "lavender menace" suggested that lesbians were unwelcome in the movement. Her attitude, however, inspired one of second-wave feminism's greatest pranks. Secretly dressed in LAVENDER MENACE T-shirts, a collective of lesbian feminists who had been active in the movement challenged homophobia by attending the Second Congress to Unite Women in May 1970. Shutting off the auditorium lights during a plenary, twenty women then reassembled onstage, appearing with T-shirt slogans

LESBIAN BATTERING
A COMMUNITY WORKSHOP

9 A.M.   5 P.M.

Lesbians gathering to explore and define the issue of lesbian battering and the ways it affects all of our lives.

NOVEMBER 23, 1985   9 A.M.~5 P.M.

EMMANUEL BAPTIST CHURCH
275 STATE STREET
ALBANY, N.Y. 12208

Childcare provided • wheelchair accessible • interpreted for the hearing impaired • bring your lunch • beverages provided

The Workshop is free, but pre-registration is required by NOV. 15. Please detach and send the following information to:

LESBIAN SAFETY NETWORK (LSN), P.O. Box 743, Albany, N.Y. 12201

Check if you need: ☐ childcare ☐ interpreter ☐ wheelchair accessibility

Sponsored by LSN through a grant from
Holding Our Own, a fund for women

Meg Christian
I know you know

OLIVIA RECORDS

DE PRINSES ONTWAAKT
lesbian nation

Warm Fuzzy Dyke

AN END TO ALL DISCRIMINATION AGAINST LESBIANS

Clockwise from top left: This 1985 flier for a workshop in Albany, New York, is testament to the prejudice lesbians faced both outside and inside the women's liberation movements.

Meg Christian's *I Know You Know* album, released in 1974, was lesbian-owned Olivia Records' first full-length release on vinyl and included both tender and humorous compositions on lesbian life: from "Valentine Song" to "Ode to a Gym Teacher." The album launched Olivia's success as an independent collective, and later a company, that was run by lesbians to market to lesbians.

This 1981 sticker celebrates the Netherlands as a lesbian nation.

A pin issued c. 1984 sends out a softer message in contrast to a more militant or revolutionary lesbian stance.

An End to All Discrimination against Lesbians was part of the sixth demand of the British Women's Liberation Movement, although lesbian politics and sexuality could at times generate tension within the movement as a whole.

Below: A demonstration in Finland for gay rights on May 29, 1976. The placard on the left of this image proclaims in Swedish, "Lesbians' struggle is women's struggle," while the placard on the right states in Finnish that "gay is not sick—oppressing society is."

displaying a powerful visual of the many energetic thinkers, writers, and activists who had been marginalized within their own liberation movement. Within a year, NOW passed a resolution naming "the oppression of lesbians as a legitimate concern of feminism."

Rita Mae Brown, Karla Jay, and other members of the US Radicalesbians group from this incident produced one of the most famous documents of the early 1970s, "The Woman-Identified Woman." It began, "What is a lesbian? A lesbian is the rage of all women condensed to the point of explosion," continuing, "for in this sexist society, for a woman to be independent means she *can't* be a *woman*—she *must* be a *dyke*."[4] Women soon formed their own coalitions and began to produce affirming viewpoints of lesbian love and politics through music and writing, including lesbian concerts and women-only music festivals and discos, radical poetry readings and events at women's bookstores, and publications such as *Dyke*. The first albums celebrating lesbian identity were Maxine Feldman's "Angry Atthis" (a 45rpm single, released in 1972), followed by Alix Dobkin's full-length *Lavender Jane Loves Women* in 1973, and Meg Christian's *I Know You Know* on the new Olivia Records label in 1974.

In contrast, within British society in the late 1960s and early '70s, lesbians were still largely invisible, marginalized, and often regarded as mentally ill. Being a lesbian had consequences. Some women were refused legal custody of their children in divorce settlements; this issue was addressed by Action for Lesbian Parents and dramatized by Gay Sweatshop in their play *Care and Control* (1977).

To challenge this stigma and oppression, some became politically active in the Gay Liberation Front (GLF). The GLF was established in Britain in 1970, inspired by the Stonewall Riots and the revolutionary activism of the Black Panthers. Gay men and women within the GLF often had different political priorities, and many lesbians

Lesbian sex wars

D-M Withers

"The Right to a Self-Defined Sexuality" was the sixth demand of the British women's movement. Sexuality became a crucial topic of debate and struggle within feminism from the late 1970s onward, as activists sought to reclaim female sexuality from man-made images and idealizations.

The lack of cultural resources to describe women's sexuality—whether lesbian, bisexual, or heterosexual—in the late 1960s and early 1970s cannot be overstated. Lesbians were invisible (or sick or perverted), *lesbianism* itself a dirty word. Heterosexual women were tethered to and by male-defined desire. Bisexual women were caught within stereotypes that painted them as selfish and indecisive. The women's movement provided an antidote, as activists invented social spaces and cultural forms that helped women explore sexuality in new public and political contexts.

Self-defining women's sexuality was no easy task given the prevalence of porn within culture. Pornographic images, some feminists argued, were not only a form of violence against women; they *were* violence against women. By the late 1970s, pornography was no longer a niche interest, consumed by freaks and perverts in shady shops or private bedrooms. It had become part of mass culture and "entertainment," from the page three girls of British tabloids to slasher movies. It was how, Jo Spence argued in the 1985 *The Picture of Health?* exhibition, the female body "is *fragmented* through representation (adverts/pornography)."[5]

Angry Women was a national network of militants who fought back against pornographic representation using any means necessary. The group hurled paint-filled eggs at cinema screens that displayed "obscene and sadistic portrayals of women."[6] Violence against porn shops was common. Locks were glued, windows smashed, and, in some cases, entire shops burned down. Porn magazines were gathered from newsagents and burned, followed by vigils for victims of male violence.

Other anti-porn groups, such as Women against Violence against Women (WAVAW), met to discuss common sexual fantasies, and uncovered shared imaginaries of rape, domination, and power. "Desire" to be violated was, they argued, the logical consequence of how female sexuality was conditioned by a pornographic, male-dominated culture. Such fantasies, they argued, could only ever subjugate women and deny them sexual power.

Despite the intensity of lesbian activism in the early 1980s, lesbian sex and sexuality remained a private and somewhat taboo issue. Lesbian conferences remained "talk shops about the things which *determine* sexuality" but became caught up in "how frightening it is actually to talk about sex."[7] They weren't, in other words, particularly sexy. What did lesbians do in bed, anyway?

In the early 1980s, this all changed when the US "lesbian sex wars" began to influence lesbians in Britain. Enter the sado-masochist (SM) "Rebel Dykes,"[8] a group of mostly London-based sex radicals who explored the tensioned point where sexuality meets pleasure, eroticism, violence, power, domination, fantasy, subjection, and control.

Lesbian SM was deemed controversial because it eroticized power imbalances and violence *between* women. It was antithetical to the nonviolent, peaceful—yet often desexualized—lesbian feminism that had prevailed during the women's liberation movements. This, along with the use of chains and whips during play scenes, a strong preference for leather, and "reported sightings of SM dykes wearing swastikas in various lesbian and gay clubs,"[9] raised concern for some activists that SM dykes were not taking seriously the racism that black and other women of color experienced in everyday life, and SM remained a contentious issue in the lesbian and gay community throughout the '80s.

Other groups, such as revolutionary feminist–inspired Lesbians against Sado-Masochism, condemned SM dykes as "walking repositories of racism, fascism and male violence."[10]

Advocates of SM viewed it as a way for lesbians to redefine and explore their sexuality. "Part of our discovery of lesbian sexuality has been an on-going exploration of darker sides, confronting our fears and desires, to give and

"Women are angry at the pictures, magazines, advertisements and films which show us as objects for men to possess, use and abuse. These foster a climate in which male violence against women is seen as acceptable, normal, amusing, a proof of manhood."

"Women Are Angry," press release, December 11, 1980

Above: The remains of a protest by the Angry Women, who aimed to sabotage fashion photographer Helmut Newton's exhibition *31 Nudes*, which was displayed at the Olympus Gallery, London, in 1983. Newton was renowned for making controversial and hypersexualized images that into the 1990s raised the concern of some feminist activists.

Far right: Photo from the first night of a Chain Reaction event in 1987.

Right: Brixton Lesbian Collective members attend a festival during the 1980s.

take power in sexual situations, bringing out into the open both the contradictions and conflicts which are usually suppressed. For us, therefore, lesbian SM is both a liberating process and puts the pussy back into politics,"[11] explained a member of Chain Reaction, an SM group "for proud women perverts," active in London during the 1980s.

At the time, debates between the pro- and anti-SM lesbians proved bitter and irreconcilable. "There is no dialogue. Just two entrenched positions screaming offensive monologues at each other over the heads of the majority of lesbians who occupy that broad middle ground."[12]

Anti-porn and SM feminism may, on the surface, seem like uneasy bedfellows. Yet perhaps they are opposite poles in the complex and historical struggle to reclaim a self-defined sexuality, instigated by the women's movements of the 1970s and '80s.

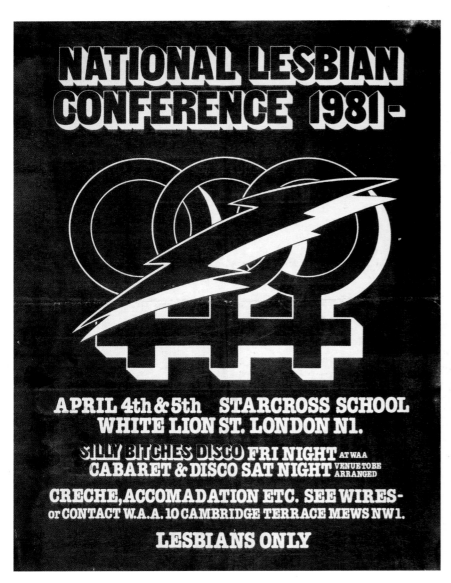

NATIONAL LESBIAN CONFERENCE 1981-

APRIL 4th & 5th STARCROSS SCHOOL
WHITE LION ST. LONDON N1.

SILLY BITCHES DISCO FRI NIGHT AT WAA
CABARET & DISCO SAT NIGHT VENUE TO BE ARRANGED

CRECHE, ACCOMADATION ETC. SEE WIRES-
or CONTACT W.A.A. 10 CAMBRIDGE TERRACE MEWS NW1.

LESBIANS ONLY

LONDON LESBIAN LINE

837 8602/3

Mon–Fri. 2pm–10pm. Tues. Wed. Thur. 7pm 10pm
Info. about, Clubs, Events. Disco's,
Lesbian mothers, Young lesbians, Jewish le
Irish lesbians, Lesbians with disabilities,
Black lesbians, Working Class lesbians, Ol

split from the group in 1972 to join the Women's Liberation Movement.[13]

As in the US, relationships between lesbians and heterosexual women in the British women's movement were not always harmonious. During the first half of the 1970s, some lesbians felt the early campaigns and focus of the movement reflected a "heterosexual outlook."

"Our presence within the movement has been implicit," wrote attendees at the UK's first national lesbian conference, which took place in Canterbury in April 1974. "We have struggled and discussed issues which have not been clearly relevant to our own oppression as lesbians. Now we wish to have our presence explicitly recognized, and have the movement en masse join us in the struggle for greater autonomy for female sexuality, the right of women to love other women, and a generally broader concept of sexuality."[14]

Events at the conference were deemed a "rousing success," with workshops on separatism, radical feminist lifestyles, monogamy and jealousy, lesbians and the women's movement, lesbians and the gay movement, lesbians and the revolutionary left, lesbians in the US, and lesbian mothers.

"The atmosphere was incredibly together and friendly and it lasted through to the disco on the Saturday night,"[15] with one participant reflecting that "it was the least sexist disco I have attended." Serenaded by the London Women's Liberation Rock Band, "the closeness generated by the workshops simply carried through into a more physical rapport."[16]

Still, tensions between some lesbians and "straights" in the women's movement remained and came to a climax at the end of the 1970s with the arrival of a new tendency within the women's movement—revolutionary feminism.

Above left: Conferences created important social and political spaces, especially for groups who were marginalized by the dominant discourses of women's liberation.

Above right and inset: The London Lesbian Line offered a confidential service where women could discuss their sexuality and the issues they faced.

Political lesbianism

"Political lesbianism" is a term often associated with women's liberation movements. It was coined by the British Leeds Revolutionary Feminist Group in its 1979 paper "Political Lesbianism: The Case against Heterosexuality":[17] "All feminists can and should be political lesbians. Our definition of a political lesbian is a woman-identified woman who does not fuck men."[18] The group stated that the political lesbian need not necessarily have a sexual relationship with women, but she must withdraw all her social and sexual energies from men.

For revolutionary feminists, becoming a lesbian was "a necessary political choice, part of the tactics of our struggle, not a passport to paradise."[19] It was an equivalent protest, the group argued, to not buying South African Cape apples in order to contest apartheid. According to the group, women who lived with men faced a "glaring contradiction" in their feminist politics and that through collaborating with "the enemy," heterosexual women fundamentally failed to unite the personal with the political. British revolutionary feminists also distinguished themselves from lesbian feminists who had been active in the Women's Liberation Movement since the split from the GLF. These (often socialist) lesbians were deemed not to be fully "woman-identified" because they sometimes worked with left-wing men. As a result, revolutionists claimed that their actions could only

ever make a small dent in "male supremacy," "the system by which men as a class oppress and control women as a class."[20]

In practical terms, political lesbianism saw women create self-sustaining collectives, businesses, and events by and for women only. In the US, experimental living communities sprang up across America, including the Oregon Women's Land (OWL) group and Washington's The Furies Collective, which produced a magazine and whose members eventually played key roles in starting Olivia Records. Labyris, the first women's bookstore to open in New York's Greenwich Village, marketed buttons, shirts, and stickers with its slogan "The Future Is Female."

In Europe, political lesbianism saw the establishment of groups such as Italy's Identità lesbica, which sought to determine its own agenda away from the male-dominated gay group FUORI! and the predominantly heterosexual women's liberation movement in the country, among whom lesbians often found little acceptance. Consequently lesbianism was far less visible in Italy than in other European countries.[21] In France, for many it was the radical lesbian writer Monique Wittig who embodied the political lesbian movement, founding groups such as Petites Marguérites, the Gouines rouges, and the Féministes révolutionnaires. She also wrote the groundbreaking

Below left: A sign at the International Women's Day march, New York, March 12, 1977, photographed by Bettye Lane. Lesbian feminism had become an entire movement of its own by this time, with slogans such as "Feminism is the theory—lesbianism is the practice," and some leaders arguing that women who continued to have male partners were in fact sleeping with the enemy. Other lesbian activists turned to separatism, focusing their energies and lifestyle entirely around women.

Below left, inset: Button encouraging American gay women to exercise their vote to improve homosexual rights, c. 1970s.

Below right: Bisexual centers offered important social spaces for women who identified as bisexual.

Lesbian roles in film and television

Bonnie J. Morris

Traditionally in Hollywood, female roles were typecast as mothers, wives, and heterosexual lovers—but a determined set of avant-garde directors, producers, scriptwriters, and actors were set to change that.

As per the question "What is a lesbian?" posed by Rita Mae Brown et al. in "The Woman-Identified Woman,"[22] Americans had to learn that a lesbian could also be a neighbor or coworker, mother or daughter, artist or athlete, or ally. For Western audiences in the 1960s and '70s, before the Internet and the broader reach of cable television programming, the few images of lesbians in popular culture were often designed to titillate rather than educate—or they warned young women of the "dangers" in becoming too sexually liberated, or too strident a feminist. Paperbacks, sensationalist women-in-prison films, and a few late-night television scripts were all that a questioning youth or awakening housewife might find. Examples from the 1960s included *The Children's Hour* (ending with one character's lesbian confession and suicide), *The Fox* (ending with one character's death by falling tree), *The Killing of Sister George* (heavily reliant on butch-femme stereotypes but partially filmed in an actual lesbian bar, Britain's famous Gateways Club). Some lesbian roles were intended to titillate men: the icy Pussy Galore, in the James Bond film *Goldfinger*, melts into the hero's arms by the end. But with the emergence of the lesbian and gay rights movement after the 1969 Stonewall Riots, and NOW's gradual acceptance of a pro-lesbian rights platform, visibility increased and authentic storylines began to emerge in mainstream media.

The first television script to examine a lesbian mother's custody battle was *A Question of Love*, starring Gena Rowlands, in 1978. Lesbian characters appeared in the plot twists of *All My Children*, and in historically researched productions, including *The War Widow* and *The Bostonians*.

Films in the 1980s could and did reinforce fears of the lesbian as a vampire who preyed on young, beautiful women (1983's *The Hunger*, in which a soft-porn lesbian love scene was a point of entry to misery and murder in the "undead" lifestyle—a warning not lost on the aroused viewer). But more realistic, complex, and sensitive storylines about lesbian lives and partnerships began to appear in television and film. *Personal Best* (1981) followed the careers of two fictional Olympic track stars whose love affair succumbed to their athletic rivalry. Although in the end one of the two athletes found new love in the arms of a man—a common resolution in earlier "lesbian" films endorsing heterosexuality—*Personal Best* broke ground as a mainstream film showing both naked lovemaking and a definite range of strong female bodies competing for athletic rather than romantic goals. The Canadian production *By Design* (1982) followed two fashionable women lovers trying to conceive a child. *Lianna* (1984) explored the awakening of a married housewife and mother who leaves her husband for an older female professor at the local university; the plot included realistic aspects of divorce and coming out, from the shocked best friend who becomes distant and judgmental to the main character's tentative hookup night in a lesbian bar. In one of *Lianna*'s best scenes, the likes of which had never before appeared on commercial screens, Lianna simply walks through a market street in her university town's pleasant upper-middle-class neighborhood and—having made love with a woman the night before—gazes appreciatively at every woman in her path, experiencing their female appeal in a new light. The film's lovemaking scene included realistic physical intimacy; yet it was the "day after" stroll that reversed decades of gay and lesbian shame and denial by showing a character comfortably settle into her new identity and speculate about which other ordinary women in the neighborhood might be just like her. *Lianna* was directed by John Sayles, who emerged as a prolific filmmaker with strong roles for women in each of his independent and critically acclaimed features.

Though lesbian-themed films produced as commercial Hollywood movies were almost all directed by men, audiences in 1986 enjoyed a new feature directed by a

> "Not all women are raving bloody lesbians, you know."
>
> "That is a misfortune I am perfectly well aware of!"
>
> The Killing of Sister George, 1968

Opposite, left: *Lianna* opened in theaters in 1984 with a sensitive, realistic storyline about a woman's departure from a failing marriage and her further awakening through a lesbian love affair. The film, directed by a progressive man (John Sayles), netted positive reviews and was one of the first screened in mainstream theaters to portray intimate sexuality between women—including oral sex.

Above right: *Desert Hearts*, a 1986 feature directed by Donna Deitch, was based on the thoughtful novel by lesbian author Jane Rule. The film's witty, intelligent dialogue—combined with one of the hottest lesbian lovemaking scenes yet seen in a mainstream film—electrified audiences. Many lesbians could relate to the seductive cowgirl's strong declaration, "I don't act like this to change the world—I act like this so the God-damned world won't change ME." Other viewers identified with the inexperienced professor character, who during her first experience with a woman confesses, "I'm not used to feeling like this at eleven o'clock in the morning."

woman, Donna Deitch. Based on lesbian author Jane Rule's novel, *Desert Hearts* was set in the divorce subculture and casinos of 1950s Vegas, with a staid intellectual divorcee seduced by a brash younger cowgirl. This film had a prolonged lovemaking scene set in a hotel room in broad daylight, with one character saying to the other, "I'm not used to feeling like this at eleven o'clock in the morning."

It took time for the media to offer ongoing roles to actual lesbians like Ellen DeGeneres. Television series offered brief sub-plots for humor (the divorced mothers in *Kate and Allie* pretend to be gay to get a better rent deal from their lesbian landlady). Hollywood critics applauded straight actresses who dared to accept and portray lesbian roles, as Cher did in *Silkwood*. The practice of praising straight allies to the LGBT community often put heterosexuals on the cover of magazines like *The Advocate* in an era when very few working lesbian actresses were willing to come out. But many feminist

viewers felt betrayed by the icepick-wielding, killer-bisexual role Sharon Stone portrayed in *Basic Instinct*. Viewers and fans who were pretty sure Lily Tomlin and Jodie Foster were lesbians searched in vain for words to that effect in the actresses' interviews and publicity. And, as usual, lesbian or bisexual roles for nonwhite actresses were even scarcer, with a few blockbuster exceptions, such as Whoopi Goldberg in *The Color Purple*.

By the mid-1980s, gay and lesbian film festivals were showcasing important new works by independent documentary filmmakers and historians, so that activist and academic audiences (and audiences at women's music festivals) were introduced to historic material like *Before Stonewall*. Most women coming out in the 1960s, '70s, and '80s, however, had to do their own sleuth work to find positive images of their lives on screens of any size: a reason why concerts and bookstore events were so life-sustaining.

Le corps lesbien in 1973, which was then translated into English and published in 1975, and sought to frame a unique language for female desire.

The views of the Leeds Revolutionary Feminist Group were certainly controversial, but they were also very influential and inspired women to make drastic change in their lives. One participant at the British 1979 Revolutionary Feminist Conference remembers the impact it had on her: "It crystallised it for me, it was like a kind of 'eureka' moment, an absolute guillotine that came down, and that was it! I came back saying, 'I'm a political lesbian.'" Friends were concerned "that I'd got some sort of missionary zeal about being a lesbian, but I never changed my mind and twenty-five years later, I'm still here, a lesbian."[23]

For some black lesbians, the arguments of the Leeds Revolutionary Feminist Group were also important. "We read this pamphlet 'Love Your Enemy' [a pamphlet that originated from a paper given by the Leeds Revolutionary Feminist Group and published in 1981 by Onlywomen Press]—a discussion between many different kinds of lesbian and heterosexual feminists—which we'd never seen the likes of before . . . we settled down with this book, and talked through every argument and personal experience for four days. By the end of it we couldn't bring any reasons forward for continuing relationships with men and that was it. But we felt very isolated because in that part of London, we didn't know any other Black lesbians at all."[24]

For other black activists, lesbian separatism was a single-issue "luxury" that could never address intersectional oppression. "While my sexuality is a part of me, it's not the only thing. My race and class are equally important and this has an implication for me in the way I organize, or want to organize, politically."[25]

Certainly, within the British Black Women's Movement, lesbianism could be a fraught issue, despite the fact that founding members of key organizations such as the Brixton Black Women's Group and OWAAD were lesbians.[26] At the 1981 OWAAD conference, a tense

Far right: *Love Your Enemy?* captured the occasionally incendiary debate between heterosexual feminism and political lesbianism.

Right: Classic button design, openly declaring solidarity with the lesbian community, c. 1970s.

Button produced by the Organisation of Lesbian and Gay Activists (Cape Town), date unknown.

Below left: As lesbian feminism became a clearly distinct movement within a movement, it drew charges of being "too white," but in fact its adherents emphasized diversity and unlearning racism at conferences, concerts, and workshops.

Below middle: The Hackney Lesbian Group's calendar of events displays the ways in which lesbian women came together for socializing and solidarity.

Below right: *Rites* magazine was published from 1984 to 1992, catering to Canada's bisexual, gay, and lesbian community.

CAMDEN LESBIAN CENTRE PROJECT
2 MALDEN RD. LONDON NW5 267·1402

LESBIANS IN CAMDEN

Do You Want a Centre ?!!

There is a group of us meeting to make this possible !!!!

contact Janet or Laura 267-1402
or come to the next meeting

at : HARMOOD COM. CENTRE   1 FORGE PLACE
                             FERDINAND ST. LONDON NW 1

time + date OCT. 11, 1984 8 pm. to 10 pm.
             OCT. 23, 1984 8 pm. to 10 pm.

access : Level entrance,,parking, babysitting fees available,
         Toilet w/c accessible, signer by arrangement.

funded by the Camden Women's Committee

In conjunction with Camden Women's Committee Lesbian Working Group.

Far left: The Camden Lesbian Centre was co-run by the Black Lesbian Group and was the first center in Britain established specifically for lesbians. Opened in 1987, it provided a home for groups such as black lesbian organization Zamimass; GEMMA, a lesbian disability group; and many other activities.

Left: The intertwining of the feminist symbol in this blue button, c. 1970s, indicates lesbian solidarity.

This "Viva là vulva!" button, c. 1970s, was not only worn by the lesbian community, but the slogan was also adopted by those seeking to promote an open attitude toward women's sexual health and exploration.

What to do if the police raid

At all stages of a raid :
* Keep calm
* Don't be provoked
* Take notes and sign and date them (you may be able to use them in court)

Put your solicitor's number here:

Points To Remember
The police have wider powers of Search and Seizure under the new Police Act; they can enter more or less any premises for anything.

* * *

The police have more powers to arrest/search under the prevention of terrorism act and the immigration laws.

* * *

Questions-you do not have to answer any questions, except to give a name and address. Use your discretion.

They Are Outside/At TheDoor Let everyone else there know what's happening.

Phone your Solicitor

Find out why they're there
Check their ID.

What can they look at take away search for?

without a warrant
or with a warrant

Anything which could relate to why they're there.

Anything which has anything to do with any offence.

If they have a warrant read it carefully, you may only get one chance
Ask for a copy of it

A warrant could be for search, seizure or arrest.

They don't need a warrant if:
- The occupier has already been arrested
- They suspect a breach of the peace is about to be committed, (which can mean almost anything)
- They claim to be chasing someone who they want to arrest/recapture
- They've been invited in
- To prevent 'serious damage to property'
- To save 'life or limb'
- There are public pool tables pinball machines etc. or if it is a licensed gambling hall

For out of hours drinking on licensed premises

They suspect a 'crime' has been or is about to be committed

Can I Be Searched? inside the premises only if the warrant includes it, (e.g. a search warrant for drugs) or if you have been arrested.

They do not have to wait for your solicitor to arrive before they search you or the premises.

Get witnesses from outside. (Use your discretion)

Every police officer should be followed around.

Take notes of what they say and do. (Use a tape recorder if you can)

Object to them looking at any thing that could not possibly relate to an offence. Make notes of your objection and their response.

It is a good idea to keep 'sensitive' information away from places that are likely to be raided.

"Nothing here same"

Never leave children alone with police.

They must give you a list of everything that they take away. (Make sure that you sign for your property)

Don't go outside with the police Outside the premises they have even wider powers to search/arrest

Can they take me to the police station?
Only if you've been arrested.

What Can They Arrest Me For?
You can be arrested on the spot (without a warrant) if:
* They suspect you have committed or will commit an 'arrestable offence' (anything)
* They doubt your name and address
* You're commiting an offence
** They have to protect a child/vulnerable person from you
* You're 'obstructing the highway' (so don't go outside!)

Remember you can be held under S 136 of the Mental Health Act for up to 72 hours.

If you are arrested
Keep Calm
Do not answer any questions/make a statement without a solicitor being present
The only information you have to give them is your name and address.

You are entitled to
● A doctor if you are in need of medication / injured
● A pen and piece of paper
● A police woman being present when you are searched
● A sign language interpreter if you need one

When they take your belongings away sign for them Directly underneath the last item on the list.

Designed by: **Kris Black**
(Reproduction by permission only please!)

Printed:
with the help of WOMEN IN PRINT

For more info about the project etc. write to
**The Lesbians & Policing Project
38 Mount Pleasant,
LONDON,
WC1X 0AP.**

(01)- 833-4996
(24 hrs ansaphone)
or **833-4999**

produced by the Lesbians and Policing Project

FUNDED BY THE GREATER LONDON COUNCIL

> "We're told separatism is the ultimate guilt-trip where separatists use the heterosexual:lesbian split to condemn other wommin. We're apparently convinced we're 'more right-on,' and reek of being 'holier-than-thou.'"

Nessie—Thi Radical Raddish Frae Scotland 1, May 1979

atmosphere arose when black lesbians demanded separate workshop space. A positive outcome resulted, however, with the formation of the first black lesbian group in Britain. Despite being London-based, it had members from all over the UK.

In the 1980s, "black lesbian activity flourished throughout Britain."[27] In 1983, the Chinese Lesbian Group was launched and in 1985, a group for black lesbians of Asian descent (BLAISA) was founded.[28] The Lesbians and Policing Project (LESPOP), established in the mid-1980s, provided legal support and advice to women involved in legal procedures, from victims of hate crime to those caught up in the immigration system. In 1984, the Camden Black Lesbian Group was established at the Camden Lesbian Centre. In October 1985, over two hundred women attended Zami 1, the first British Black Lesbian Conference in London. Zami 1 "paved the way for further conferences, gave confidence to those lesbians who were frightened of coming out, and most of all it told the general public that black lesbians do exist, and in numbers."[29]

Although much of the activity in Britain was centered on London, during the latter part of the 1980s black lesbian groups were formed in Birmingham, Manchester, and Bradford. Groups and organizations for lesbians of color, such as the Black Lesbian Support Network, were often short-lived—especially if reliant on funding and limited volunteer labor—yet "the foundations of black lesbian and cultural activity" were laid in the 1980s to "be built upon and revitalised at any time by new black lesbians."[30]

Revolutionary feminists on both sides of the Atlantic continued to be accused of dividing the women's liberation movement. Others questioned the wisdom of their political strategy: "Whilst I do see it as a positive that feminist women are deciding to put more and more energy into supporting women emotionally and sexually . . . I do not see that becoming a lesbian . . . necessarily makes a woman more right-on in her feminist politics."[31] Some criticized political lesbianism because it desexualized lesbianism and defined lesbian sexuality in (non)relation to men, rather than to women.

Indeed, in the US, tensions over issues of identity and separatism were evident at a large West Coast Lesbian Conference held at UCLA in 1973. Journalist Jeanne Cordova later recalled, "Bringing together the largest dyke conference in history was politically explosive.

Hundreds of lesbians favored a total separatist withdrawal from the world of men while hundreds of others simply wanted to be open about being gay at their jobs without being fired."[32] This conflict foreshadowed ongoing division between a woman-identified feminism (and the quest for autonomous, women-only spaces) and the eventual rise of advocacy for more inclusive, trans-positive, and fluid definitions of gender. In her memoir *When We Were Outlaws*, Cordova also shared her discovery, many years later, that the FBI had sent undercover informants to that 1973 conference—and to many other lesbian events throughout the 1960s and early 1970s.[33]

Other lesbians did not care to identify with separatism or with lofty political theory. Many, particularly in the US, who could not afford legal representation suffered from biased interactions with police, who segregated butch-looking women into so-called daddy tanks of women's jails, both in California and New York. Still bound by homosexuality laws defining their relationships as illegal in most states, gay women were especially at risk of losing child custody and/or jobs that put them in contact with children. Since a huge percentage of working women earned a living as teachers, homophobia was not just a personal burden but a clear economic threat. These issues became visible to the American public in the years 1977–78, which saw the emergence of the first well-publicized backlash against gay rights led by a conservative evangelical woman, Anita Bryant. Bryant's "Save the Children" campaign sought to overturn a new gay rights statute in Florida on the grounds that homosexuals aggressively "recruited" children; soon afterward, the proposed Briggs Initiative in California attempted to ban teachers from the classroom even if they merely supported gay rights. Lesbians fought back through street protests, recordings, and campaigns; much of the credit for defeating the Briggs Initiative belongs to activist professor Sally Miller Gearhart, author of the lesbian sci-fi novel *The Wanderground*; and Olivia Records made its statement against Anita Bryant (who had long been a model in Florida orange juice ads) by releasing a compilation album called *Lesbian Concentrate*. Featuring an orange juice can on its cover, this album connected lesbian lives of the 1970s with those of black and white women from earlier eras, via Teresa Trull's version of the Ma Rainey hit "Prove It on Me Blues" (and her own composition, "Woman-Loving Women").

Meanwhile, in Britain many homosexuals challenged the infamous 1988 Section 28 rule implemented by Margaret Thatcher's Conservative government. This banned local authorities from "promoting" homosexual lifestyles within schools and was effectively an act of censorship. The act, repealed only in 2000, created a climate of fear among schoolteachers, librarians, and education staff, who worried about losing their jobs or state funding if they discussed homosexuality with pupils.

Few lesbians of the 1970s believed they would see gay marriage in their lifetime, and some actively opposed the idea, criticizing monogamy as too imitative of male-female coupledom, and experimenting with threesomes, non-monogamy, and group living. Others created their own commitment ceremonies regardless of whether lesbian "marriage" was recognized in law books. The lack of legal protections for long-term partnerships was illustrated in one American court case that sent chills through the lesbian community of the early 1980s. Longtime lovers Karen Thompson and Sharon Kowalski were torn apart when a tragic accident left Sharon paralyzed and under the legal control of her father, who promptly removed Sharon from all contact with Karen. This case prompted many lesbians in the US to display the bumper sticker "Why can't Sharon come home?" on cars and windowsills, and it led to new efforts to secure lesbian couples the power of attorney and decision-making in their relationships. A legal victory reuniting the long-separated couple was celebrated when, at the 1987 March on Washington for Lesbian and Gay Rights, a symbolic lesbian street wedding included Thompson and Kowalski.

By the mid-1980s, women who had spent their coming-out years pursuing issues specific to lesbian feminism were rejoining gay men in the struggle against AIDS. Long marginalized in gay political groups run by men, now appreciated for their tireless energy in rallying around the dying, lesbians were rewarded with broader recognition in activist coalitions. For example, as the Reagan administration introduced new anti-gay rights bills in the US, both the Gay Activists Alliance and the National Gay Task Force added "lesbian" to their organizational titles.[34] But not all lesbians saw increasing unification as progress. While they had marched for AIDS funds with gay men, and with straight women for abortion rights and family planning funds, would gay men march with lesbians for breast cancer research? Would women's health clinics make lesbian health a platform in fundraising?

Nevertheless, the politicization of sexuality in the women's and black women's liberation movements transformed personal lives and wider society. The feminist movement dared women to experiment and question what and who they desired, and it challenged heterosexual feminists to withdraw sexual energies from men in order to be "authentic" revolutionaries. Through visibility, defiance, and sacrifice, these women opened the door for queer, lesbian, bisexual, and trans freedoms that many continue to struggle for today.

Opposite top: California's proposed Briggs Initiative (1978) terrified the gay and lesbian community; it would have banned gay and lesbian teachers from teaching in public schools (and silence those who defended homosexuality in the classroom regardless of their sexual identity). This initiative was defeated thanks in large part to the hard work of activists Sally Miller Gearhart and Harvey Milk.

Opposite bottom left: A group takes part in Britain's Lesbian Strength march, c. 1980s.

Opposite bottom right: Members of Rebel Dykes lift high this beautiful banner at Gay Pride in the 1980s.

Below: This sticker was created to support the campaign against the seizing of imported gay and lesbian works by the British customs authorities in 1985.

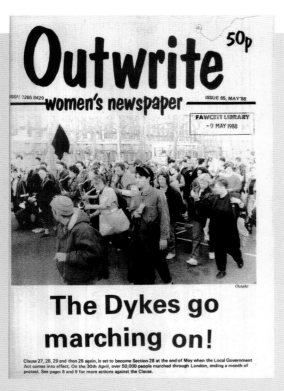

Far left: Feminist newspaper *Outwrite* leads with London's lesbian marches in protest of Section 28 legislation stating that people "shall not intentionally promote homosexuality or publish material with the intention of promoting homosexuality" or "promote the teaching in any maintained school of the acceptability of homosexuality as a pretended family relationship."

Left: In 1977, former beauty queen and orange juice spokeswoman Anita Bryant launched an anti-gay campaign in Florida. In response, Olivia Records released a stellar album celebrating lesbian identity, with the title and logo slyly mocking an orange juice can.

Women together worldwide: lesbian collectives

The 1970s and 1980s saw lesbian, gay, and bisexual rights become a key part of the struggle for liberation across Europe and America. For many, though, solidarity was found in small groups that defined their own way of being.

Lesbian-only collectives were seen as a way in which lesbian women could seek to define their relationships and lives free from the prejudice of society. Collectives ranged from small groups of women who would meet regularly, sometimes with a specific purpose, such as publishing their own work or practicing performing arts, or entire communities where women could live and practice their sexuality openly. The aims of such communities were often deemed as follows:

- to create a safe space for women;
- to develop a viable feminist economy;
- to recreate female identity free from patriarchal influence;
- to dismantle the patriarchy through separatism.[35]

In the US, such communities became known as "womyn's lands" and were often founded in rural areas where women could live an existence rooted in nature. To this day, there are around a hundred such communities throughout America.[36]

Elsewhere, collectives took more of an umbrella form, with a loose organizing structure that smaller groups operated within. Typical of this type of collective was Denmark's Lesbian Movement, formed in 1974, which published *Kvinder-Kvinder* to encourage lesbians to fight for their freedoms, but came together en masse only for annual summer retreats on the islands of Femø and Sejerø. The movement disbanded in the mid-1980s, but women's

> "There was a real sense of the need to strongly identify as a woman and have women's space. . . . We really felt the need to be apart, to draw on our strength and our own empowerment."
>
> **Dr. Jane Dickie** quoted in "My Sister's Keeper," Sarah Kershaw, *New York Times*, January 30, 2009

Left: The Leaping Lesbian Collective. The collective published "The Leaping Lesbian" newsletter for three years starting in 1977.

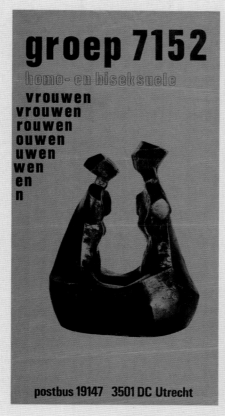

Målningar av Benedicte Bergmann

camps still continue every year on Femø with an "international" week devoted to bringing women together from all over Europe.

One of the most well-known lesbian collectives of the period was the Combahee River Collective, formed in Boston by and for black lesbians. The collective held retreats for its members to table and debate issues relevant to black lesbians. From these discussions, the famous Combahee River Collective Statement was born. The statement powerfully defined the collective's view of black feminism and black lesbianism.

This desire to create an identity that was not carved from heterosexual viewpoints was common to feminist lesbian collectives across the world. In Italy, the name of collective Identità lesbica speaks for itself, and conferences such as that organized by Vivere lesbica (Living Lesbian) in Rome in 1981 were dedicated to exploring the notion of lesbian identification.

The collective itself was a compelling way for lesbians to explore and discover how their sexuality could be a liberating force in its own right for them and those around them.

"A WOMAN'S PLACE IS . . ."

Reinventing culture in and out of the workplace

The women's movements of the 1970s and '80s lifted the ideological veil on the patriarchal truism that "a woman's place is in the home."

The so-called gendered division of labor, which imagined a symmetrical relationship between women's work in the home and men's paid work outside it, had been eroded by postwar economic and social change.

As women fought for opportunity, recognition, and equal pay for their labor in the work world, they were not only shaping present-day society, whether in the classroom or in the streets; feminists were also creating a new awareness of how working women had been taken for granted and underpaid across history. Scholars and activists alike pointed out that women's work and inventions remained invisible in standard history books. Moreover, men and women who depended upon female teachers, nurses, secretaries, and domestic workers saw no apparent contradiction in belittling "career women"; in one of the greatest ironies of the feminist revolution, American conservative lawyer Phyllis Schlafly made a professional career out of opposing professional careers for women.

Such attitudes helped keep traditional female service roles poorly paid, with limited possibilities for promotion. Although some teachers and nurses in Western democracies had access to union organizing, housewives and domestic servants did not; and powerful male-led unions in the trades were often anything but progressive when talented women sought training as welders, carpenters, plumbers, or engineers. Nevertheless, women did make their presence felt within the trade union movement. In the US, feminist caucuses were formed within existing unions and in 1974, thirty-five thousand women attended the first convention of the Coalition of Labor Union Women (CLUW).[1] In Turin, Italy, 1974 and 1975 were landmark years in union feminism with the establishment of the Coordinamento donne intercategoriale—a feminist group specifically aimed at addressing women's issues both within the workplace and the union. The group also played a major role in Italy's "150 monographic courses." Aimed at offering one hundred and fifty hours of free education—including basic literacy and the opportunity to study for school diplomas—to workers, feminists used this scheme as a platform to disseminate their ideas.[2] These examples are testament to the ways in which women mobilized within

Page 124: This illustration is taken from a c. 1978 Red Women's Workshop poster. The original carried the slogan, "Bite the hand that feeds you," publicizing the cutbacks in public services.

Far left: The women's movement provided a fertile context to interrogate the concept of work from a feminist perspective, often highlighting the unpaid work women undertook in the home, as well as the unequally paid work done outside of it.

Left: Activist Carol Giardina at the August 26, 1970, equality march in New York, photographed by Freda Leinwand. Throughout the 1970s a huge percentage of American working women were employed in clerical work as secretaries and typists, in service to powerful men (and often subject to sexual harassment) but without paths to executive power themselves.

their contemporary workplace and union structures, as well as seeking out ways to reinvent or reshape them.

As feminists in Britain, Europe, and the US demanded greater access to professional training and leadership roles for women, they were changing the rules for how and where women held power in the workforce and public life. But the title of US labor historian Alice Kessler-Harris's book *Women Have Always Worked* is a cautionary rebuke to those who, looking back at the gains of the feminist movement, think that no women worked outside the home until the 1970s. That was never true for women whose families depended on their labor in every era.

On a purely pragmatic level, there had been a steady rise in women in employment since the 1950s and, by 1971, in Britain 53 percent of women aged sixteen to sixty-four were in paid work outside the home. Nevertheless, cultural perceptions remained rooted in the idea that women's work—whether in the home or in the workplace, skilled or unskilled—was of less value than men's. Even in Communist or Socialist countries, such as the USSR and the German Democratic Republic, where all workers were deemed "equal," women routinely still ended up in more menial jobs and were expected to carry out the majority of domestic tasks alongside their "careers." Indeed, gender stereotyping in men's and women's career options, and in workplace structure itself, presented such a vast barrier that it had to be confronted at every stage of women's lives from infancy to retirement.

Sexism in toys, games, and language

As soon as newborn babies were tagged boy or girl at delivery, their very first toys put them on separate paths to sex-typed occupations. Advertisers promoted tiny homemaker ovens and tea sets for girls, and sports, miniature cars, and building sets for boys. During the peace movement ethos of the 1960s, many parent-led

Above this photo, various signs and toy packaging are visible:

= EQUAL TOYS for Girls and Boys Truth in Packaging

Toys let a child experiment with the questions: What shall I be? What is this world like? Stop toy packaging that limits any child's horizons

MATCHBOX STEER-N-GO

PLAYSKOOL Wiggle Wagon — Unique! Self propelled "GLIDE ACTION" RIDING TOY

BIG JIM SPORTS CAMPER with 15' BOAT

SUNLIGHT

MAGNETEL game for 2 to 4 players — 11 Big Shootin', Slidin', Scorin' Games Packed with MAGNETIC ACTION

ALL BAD Examples

Sleeping Beauty

organizations began to question the wisdom of war toys and violent games for boys, but it took *Ms.* magazine's "Toys for Free Children" feature in 1974 to raise feminist critiques of girls' domestic- and popularity-based games in the US. Fashion-centered Barbie dolls, card games like "Old Maid," and the board game "Mystery Date" emphasized that for girls, future security depended on attracting a successful man. Few science kits, Erector Sets, or sportswear ads featured a girl on their packaging, except as a passive spectator admiring active boys.

The low wages paid to working women forced many women to depend on attracting a higher-salaried man to keep a roof over their heads and maintain a certain lifestyle. The assumption that the male should be the breadwinner was also reinforced through many regulations requiring women to quit their professional jobs at marriage.

Toy manufacturers, school guidance counselors, youth and church groups, and television commercials were all complicit in steering young women to goals of popularity and marriage, with gifted girls often locked out of

programs and schemes recruiting boys into accelerated math and science. Ambition itself might be presented as a freakish quality in a girl; Dr. Grayson Kirk, former president of Columbia University, declared, "It would be preposterously naïve to suggest that a B.A. can be made as attractive to girls as a marriage license." Ambitious young women might be steered toward babysitting and remain relegated from pre-professional internships and training programs—girls in America were forbidden even to become Senate pages (general helpers in senators' offices, who might run errands or do administrative tasks for the senator, often on an intern basis).

At the same time, women who gained employment in what were considered at the time glamorous (though demanding) careers such as flight attendants or news reporters could be forced to retire in their early thirties, on the grounds that men did not wish to see them age. Few American middle-class girls were taught about other realities of womanhood that existed throughout the 1960s: the dangerous toil of white and black women coal

Above: A toy display at the February 1973 NOW conference photographed by Bettye Lane. This exhibit showcased a variety of active, skills-building toys featuring boys, but not girls, on the outside packaging—pointing out that children were sex-segregated by job skills and aptitude early in childhood. Feminists asked manufacturers to "stop toy packaging that limits any child's horizons."

Below left: British *Women's Voice* poster from the 1980s urging women to demand their working rights.

Below middle: The Working Women's Charter was a collaboration between trade unionists and women's liberation activists in Britain. Launched in 1974, it included a list of ten demands related to equal pay and equal access to education, reproductive rights, maternity leave, and greater representation of women in public and political life.

Below right: This October 1986 *Nurses Action* newsletter from Australia reveals how the debate over sexual discrimination in pay gradings was an issue for working women throughout the Western world.

miners surviving in desperately poor Appalachia, or the scientific brilliance of black women engineers and mathematicians in the space program. But as educators pointed out bias in schools, paving the way for the US's Title IX reforms, an entire nation soon learned—if reluctantly—to say "police officer" rather than "policeman," "firefighter" rather than "fireman," and, in more than a few companies, to respect the title "chairperson of the board."

The women's strikes during the late 1960s and early 1970s practically sought to challenge the ongoing problem of women's wages in a male-dominated workplace. Clever satirical essays such as Judy Brady's "I Want a Wife!" (published in *Ms.* magazine, 1971) and Lisa Leghorn / Betsy Warrior's handbook *What's a Wife Worth?* (New England Free Press, 1974) exposed the issues of living in a society where mothers were often responsible for finding and paying for private childcare.

The working women's dilemma

In Britain, the 1968 Ford Dagenham sewing machinists strike led by Rose Boland, Eileen Pullen, Vera Sime, Gwen Davis, and Sheila Douglass saw women halt car production in a major factory because their work and pay was downgraded compared to their male counterparts. The fallout from their stand against workplace

discrimination led to the founding of the National Joint Action Campaign Committee for Women's Equal Rights (NJACCWER), which placed growing pressure on the British government over the issue of equal pay. Labour MP Barbara Castle's response was to introduce the 1970 Equal Pay Act, which enabled women in private and public sectors to make an equal pay claim if they were employed in the same or broadly similar work as a man. The act itself was not implemented until 1975, and by this time employers were able to navigate its terms, mostly by regrading male jobs if the work they did was the same as a woman's.[3]

Many British women's liberationists perceived the 1970 Equal Pay Act to be a charade. The London Women's Film Group's 1974 film *The Amazing Equal Pay Show* presents Castle as a con artist, skilled in playing games of smoke and mirrors, with the Equal Pay Act reduced to political jargon that had no impact on women's economic and social position. Even the original inspiration for the act—the Dagenham sewing machinists—had to wait until 1984 before their jobs were regraded, which meant they never actually received equal pay in their lifetime.[4]

Fundamentally, "Equal Pay for Equal Work" remained one of the initial demands of the women's movement in Britain, yet feminists' interrogation of work and labor far exceeded the question of equal pay.

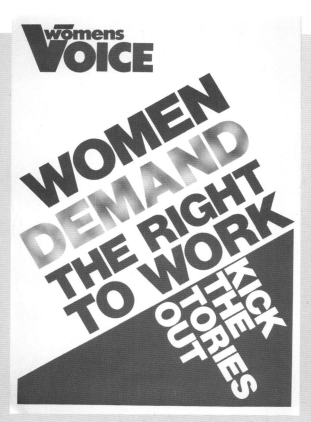

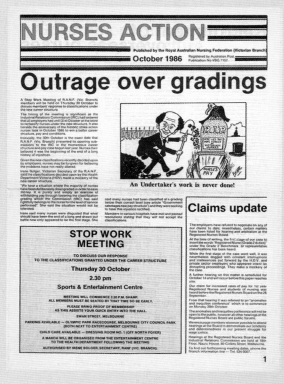

The night cleaners

D-M Withers

In the early 1970s, women's liberation activists put their politics into practice as they built links with working-class women involved in industrial struggles.

British night cleaners had been involved in an industrial dispute since the early 1960s, in response to the UK government's decision to outsource cleaning to contractors, who were making huge profits. "That is why one firm gave up most of its rubber plantations to become Mr. Mopps," wrote one of the militants. "In some respects I've got more respect for the Mafia than for some cleaning contractors. At least the Mafia never exploited innocent cleaning ladies."[5]

Cleaners were forced to accept lower wages, job insecurity, and no benefits. Contractors offered no holiday or sick pay, routinely fired workers on the spot, and employed fewer women to do the same amount of work. This made the hard, physical work of night cleaning ever harder. Women would arrive at 10 pm and leave at 6 am, arriving home to prepare breakfast before their children went to school. "When everyone else is in bed, the night cleaners start their 'day.' Scrubbing floors and washing walls."[6]

The first night cleaners' strike happened in 1962, after a racist supervisor dismissed a West Indian cleaner called Effie.[7] The following day cleaners went on strike, Effie was reinstated, and the supervisor lost her job. In London, over half the estimated 1,800 night cleaners were black or immigrant women, and they were at the forefront of the struggle to achieve better conditions and pay. Most had children and were between the ages of twenty and sixty.[8]

Night cleaners were always facing an uphill battle. They received little support from male-dominated trade unions that classified their work as "unskilled" and "casual." This meant night cleaners had to organize themselves, but this was difficult. A known militant could be fired and excluded from future employment, and many simply could not afford to lose wages. Cleaners worked in small groups in buildings across London, which meant they were isolated from each other. As night workers, it was difficult to organize union meetings.

A key figure in the night cleaners' dispute was May Hobbs, who had been involved in the initial 1962 strike and was repeatedly fired for militant activity. Hobbs became a bridge between activist groups, trade unions, and the cleaners. In October 1970, she approached international socialist and women's liberation groups to ask for help with the campaign. The Cleaners' Action Group (CAG) was formed and the struggle escalated.

CAG printed and distributed leaflets that explained to cleaners the benefits of unionization. By July 1972, the CAG had helped unionize a significant number of London's night cleaners.[9] Through their newsletter, the "Cleaner's Voice," they reached night cleaners in Birmingham, Newcastle, Lancaster, and Coventry. In over ten years of struggle, there had been little improvement in working conditions for night cleaners. Small victories negotiated between unions and contractors—such as wage increases or holiday pay—became irrelevant when contractors changed,[10] and they changed regularly.

The night cleaners' campaign was captured in the film *Nightcleaners*, made by the Berwick Street Collective. Now regarded as an important piece of experimental left-wing cinema, it was nonetheless far removed from the short campaign film the cleaners had hoped for. The film was finished at the end of 1975, two years after the campaign had lost momentum.

The night cleaners' campaign is often remembered as an example of how the women's movement supported working-class women in industrial struggles. Yet it was clearly also a campaign spearheaded by black, immigrant, and working-class women who fought against casual, insecure, and debilitating work conditions that regrettably still continue in many cases to this day.

Above: A still from the *Nightcleaners* film by the Berwick Street Collective, 1975. It shows the campaigners aligning with the Women's Liberation Movement as May Hobbs delivers an impassioned speech.

"Black girls are victimised through sackings and through giving them the worst jobs. . . . We must resist every attempt by the companies to victimise cleaners because of their colour, for an attack on one cleaner is an attack on us all."

"Cleaner's Voice," *1972*

In the US, it was a similar tale, with the Equal Pay Act of 1963 only covering a small section of the jobs that women might undertake with roles such as those in an "executive, administrative or professional capacity, or as an outside salesperson" being excluded. In 1972 Congress enacted the Educational Amendment of 1972, which rectified this. Nevertheless, in practice women's pay still has not reached parity with men's.

The same story rings true for many countries worldwide, with a raft of European countries enacting equal pay legislation either prior to (such as France in 1946 and Germany in 1949) or after joining the European Economic Community, including: Greece (1975), Denmark (1976), Italy (1977), Norway (1978), Austria (1979), and Sweden (1980). In Australia, legislation to regulate pay was introduced in 1969 and anti-discrimination in the workplace laws in 1984. Yet, in many cases the reality was, and still is, that the gendered pay gap was not breached.

Alongside issues of pay, downing the household tools and going out to work presented moral and practical difficulties for women. On the moral side were guilty feelings. How would children cope if they were left with a childminder, and would the husband be able to cook his own dinner? Taboos also had to be shattered, as women spoke out about their rejection of housewifery.

Lack of daytime nurseries and workplace childcare provision meant women were unable to go to work, even when they desperately wanted or needed to. For the black woman who "ha[d] to go out to work to supplement her husband's income, and also the mother who [was] the breadwinner of the one-parent family," she was "super-exploited," as she was forced to pay extortionate childcare fees that accounted for a large part of her wages.[11] Indeed, with the rising divorce rate, women struggled to find adequate housing for themselves and their children, additionally bruised by a media that blamed single mothers and "welfare queens." Gloria Steinem declared that, "We are all one man away from welfare,"[12] but the US government remained firm in refusing to create affordable day care options for working mothers. And in many cases, across Britain, America, and Europe, there was still a stigma attached to any form of role reversal with few fathers being willing to become stay-at-home dads. While the question of men sharing housework and childcare was constantly raised in feminist writing and discussion groups, the 1980s American film *Mr. Mom* reinforced mockery of the clueless, unemployed male forced by circumstance to switch roles with his working wife.

Across Europe and the US, many women's groups and centers sought practical ways to address the issue. One such example in Britain was the Women's Liberation Playgroup in Birmingham, which decided to set up communal childcare to address scarce nursery provision.

> "Another question I am asked is how do you manage to find time to do the housework? The answer is, of course, that I don't. I dislike housework intensely and really do the bare minimum that standards of hygiene require. It's a question of your priorities really, and as long as the place isn't actually ankle deep in dirt, I don't mind."
>
> "Working Mothers," *Shrew*, February 4, 1971

de achturige werkdag

8 UUR WERK · 8 UUR VRIJ · 8 UUR RUST

Far left: Women mobilized through a variety of networks, both inside and outside the trade union system, to fight against workplace discrimination and benefit cuts, as shown by this undated (likely c. 1970s) British poster.

Left: A Dutch poster designed by Joke Dallinga, c. 1975, reveals how a woman's eight-hour "working day" is never really done.

Above: The Hackney Flashers created agitprop exhibitions that invited audiences to learn about social issues, such as childcare, and take action in their local communities.

Far right: A demonstrator at a women's work and welfare rally speaks her mind to a male onlooker in 1977.

Right: The issue of day care was central to women's liberation, as this poster, exhibited at the first women's liberation rally in Washington on August 26, 1970, shows.

Feminist religion and spirituality

Bonnie J. Morris

In America, as elsewhere, women's feminist beliefs affected every realm of their life, including the spiritual and the religious.

"Girls can do anything." "Biology is not destiny." "The best man for the job may be a woman!" These slogans, on buttons and stickers, summed up feminists' confidence that all sex discrimination in the workplace could be contested under new American laws like Title VII of the Civil Rights Act and Title IX of the Education Amendments. But in the US, separation of church and state meant that religious institutions had special protections to discriminate as they saw fit.

Churches, mosques, and synagogues, as well as their networks of schools, charities, hiring boards, and counseling centers, were not bound by the same laws as public employers or schools. Private parochial schools in particular could even exclude students based on race or ethnicity (or if the student's parents were gay), as well as restricting or disciplining girls in ways that were already illegal in the public school system. Enjoying tax-exempt status that supposedly barred them from political endorsements, religious institutions could and did lobby for or against policies they felt reflected their ideals of woman's place in society. The more that second-wave feminists located the source of female oppression in patriarchal religious practices, the more church leaders fought back with charges that feminism was anti-family, anti-life, and anti-God.

From the ancient stigma that Eve had tempted Adam and thus caused the Fall of Man, to biblical metaphors of Jezebel and harlotry, some religious doctrines had long kept women subservient to men, submissive to husbands, silent in church, and bound to the sex role behaviors and codes that male clergy upheld as correct. Most women throughout history were pious but uneducated, few daring to object to the decisions of their community's religious leadership. Those male councils had the power to render decisions on every aspect of family life: birth, circumcision, contraception, abortion, divorce, fertility, marriage, sexual practices, and childrearing.

Had spirituality always been so masculine? Across Europe, the Mediterranean, and North Africa, from Egypt to Iceland, ample evidence suggested that goddess worship had once defined daily practices, beliefs, and art.

The divine female, a life-giving force of nature, had inspired human spirituality well before the monotheism of one God the Father. But after most of Europe adopted Christian beliefs, and the Inquisition introduced torture to punish suspected nonbelievers, women and girls accused of carrying on older folk traditions were likely to be burned at the stake. Accusations of witchcraft fell heavily on midwives (who eased the pain of labor and offered birth control advice), leading to an era of fiery public trials that scholars now call the Burning Times. In the new American colonies, witch trials, stoning of adulterers, and other physical punishments awaited women who misbehaved or who were believed to have committed blasphemy at any level. And while nineteenth-century feminists applied their personal Christian beliefs to fighting the slave trade, they were limited—as women—in their religious protest of enslaved women's abuse.

Not surprisingly, some first-wave feminists blamed religion more than any social force for keeping women oppressed and unable to speak. In reaction, Elizabeth Cady Stanton wrote her blisteringly critical *The Woman's Bible* (1895, 1898). Abolitionists Sarah and Angelina Grimke had a different approach, urging Southern white women to read the Bible, to pursue a liberation theology that included helping runaway slave families, and to become learned in the sacred texts that applied to their own sex. In short, for women to out-argue male clergy, some would need to become clergy themselves, able to translate biblical or Islamic rules for female behavior from the original language. A few women were able to become visionary leaders and enter the ministry, though most were advised to express their spiritual energy through missionary work, the Salvation Army and temperance charities, teaching Sunday School to children or (in the Catholic Church) joining a convent order as a celibate nun.

These issues raged anew during the second wave of feminism, as scholars including Marija Gimbutas, Carol Christ, Gerda Lerner, Merlin Stone, and women's music artist Kay Gardner helped popularize awareness of goddess worship in earlier times. Many feminists were drawn to goddess-based and Wiccan practices as

Top: Button declaring "My goddess gave birth to your god," c. 1970s.

Bottom: This campaigning button sought to address the discrimination against women priests within church structure.

Above left: An earth goddess workshop held in New York on December 5, 1980.

Above right: A member of the British campaign for women priests protests at how her years of dedicated service to the church have gone unrecognized.

alternatives to patriarchal religion. They eagerly read the provocative works of theology professor Mary Daly, whose books *The Church and the Second Sex* and *Beyond God the Father* threatened her job at a Catholic women's college. Through the 1960s, as male religious leaders continued to be some of the loudest critics of women's rights (with the Vatican reaffirming opposition to birth control and homosexuality), there were almost no women in the top tier of influence in any religious council from Greek Orthodoxy to the Mormon Church. But because church or synagogue activities and sisterhoods were sometimes the only place where women had established acceptable roles and recreation outside the home, with powerful church meetings sustaining the African American community throughout the Civil Rights Movement, many women found faith traditions a source of comfort. These women of faith drew back from radical feminism's interrogation of religion.

As more and more women applied their personal feminism to career goals, asking, "Why can't I be a . . . ?" (firefighter, astronaut, president), some challenged the unique "stained-glass ceiling" in the work they wanted to do. These were the visionary women of all faiths who did not want to separate from religion but to participate in it at the level of leadership. They asked, could women change centuries of tradition and became priests, rabbis, ministers, imams, and fully ordained military chaplains?

Those whose feminist beliefs informed and shaped new approaches to religious community and values yearned to lead a congregation. All over America, followers learned to accept the possibility of a woman leading them in prayer. Feminist theologians introduced non-patriarchal language in liturgy, directing believers to address God as "She" or as "Mother."

Women of faith acted on the possibility of moving their religious institutions toward greater equality by working from the inside. Some, like the many altar girls who protested, "It isn't fair!," were able to see from a very young age that unequal participation sanctioned inequality at the highest levels. As women became Episcopal priests, rabbis, and (if not priests) presidents of Catholic schools and colleges, the feminization of religion transformed the lives of women who had long felt alienated rather than saved. In 1972, when Sally Priesand was ordained as America's first female rabbi by Hebrew Union College in Cincinnati, she reflected, "I did not think much about being a pioneer. I knew only that I wanted to be a Rabbi."[13] By 1977, the first female priest was ordained in the Anglican church; and some Roman Catholic nuns dared hope—with considerable reproval from the Vatican—that they might one day serve Mass. A few began to do so in secret, meeting together behind drawn curtains, not unlike the first devout Christians of ancient Rome.

Fathers were involved, and the group tried to find ways to break down gender stereotyping through their play activities.[14] "Against natural laws"[15] that oppressed women and men, the women's movement challenged the idea that gender—whether masculine or feminine—was fixed and compulsory. Everyday statements such as "only sissies play with dolls," "girls don't climb trees," "big boys don't cry," and "don't do that, it's not ladylike" were rejected as harmful and restrictive.[16]

Across Europe and the US, many women's groups and centers sought practical ways to address the issue and for some, establishing collective responsibility for childcare was part of exploring "alternatives to the way in which we live."[17]

Despite attempts to experiment with childcare arrangements, throughout society it was largely still women who were left "holding the baby." The Hackney Flashers, a British socialist-feminist art collective whose agitprop exhibitions aimed to politically inform and motivate their audiences, explored this topic in a touring exhibition entitled *Who's Holding the Baby?* (1978) featuring photographs, cartoons, text, and appropriated imagery from advertising and other media. The exhibition explored themes of maternal isolation, birth control and abortion, the need for shared childcare, and how childcare issues varied among social classes. The exhibition juxtaposed information about ample nursery provision in World War II, a time when the state supported women's entry into the workplace, with insufficient childcare provision in the 1970s.

The Hackney Flashers' agitprop exhibitions encouraged audiences to find solutions to the problems they faced. They showed how people set up local community nurseries in order to provide affordable childcare, and included information about running costs and management, as well as the challenges faced and benefits gained.

Changing the notion of the workplace

Indeed, as more and more women entered male-dominated fields, they found sympathetic media support in unexpected places: the comics page, television episodes, weekly feminist radio programs, and the record player at home.

American cartoonist Garry Trudeau's popular liberal comic strip *Doonesbury*, launched in October 1970, championed the plight of homemaker Joanie Caucus, a character who returns to law school as an adult and eventually runs for office; the comic series addressed every issue from unfair wages to sexist law professors,

including a cross-generational conversation between Joanie and an older female politician about when and how to demand a raise: "It's not tacky to want justice!" Charles Schulz, influential creator of the *Peanuts* strip, championed Title IX both on and off the comics page, allowing tomboy icon Peppermint Patty to be both an athlete and (some felt) a prototypical gender-bender; and Dale Messick's *Brenda Starr* had long broken the mold as a comic strip journalist (alongside Lois Lane). Television examined issues of bias and sexism in series ranging from the staid *Marcus Welby, MD* to the early 1980s controversial hit show *Murphy Brown*, featuring Candice Bergen as a news journalist who, at over forty, gets pregnant and chooses to raise her baby as a single mother. Children observed the changing roles for men and women through a new feminist literature and music genre marketed to their age group: many youngsters listened to Marlo Thomas's album *Free to Be . . . You and Me* and Peggy Seeger's "I Gonna Be an Engineer"; while adults chuckled over Tamar Hoffs's fairy tale parody *The Liberated Mother Goose*.

Seated in front of the television, children of the 1960s and '70s took in the biases of advertising and news that imparted sex role stereotypes hour after hour. But it was television that also beamed positive images into every home: Jane Goodall as an animal scientist, Olympic women bringing home gold, and the gradual ascent of female news anchors.

Meanwhile, in America it became increasingly clear that with such a high percentage of women in the workforce, the nature of the workplace itself would have to change in many ways, but too often this meant making women conform to a male-dominant atmosphere and late-night work schedule with few concessions for family life. Many men resented requests to take down pornographic calendars on office walls and were uncomfortable about having women join male-only business associations, golf club outings, and team-building trips. Female firefighters especially were often considered interlopers; the bonds of "brotherhood" did not extend to them, and their presence could be resisted with acts of sexual aggression and cruelty. For these women, and their counterparts in the US police force and the military, male hostility was threefold. Some men doubted women's physical ability to meet strict

"One does not want to release women as isolated units from the care of children. One wants to bring women and men together to care for children and each other in new ways. Setting up a local playgroup . . . is one way of bringing together people who otherwise would not meet each other and who might never know at first hand what women's liberation is about."

"More Than Minding," *Shrew*, 1972

Who's holding the baby...
and often alone

THE LIBERATED MOTHER GOOSE

By Tamar Hoffs

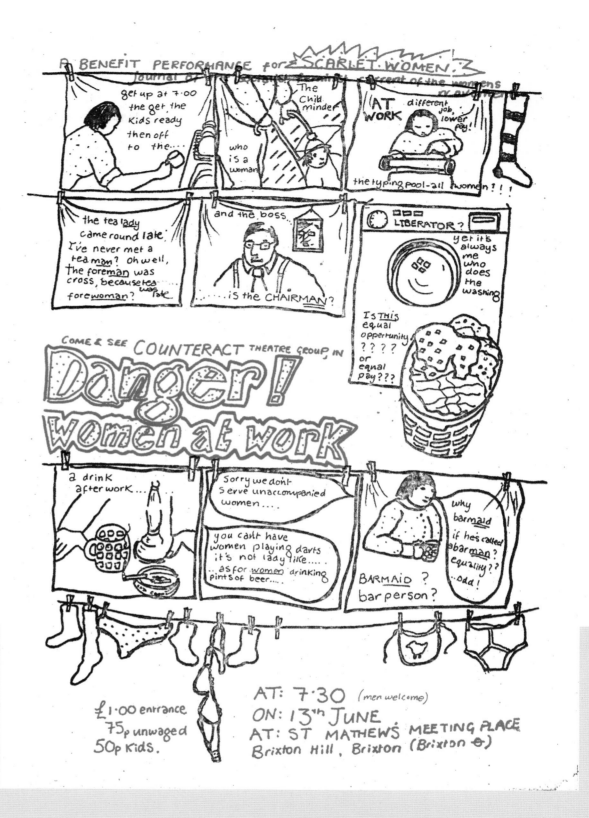

Top left: *Who's Holding the Baby?* by the Hackney Flashers explored issues related to women's work, childcare, and nursery provision.

Bottom left: In her 1974 book, Tamar Hoffs took on the traditional lessons of medieval fairy tales and rewrote popular Mother Goose fables with surprising feminist twists.

Right: This poster for a benefit performance of the British-based Counteract Theatre Group's *Danger! Women at Work* play highlights the predominantly male-led culture of the workplace.

standards and resented partnering with someone "weak;" they resented female intrusion into a male profession that signified dominance, authority, and the protection or rescue of women; and they resisted taking orders from a female superior. The first American women admitted to the US military academy West Point found their breakthrough complicated by media attention—with some male observers eagerly waiting to see them fail.

In trying to fit in, yet not offend, the "power feminist" of the 1970s and '80s was often parodied for her gender-blending style of dressing for success. But striving to appear nonthreateningly feminine while proving equal ability left the public woman with limited options for professional style. By 1987, appearing in her Broadway hit *The Search for Signs of Intelligent Life in the Universe*, actress Lily Tomlin poked fun at the feminist "power suit": "A new fashion trend where you wear something around the neck that looks sort of like a scarf and sort of like a tie and sort of like a ruffle and doesn't threaten anyone, because you don't look good in it."[18]

Businesswomen fought for access to male-only professional memberships at sites where their male peers networked (including elite venues such as Washington's private members' Cosmos Club), giving rise to the expression "the old boys' club" to sum up influential support networks traditionally excluding women.

Alongside fighting to fit into the workplace culture, Wages for Housework was an international campaign established in 1972 and coordinated by the Lotta femminista collective, founded by Selma James, Mariarosa Dalla Costa, Silvia Federici, and others to address the imbalance in work outside of the "workplace."[19] "Wages for Housework" never simply meant cleaning the house; it was a slogan used to revalue women's unpaid domestic work. Cooking meals, doing the laundry, cleaning the house, bearing and raising children, shopping, and providing sexual services to male partners were just some of the difficult emotional and physical types of work women did everyday under the banner of "housework." Without women's contribution, the group argued, the whole system would not function. Wages for Housework would pay working-class women for the work they were *already* doing, and would help poor and low-waged women become economically and socially independent. In France, the Wages for Housework movement had been precipitated by a series of national surveys on the "time-budgets" of the

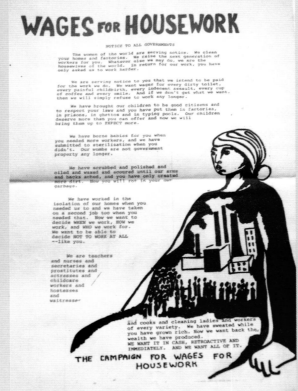

Far left: Wilmette Brown was a key figure in the international Wages for Housework campaign. Her book, *Black Women and the Peace Movement* (1984), offered an important commentary on militarism, anti-racism, and class inequality within the feminist movement.

Left: Wages for Housework was often discredited in the British Women's Liberation Movement as offering a reductive analysis of domestic labor and capitalism. Yet the campaign resonated internationally with many working-class women, immigrants, and women of color.

Right: The international campaign Wages for Housework grew out of the International Feminist Collective in Padua, Italy, in 1972, led by Marxist women who contested that most of women's work in the home was noncompensated, nonunionized, and yet supported industry, capital, and national economies in countless ways. Wageless Women's Day was one facet of the campaign in which women were encouraged to strike from their "domestic" jobs for better (or any) pay and recognition.

French population, conducted by the Institut national de la statistique et des études économiques (INSEE). Initially, these surveys did not detail domestic work or the gender imbalance in the home, but in the 1974–75 and 1985–86 surveys, the division of domestic tasks was broken down. For example, the 1974 survey revealed that for people in the eighteen to sixty-four age range, employed women spent nearly thirty-three hours (thirty-two hours and fifty-four minutes) on domestic work per week, whereas men spent around half of that (sixteen hours and twenty minutes); "unemployed" women were shown to be engaged for fifty-four hours and twenty-nine minutes in domestic tasks.[20]

For many activists in the British Women's Liberation Movement, Wages for Housework was viewed as a controversial and reductive approach that would keep women forever locked in the home. Nevertheless, for those involved in the campaign, Wages for Housework was never meant to be an end in itself, but was perceived as a temporary strategy—a way for women to reclaim economic power from a system that was indebted to them.

Industrial struggles and manual work

In the 1970s, Britain suffered general industrial unrest, and many women took part in strikes for better pay and working conditions. In 1972, women workers at Sexton's Shoe Factory, Fakenham, Norfolk, staged a six-month "work-in" to protest against their redundancy. They occupied the building, worked cooperatively to keep the factory open under their own auspices, and carried on working "with an air of almost cosy domesticity," challenging the image of militant, male-led industrial struggle.[21] Other strikes were organized by textile workers in Leeds (1970), at Imperial Typewriters, Leicester (1974), Crosfields Electronics, London (1975), and Trico-Folberth factory, Middlesex (1976). Black and Asian women often took leading roles in strike actions, probably the most famous being Jayaben Desai, who spearheaded the epic two-year strike at the Grunwick Film Processing Plant, North London (1976–78), a struggle that challenged the racism and sexism of trade union movements and employers. Similarly, across Europe women mobilized as part of the trade union organizations; for example in

France, feminist movements aligned with the CGT (Confédération générale du travail) and the CFDT (Confédération française démocratique du travail) to lobby for working women's rights.[22]

Industrial struggles propelled women into public life in many different ways. Women against Pit Closures (WAPC) was set up by a group of working-class women in Barnsley in 1984 to campaign against the closure of the local coal mine. Similar miners' support groups were established across the UK. Their aim was to "organise women in the coal field against pit closures" and ensure "victory for the miners" during the strike of 1984–85.[23] WAPC set up communal food kitchens, raised funds, organized marches, spoke at rallies, and endured police brutality on picket lines. Inspired by activism at the nuclear site Greenham Common, they set up temporary camps at threatened pits. WAPC transformed the lives of women involved, and even after the official end of the strike in 1985, WAPC continued to organize and

campaign. Before the strike many of the women had rarely traveled beyond the Yorkshire border, but the group's activities were so renowned they led to international recognition and speaking invitations:

We went to Russia, we went to a coalfield, we were in this coal yard and these men and women, they asked us to speak. I said I'm not going to speak, but Margaret did, and I tell you at the finish they were crying for us. Over in Russia where they've got nowt to begin with. It was astounding, you took a woman to a meeting and you shoved her up in front of maybe a thousand people and she was so nervous, but she started speaking and her emotions took over that much that she'd go on for an hour.[24]

Within the women's movement, women gained confidence to make incursions into just about every area of male-dominated life. In the world of work, this

Below: Women gather on the picket line at the Grunwick Photo Processing plant, Brent, London, in October 1977. The Grunwick dispute was one of a number of high-profile industrial struggles that took place in Britain during the 1970s, within which black and Asian women took on important leadership roles.

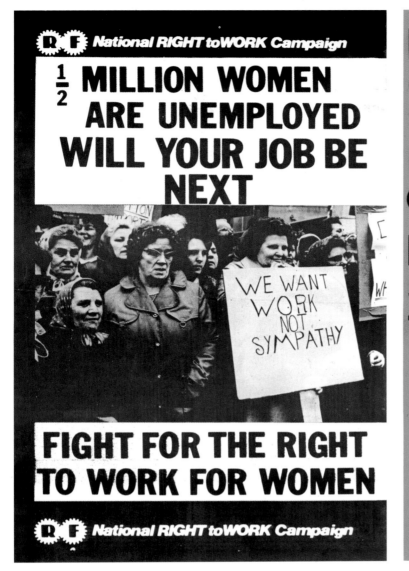

National RIGHT to WORK Campaign

½ MILLION WOMEN ARE UNEMPLOYED WILL YOUR JOB BE NEXT

WE WANT WORK NOT SYMPATHY

FIGHT FOR THE RIGHT TO WORK FOR WOMEN

National RIGHT to WORK Campaign

Pour l'amélioration des conditions de travail. Pour le respect de la dignité des travailleuses.

NON à la surexploitation sous toutes ses formes.

CGT «..changer notre vie..!»

1975 Année Internationale de la Femme

Above left: The British Right to Work campaign sought to address the issues of unemployment in general and, particularly, the high rates of unemployment among women.

Above right: France's CGT trade union fought for better working conditions and for recognition of all forms of work, as well as campaigning against exploitation in all forms. The women's liberation movement in France found in the CGT a champion for their fight for working rights, as demonstrated by this poster (one in a series) created to mark International Women's Year.

Right: A CGT demonstration on May 29, 1968, campaigning for equal pay classifications, a forty-hour working week, and equal recognition of women's contribution to the workplace.

included learning manual skills, such as carpentry, roofing, bricklaying, and plumbing.

For women to learn "traditionally male" skills, significant cultural barriers had to be broken down because practical skills were "something you've always learned you can't do (because that's what you've always been taught)."[25] Once fully trained, isolation could be a problem, because there were so few women employed in manual industries. Women and Manual Trades was established in Britain during 1976 and functioned as a support network, organized conferences, and distributed information with the aim of getting more women "on the tools."

Women's workshops were also established to train women in practical skills. In Britain, the Bristol Women's Workshop and the East Leeds Women's Workshop were both set up in 1981. East Leeds provided vocational training in carpentry and joinery, and electronics and computing. They prioritized women who were socially disadvantaged due to disability, race, ethnicity, class, and educational background. Workshops enabled women "to have a thought or design in their own minds and realize it in three dimensions, and that's an opportunity women don't often get. Women are on the receiving end, the buyers of someone else's design," reflected the founder of the Bristol Women's Workshop.[26]

Top left: East Leeds Women's Workshop provided training for women in "male-dominated" occupations, such as carpentry and computing, with a particular emphasis on training women who were disadvantaged due to class, ethnicity, sexuality, or disability.

Top right: This c. 1980s poster from Australia's Women's Directorate advocated trade training for women.

Bottom left: Women's Design Service (WDS) was set up in London in 1984 as a worker's cooperative dedicated to improving the built environment for women. WDS provided advice to women's groups, and created a body of research that applied a feminist analysis to architecture.

Bottom right: Film still taken from an excerpt of Pat Fiske's documentary *Rocking the Foundations* (1985) included in Alex Martinis Roe's film *It Was about Opening the Very Notion That There Was a Particular Perspective* (2017). Shown here are female members of the N.S.W. (New South Wales) Builders Labourers Federation—a radical union in Australia, which in the early 1970s set a mandate that women would be prioritized for getting jobs in the building industry.

Women who were the first in their field to break barriers or whose stance and personality made them particularly memorable drew acclaim in the feminist era: Valentina Tereshkova became the first woman in space in 1963; Sarah Caldwell became the first woman to conduct New York's Metropolitan Opera; Diane Crump, the first woman jockey in the Kentucky Derby; Elaine Noble was the first openly lesbian councilwoman elected to office in Boston; Simone Veil became the first woman president of the European Parliament; Barbara Jordan, the first black member of the Texas state senate since the nineteenth century; Shirley Chisholm, the first black woman to run for president; Nilde Lotti, the first female leader of the Italian House of Commons in 1979; Geraldine Ferraro, the first female vice presidential candidate on the Democratic ticket; Sandra Day O'Connor, the first woman appointed to be a Supreme Court Justice; Barbara McClintock, the first woman to win

an unshared Nobel Prize in Physiology or Medicine; Junko Tabei, the first woman to reach the summit of Everest—to name but a few. By the early 1980s, symbolic "firsts" stretched even more boundaries, as Britain saw its first female prime minister in Margaret Thatcher and Vigdís Finnbogadóttir became Iceland's first female democratically elected president. Wilma Mankiller became the first female chief of the Cherokee Nation, and Sally Ride, the first American woman to enter space as an astronaut. But as late as the 1990s, Walmart stores in the US stopped selling a T-shirt that showed Margaret, a character from the cartoon series *Dennis the Menace*, proclaiming, "Some day a woman will be President!" after complaints from some customers that they found it "offensive." In an era that saw Christian fundamentalists reinforcing the role of husbands' male authority, a baby-sized T-shirt promoting female leadership still had the power to offend.

"WOMAN MUST WRITE HERSELF"

Publishing and the media

Feminists were both wordy and word-critical and began to take control of the media and the printing presses to define their own language.

The women's liberation movement famously introduced new catchphrases, slogans, and theory, asking one and all to consider the weighted meaning of language such as *chick*, *bird*, and *slut*; *fireman*, *policeman*, and *chairman*. Rallying cries of the era—*Sisterhood Is Powerful*; *Reclaim the Night* and *Take Back the Night*; *Uppity Women Unite*; *The Personal Is Political*; *Woman Loving Woman*—drew new participants to a revolution engaging the minds of millions of women. Women changed spellings to define themselves separately from men: using *womon* or *womyn*, and returning to maternal lineage with new last names such as Sarachild. In France an entire feminist philosophy was founded on the concept of *écriture feminine* that sought to emphasize female difference through the written word.

Theorists, writers, and speakers whose broadsides exhorted their audiences to action were swiftly introduced via pamphlets, posters, and poems. This shared rhetoric both spread the ideas of feminism and encouraged others to narrate their lived experiences: as American historian Ruth Rosen points out, "No area of graphic expression proved livelier than poster art."[1] However, some printing shops and established presses did not care to serve a radical feminist client, rejecting orders to publish "offensive" material, particularly work that celebrated a woman-loving sensibility. Cultural barriers needed to be overcome, from the sexist idea that "normal" women couldn't be writers to the basic fact that women were marginalized in every aspect of the publishing industry. Feminist activists responded in a characteristically proactive manner.

> "Woman must write herself: must write about women and bring women to writing, from which they have been driven away as violently as from their own bodies. . . . Woman must put herself into the text—as into the world and into history—by her own movement."
>
> Hélène Cixous, "The Laugh of the Medusa," 1976

A WOMANS WORK IS NEVER DONE

Page 144: The logo illustration for Onlywomen Press. This all-female publishing company was founded during the 1970s and was based in London. It continued publishing through to the 1990s. The press's mission statement was: "Onlywomen Press is a women's liberation publishing and printing group, producing work by and for women as part of creating a feminist communication network and, ultimately, a feminist revolution."

Left: Britain's Red Women's Workshop was established in 1974 with the aim of producing positive and "truthful" images of women and women's lives. The collective went on to become one of the defining visualizations of the Women's Liberation Movement with their distinctive silkscreen-printed style, accompanied by provocative and punchy slogans.

Right: Local newsletters were an integral part of how regional women's liberation groups organized. Newsletters contained informal discussions, campaign information, and listings of activities taking place in the area. This undated pamphlet (possibly c. 1970s) from Bristol-based women's liberation group clearly identifies that these works were produced by women for women only.

BRISTOL WOMEN'S LIBERATION NEWSLETTER

FOR ♀ ONLY PLEASE RESPECT THIS.

♀'s CENTRE 44, THE GROVE PRINCE ST. BRISTOL TEL. 22760.

Women-only publishing companies, printing cooperatives, typesetting collectives, and bookshops were all launched during the 1970s. The women's liberation movements gave women confidence to learn new skills that would be vital to support the eruption of women's writing that began to fill bookshelves, libraries, and newsstands during this period.

In the early 1970s, the Women's Liberation Movement in Britain did not have a literature of its own. As the movement grew, British activists began to publish their own thoughts, feelings, and ideas about women's liberation.

The first writings to emerge from the British women's movement were local newsletters and low-cost pamphlets. Women's liberation newsletters were the "internal organ"[2] of the movement, and provided information about local activities and groups. These publications featured short articles and letters, and acted as an informal forum in which women could develop ideas. Newsletters were often only available through subscription and were really aimed at women who were already active in the movement.

Pamphlets, as low-cost, short publications, were also an important way in which the ideas of the movement were circulated. Publishing a pamphlet was quicker and required less knowledge and resources to produce than a "proper" book. Pamphlets often contained writing of an "exploratory and tentative nature,"[3] or provided practical advice on specific issues, such as health or domestic abuse.

Women's presses

Soon these initial forays into publishing became formalized and women-only publishing companies were key to the development of women's writing in the 1970s.

Women's publishers had a practical function in the movement. They were "not a temple of culture, [but] a forum for discussion and creativity; women have and are producing much literary, theoretical and visual work, and it is the job of a woman's press to give them the network of communication they need."[4]

In 1970, in Italy, Rivolta femminile created its own publishing house, the Scritti di rivolta femminile. It published Carla Lonzi's influential works *Let's Spit on Hegel* (1970) and *The Clitoridian Woman and the Vaginal Woman* (1971). A 1978 catalog stated that "to reject the support of an editor reflected our symbolical, as

> "Most of us were women writing in the isolation of our own homes who wanted to share our experiences, communicate our ideas. All of us were women who felt the need for our movement to generate its own body of literature in response to our situation."
>
> Women's Literature Collective, *Women's Liberation Review* 1, 1972

Special Issue: Lesbian Community

FEMINARY

WHOLE WOMEN CAROLOGUE

$3

Far left: *Feminary* was a feminist journal particular to the vision of feminist and lesbian concerns in the American South. Founded in 1978, it expanded on a previous newsletter organized by women of the Durham–Chapel Hill Triangle Area, who were living in a collective household, exploring the women's music movement, and publishing on lesbian issues.

Left: A staple of American counterculture and the back-to-the-land movement, the *Whole Earth Catalog* sold millions of copies between 1968 and 1972; this feminist version appeared in 1973 as the *Whole Women Carologue*. Diana Press, which specialized in books by and for women, printed three thousand copies.

The International Feminist Book Fair

D-M Withers

By the early 1980s, feminist publishing had evolved from humble beginnings into an industry of its own.

A new reading public, hungry for feminist ideas and women authors, was part of this expansion.

At the heart of this growth was an ambitious cultural event—the First International Feminist Book Fair, held at Jubilee Hall, Covent Garden, London, from June 7 to 9, 1984, funded by the socialist-run Greater London Council (GLC). The book fair was followed by a "feminist book week"—ten days of readings, discussions, and debates in bookstores and community centers throughout the UK and Ireland.

The International Feminist Book Fair began as a "conversational fantasy" between women involved in feminist publishing in the early 1980s.[5] By April 1983, fifty-five women were enlisted to make the fantasy become a reality. Over a year later, the event brought together authors, publishers, illustrators, designers, production workers, booksellers, and readers to celebrate women's writing, and the industry that supported it. Around 4,500 people attended the London fair, spending an estimated £28,000 on feminist books (equivalent to £86,645 today).[6] In excess of a hundred publishers from twenty different countries exhibited their books. Participating authors included Alifa Rifaat, Adrienne Rich and her partner Michelle Cliff, Alice Walker, Mary Daly, Eavan Boland, Toni Cade Bambara, and Madhu Kishwar (founding editor of the Indian feminist journal *Manushi*).

Politically, the International Feminist Book Fair was imagined as a space to build a truly global women's liberation movement. Through the power of writing and story sharing, feminists from different countries could forge a common culture. The closing session explored "Different Concepts of Women's Liberation, Internationally." The book fair hosted a number of discussions such as "How can women write about sex? Should we be explicit? Should we describe lesbian sex in mass market books?" "Is feminist publishing a first world luxury?" and, for booksellers, "How do we sell our books and to whom?" An exhibition entitled "Notebooks" celebrated marginal forms of women's writing: "Women have much to say whether it be on the back of shopping lists, bus tickets, diaries and other scraps of paper."[7]

The fair was not without its critics. Black feminists questioned how "international" it really was and criticized white organizers for inviting crowd-pulling black and Third World women writers such as Alice Walker, Flora Nwapa, and Nawal El Saadawi to the neglect of British black women authors. Audre Lorde echoed these points when she said the organizers "totally objectified black women by choosing not to deal with the black women in their own communities."[8] This criticism extended to subsequent book fairs, and some women of color boycotted the Third International Feminist Book Fair, held in Montreal in 1988.

If the book fair was a political project, it was also clearly trade-orientated. In fact, as a promotional activity, the fair was the moment when feminist publishing steamrolled the mainstream. Perhaps what is most surprising is that the mainstream was firmly behind it. The Publishers Association of Great Britain backed the event, and WH Smith, a high street chain, was a key partner. WH Smith gave over ten days of window displays to promote Feminist Book Week and stocked many of the

Above left: T-shirt from the Second International Feminist Book Fair, held in Oslo in 1986.

Above right: Brochure cover for the Fourth International Feminist Book Fair, held in Barcelona from June 19 to 23, 1990.

> "It is indicative of the power of the movement that 1984, the most pessimistic of years, sees the First International Feminist Book Fair: an event that has the confidence, strength and *audacity* to call for a celebration."
>
> Press release for the First International Feminist Book Fair

Above: Attendees at the busy First International Feminist Book Fair in Jubilee Hall, Covent Garden, London, share the excitement and energy of the event.

Right: A woman browses books at the First International Feminist Book Fair, while exhibition displays in the background tell the story of an emerging international women's literary culture.

two hundred and seventy-seven titles chosen by the book fair committee to "demonstrate the strength and diversity of women's writing and publishing today."[9] A spokesperson for WH Smith explained, "We are supporting this promotion because the demand for feminist books is a demand for more books—a real growth."[10]

Independent feminist bookstores were nurtured, too. London's Silver Moon Women's Bookshop opened a week before the book fair started and hosted several author events. "The adrenalin was running and it was terrifically exciting. Not only did we have the premises but we had the authors and the audience, all being brought in at the same time. In terms of launching a business, it was fantastic. You start on the crest of a wave and let that carry you forward,"[11] remembered Silver Moon founder Jane Cholmeley.

The International Feminist Book Fair went on to be a biennial affair throughout the 1980s and early 1990s. These huge events traveled to Oslo (1986), Montreal (1988), Barcelona (1990), Amsterdam (1992), and Melbourne (1994), and supported the expansion of international feminist publishing and literary movements.

well as practical, detachment from culture, making us responsible for ourselves. . . . For us the point was to gain awareness of the fact that the discovery of the self occurs through writing." The Scritti di rivolta femminile thus proclaimed a position of autonomy and separatism, not just in terms of a physical, women-only space in which to produce writings but also as a symbolic space in which to be among women, independently from men.[12]

In 1973, French psychoanalyst Antoinette Fouque founded Les éditions des femmes—a female publishing collective born out of the Mouvement de libération des femmes along with France's (and, most likely, Europe's) first women's bookstore in Paris. From the outset, the publishing arm of the liberation movement was contentious, but its ambitious mission saw it approach women's writing on an international scale, publishing

writings from Russian activists to French academic Annie Cohen. In Italy two years later, the Milan Women's Bookshop (Libreria delle donne di Milano) was opened, following the example of Les éditions des femmes. The store still exists today and remains very influential in Italy.

In the US, San Francisco was known for its alternative publisher City Lights Books and coffeehouses featuring primarily male beat poetry readings. By the early 1970s, the greater Bay Area was a hub of feminist publishing, due in large part to visionary activist Judy Grahn, whose Gay Women's Liberation Group founded the first women's bookstore, A Woman's Place, and the Woman's Press Collective. The poet Alta founded Shameless Hussy Press, publishing new works by Ntozake Shange and Susan Griffin and reintroducing readers to the lost work of George Sand. Committed to producing works by women of color as well as white

Above: Paris's famous feminist bookshop, Les éditions des femmes, opened in 1974, with branches following in Marseille and Lyon.

voices, women-owned and collectively run presses and publishing houses offered readers a library of new and provocative books. The pointedly named American publishers of radical feminist books soon included Down There Press, Onlywomen Press, Diana Press, Daughters, Inc., Persephone Press, Pandora Books, Spinsters Ink, and many, many more. Naiad Press, run by the energetic Barbara Grier, specialized in quality fiction and essays by lesbian authors. In 1976, the Olivia Records collective released a spoken-word album of poetry by Judy Grahn and Pat Parker entitled *Where Would I Be Without You?*

In Britain, Virago, Onlywomen, the Women's Press, and Sheba Feminist Publishers were four of the most significant publishers. Feminist Books, based in Leeds, published a number of influential titles in the early 1970s, and Bristol's Falling Wall Press published material associated with the Wages for Housework campaign.

Virago, which continues to thrive today, did the most to push women's writing into the mainstream, and was the most commercially minded. It published writers who are today regarded as literary giants, such as Angela Carter, Margaret Atwood, and Maya Angelou. The most enduring legacy of Virago is its Modern Classics series, which republished "lost" feminist classics from the late nineteenth and early twentieth centuries. Virago Modern Classics introduced a new generation of

readers to Sarah Grand, Willa Cather, Djuna Barnes, and many others.

Onlywomen Press espoused a more grassroots ethos, and was keen to involve the author in all aspects of the production process. Within the movement it was (in)famous for publishing incendiary books and pamphlets. The Women's Press published fiction and nonfiction, including a line of feminist science fiction novels and collections. Sheba Feminist Publishers prioritized writing by women of color, lesbians, and working-class women. It published the poetry collection *A Dangerous Knowing* (1984), which featured the work of Barbara Burford, Jackie Kay, Grace Nichols, and Gabriella Pearse, and books by American poet/visionary Audre Lorde. Sheba also published books that responded to controversial debates around lesbian sexuality, sado-masochism, and butch-femme relationships in the late 1980s, such as Joan Nestle's *A Restricted Country* (1987) and the collection *Serious Pleasure* (1989).

Though diverse, much of radical feminist publishing continued to be managed by white women. In 1980, American writer Barbara Smith decided to start a feminist press exclusively run by (and featuring) women of color. It was called Kitchen Table / Women of Color Press. Similarly, some black British women writers felt marginalized by the publishing priorities of women's

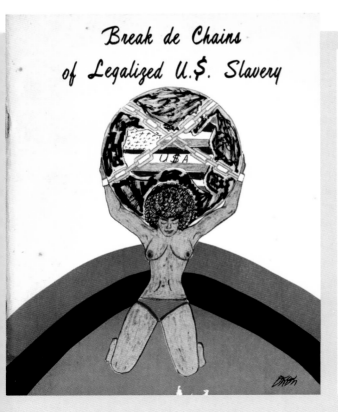

Ms. magazine

Bonnie J. Morris

Ms. magazine redefined women's mass media for the liberated woman.

From its first appearance in December 1971—as a forty-page preview inserted in *New York Magazine*—*Ms.* magazine broke the mold of male-bias journalism, making ideals and viewpoints of current feminism accessible to women from every walk of life. Up to that point, while conventional women's magazines might have offered advice to "career girls" or working mothers, nearly all featured more personal care ads than serious content. Despite the rising tide of feminist outrage visible through street protests, sit-ins, and posters, few mainstream journalists in the US took the women's liberation movement seriously—in stark contrast to the progressive media's focus on male leaders of the civil rights and anti-war factions. Women's authentic, lived experiences of sexual violence, access to political power, workplace harassment, and abortion rights did not belong in "family" newspapers, and were dismissed or simply not visible in the evening television news. With nearly all media controlled by men, any information or viewpoint that conflicted with male interests was unlikely to be broadcast. Well-respected news authorities such as Howard K. Smith belittled "women's lib" on national television, arguing that there was no problem of female income equity since "women already inherit money from worn-out husbands."[13] At the start of the 1970s, viewers with no other exposure to feminist activism were thus unlikely to gain accurate, well-rounded information about the goals of the women's liberation movement from daily news features.

Ms. filled that void. Frustrated by the condescension of top-rated male editors and reporters, and having successfully occupied the offices of the *Ladies' Home Journal* to demand the hiring of a female editor, a group of women writers led by Gloria Steinem and Patricia Carbine decided to start a feminist periodical by and for women. *Ms.* would eventually turn the familiar format of a monthly women's magazine into something not seen since Margaret Sanger's banned 1914 periodical *The Woman Rebel*: a platform for radical feminism which consumers could purchase, take home, pore over, and pass on to a friend.

As a young journalist who was both brilliant and beautiful, Gloria Steinem had already covered hot-button issues ranging from the birth control pill to women working as *Playboy* bunnies. During a historic meeting of women writers in her apartment living room early in 1971, Steinem raised the possibility of a regularly appearing newsletter or magazine that could succeed beyond one token issue. "We were simply trying to create a women's magazine that addressed real issues in women's lives, and could also publish new fiction writers and new poets and news of women in other countries," Steinem explained in a later interview. "We wanted to create something that would be like a helpful friend coming into your house once a month."[14]

Early ideas for the magazine's title included *Lilith* and *Sojourner* (both of which soon became names for other feminist publications), but *Ms.* won out as a reflection of the debate over why a woman must be defined by her marital status. The importance of racial diversity, and not shying away from critique of heterosexual romance, meant that the magazine's content might readily offend advertisers; and indeed for many years *Ms.* reluctantly ran glossy ads for cigarettes when other corporate sponsors proved to be wary of an association with feminism.

The first full-length issue appeared in March 1972, featuring topical articles that were circulated and re-read for decades: Joan Brady's "I Want a Wife," Johnnie Tillmon's "Welfare Is a Women's Issue," and the document "We Have Had Abortions," signed by many celebrity women—including Billie Jean King. These topics created considerable backlash. Patricia Carbine recalls that public libraries began to remove copies of *Ms.* from reading rooms, and on ABC *Nightly News*, Harry Reasoner jeered, "I'll give it six months before they run out of things to say."[15]

But contrary to his prediction, letters poured in from women. Poignant comments of gratitude, relief, affirmation, and shared stories filled the letters section in every issue as the magazine gained steam, and a full-length book titled *Letters to Ms.* later revealed the range of correspondence—with many letters published as "name withheld." Despite striking a chord that resounded with so many women both in the US and

> "A feminist is anyone who recognizes the equality and full humanity of women and men."
> Gloria Steinem

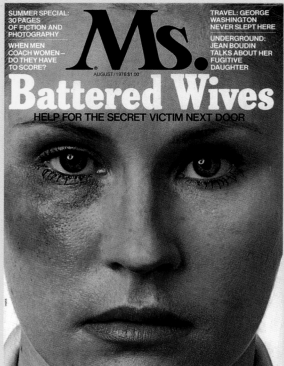

Above: Gloria Steinem did not shy away from a fight, whether in the pages of *Ms.* or in public. Here, photographed on April 20, 1979, Steinem urged a Minnesota Senate committee to provide welfare money for elective abortions. To argue her case, she displayed an article about the first woman to have an illegal abortion since public funding was cut back.

Right: The infamous cover of *Ms.* magazine's special issue on battered wives, August 1976. As Gloria Steinem later reported in her essay "Sex, Lies, and Advertising," ad sponsors for *Ms.* were livid that the issue cast such a dim light on relationships, while readers and other critics contended that the cover model seemed made up to appear far more glamorous than any actual survivor of domestic violence.

worldwide, *Ms.* struggled to stay afloat financially. Subscriptions were one challenge, as many women in abusive marriages or judgmental communities were terrified of having a feminist periodical delivered to their door. And potential advertisers continued to malign the magazine's purpose; a representative from the California Avocado Grower's Association told Gloria Steinem, "Why the hell would I want to put an ad in a magazine for lesbians?"[16] Sponsors of cosmetics and beauty products weren't happy with the magazine's critique of the beauty industry, and wanted well-made-up women on each monthly cover, objecting to a famous feature on battered wives. Much later, Steinem would review these moments in stark detail in an exposé titled "Sex, Lies, and Advertising."

Harry Reasoner's dismissive comment was not prophetic. Despite infighting among some staff, debates over racial inclusivity which led to the resignation of Alice Walker in 1986, and several changes in editorial structure over the years, *Ms.* is still published to this day, and, since 1989, has been ad-free.

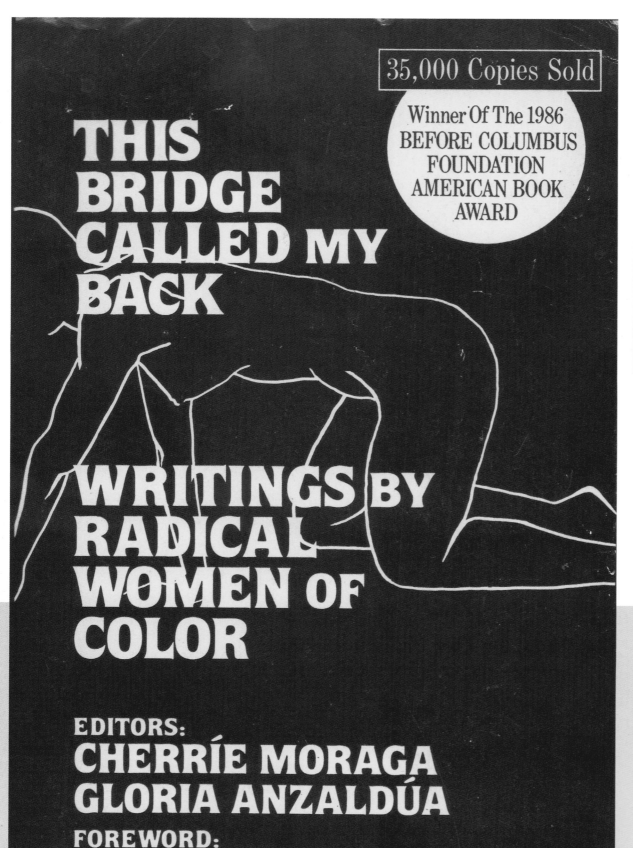

35,000 Copies Sold

Winner Of The 1986
BEFORE COLUMBUS
FOUNDATION
AMERICAN BOOK
AWARD

THIS BRIDGE CALLED MY BACK

WRITINGS BY RADICAL WOMEN OF COLOR

EDITORS:
**CHERRÍE MORAGA
GLORIA ANZALDÚA**
FOREWORD:
TONI CADE BAMBARA

Virago Modern Classics
Paule Marshall
Brown Girl, Brownstones

Above: British publisher Virago's longevity is in part due to its well-established, carefully chosen, and beautifully presented classic titles, such as Paule Marshall's *Brown Girl, Brownstones*.

Left: One of the most important feminist anthologies adopted for women's studies courses in the US, *This Bridge Called My Back* launched Kitchen Table Press (founded by black lesbian writer Barbara Smith) and offered a platform for essays by black and Chicana lesbian feminists.

Below: The early Viragos— members of one of the longest-running and most successful feminist publishers. This photograph was taken by Susan Greenhill at a party to celebrate the company's fifteenth birthday. From left to right, it shows Harriet Spicer, Ursula Owen, Lennie Goodings, Alexandra Pringle, and founder Carmen Callil. The image was chosen by Anna Ford as her contribution to the National Portrait Gallery's *Faces of the Century* exhibition in 1999 when she commented that, "The publishing firm of Virago achieved more for women's literature than any other."

presses in Britain, which privileged profitable titles by well-known Afro-American authors, such as the Pulitzer Prize–winning Alice Walker, rather than give a platform to unknown writers. During the 1980s, the Black Women Talk publishing collective responded by setting up a black women's publishing cooperative. They explained that their decision came "directly out of our experience of being excluded and/or being made invisible by white feminist publishers, as much as our commitment to seeing black women taking control and creating our own media and means of communication."[17] Such publishing groups drew on a new ethic of placing women's interests and bodies at the center of inquiry, trusting that an honest platform would attract and keep feminist customers. While readers responded enthusiastically to quality publishing that spoke to them without condescension or falsehoods about women's survival, most independent presses struggled to stay afloat after the deregulation of the book industry in the 1980s.

We own the media

Another important aspect of feminist publishing was the many different magazines, newspapers, and periodicals produced by activists in the movement.

Feminist print media helped the development of women's movements in several ways. They featured stories, news, and debate; listed events and facilitated regional and national networks; and, through the letters pages, helped create a public space where feminists could exchange views and express opinions. Like those involved in book publishing, women often worked collectively and took control of all aspects of production. In doing so, they gained new skills and independence often denied to women within the male-dominated media industry.

In the US, some lesbian publications such as *The Ladder* and *Amazon Quarterly* (first published in 1973) were sent to subscribers by discreet direct mail, arriving in plain brown wrapping or, in the case of the newsletter "Lesbian Connection" (established in 1974 and still active today), stapled shut to mask its contents.

EMMA magazine

For the past forty years, *EMMA* magazine has been a beacon of feminist mainstream magazine publishing in Europe.

Founded by journalist Alice Schwarzer, Germany's *EMMA* magazine published its first issue on January 26, 1977, and continues to be published every two months to this day. It was, and is, the only mainstream women's magazine to be published solely by women for women. Its very title is a play on the word emancipation and the content has always strived to live up to that ideal.

There are clear parallels between *EMMA* and *Ms.*, both adopting a bold design that focuses on high-quality photography and journalism, and shies away from the more cluttered and softer "feminine" aesthetic of traditional women's magazines.

Similarly in content, *EMMA* holds no punches and throughout the decades it has been at the vanguard of addressing women's issues on an international scale, from domestic violence and rape to childcare and birth control. *EMMA* has also received much controversy for pushing the boundaries, such as issues protesting against FGM in 1977 and exploring the repercussions of Islamic fundamentalism in 1979, as well as its long-standing "porNO" campaign against pornography. Such campaigns have often attracted public backlash, with the magazine's offices being broken into and covered with graffiti proclaiming, "EMMA, it's enough!" in 1997.

Nevertheless, founder and editor-in-chief Schwarzer has remained steadfast in her determination to report on the reality of women's lives across the world and it is this dedication that has kept *EMMA* relevant and revolutionary forty years on.

> "[*EMMA*] was always provocative, it didn't try to fit in with social norms. . . . It took on emotionally important and polarizing themes and was very dogmatic about it."
>
> **Dr. Alexandra Kühte**, quoted in "Happy Birthday *EMMA*: German Feminist Magazine Turns 30," © Deutsche Welle, January 25, 2007

Below: Alice Schwarzer at the *EMMA* office in January 2017 during a conference with the editorial staff.

SIMONE DE BEAUVOIR

Die letzten Fotos

Mit Kommentaren von Kate Millett und Alice Schwarzer

Scheidung: Jetzt gehen die Frauen!

Muttertag
Narzißmus
Namensrecht

Büros werden zu Fabriken
Wenn Frauen durchdrehen...
Der Wäscherinnen-Streik

G 4155 F   € 7,70 (It)   € 7,70 (Lux)   SFr 12,70   € 7,30 (A)   € 6,50 (D) / Nr. 6 Nov/Dez 2004

www.emma.de

ILLNER
Über Highheels & Jammerwessis

HASS
Ehre & Häme für Jelinek

IM VISIER
KOMMISSARINNEN MIT DEN WAFFEN EINER FRAU

TATORTE
Zwei Männer für EMMA auf den Spuren der Frauenhändler +++ Droht Freiern jetzt Gefängnis?

4 190415 506504   06

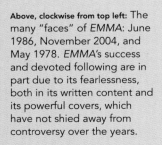

Above, clockwise from top left: The many "faces" of *EMMA*: June 1986, November 2004, and May 1978. *EMMA*'s success and devoted following are in part due to its fearlessness, both in its written content and its powerful covers, which have not shied away from controversy over the years.

"*EMMA* repeatedly uncovered grievances and criticized the exploitation and subordination of women. It moved many women to action and was able to be a powerful voice in society. A lot has changed in the country as a result."

Professor Ilse Lenz, quoted in "Germany's Feminist Magazine *EMMA* Turns 40 As Feminism Gains Ground," © Deutsche Welle, January 26, 2017

Whereas, in contrast, one best-selling feature of US feminism was *Ms.* magazine, founded in 1971 by Gloria Steinem. This was feminism sold over the counter right from a public newsstand, covering women in politics, abortion rights, and contraception, and offering regular features such as "No Comment" (highlighting sexist advertisements) and "Stories for Free Children." *Ms.* acknowledged the range of women's roles, from single mothers to women in prison, to emerging lesbians to political leaders. Nearly every issue addressed rape or domestic violence, which Steinem, as editor, later acknowledged caused great conflict in maintaining traditional ad sponsors. The usage of *Ms.* as a form of address, masking traditional emphasis on whether or not a woman was married, gradually became accepted as normal, but would not be adopted by the *New York Times* or in official government forms for many more years. However, *Ms.* was not the only trailblazer—the less well-known periodical *Off Our Backs* was founded in 1970 and remains the longest-running newspaper for women, by women in the United States.

Perhaps the most obvious European counterpart to *Ms.* was, and is, the groundbreaking German magazine, *EMMA*. In Italy, the first feminist magazine was *Sottosopra* (*Upside Down*), published in 1973. It reflected the need to create an instrument of discussion and connection between feminist groups across the country. Other famous Italian feminist magazines included *Effe* (1973–82), *DWF* (*Donna woman femme*, 1975–still published today), *Differenze* (1976–82), *Quotidiano donna* (1978–82), and *Lapis* (1987–still published today).

In Britain, publications expressed the breathtaking political diversity that evolved under the banner of "women's liberation." Some magazines reflected a political "tendency," such as the Marxist-orientated *Red Rag*, or targeted a specific demographic such as the energetic punk style of *Shocking Pink*, aimed at younger women. Other magazines addressed the concerns of particular women, such as *Mukti*, written by and for Asian feminists, or focused on specific topics, such as the music magazine *Woman Sound*. Publications could be short-lived, with one or two issues produced, or run for several years, with several hundred copies printed.

Sometimes, regional magazines took off through grassroots support and gained a national readership, as was the case for *Herizons*, Canada's feminist magazine. First published as a newspaper in 1979 and then a magazine in 1983, it continues to flourish to this day.

Despite the differing foci of publications, they were united in a concern to make print media written by women, for women. *Spare Rib*, Britain's iconic feminist newsstand magazine, was established in 1972 with its final issue published in 1992. The magazine aimed to challenge stereotypical images and stories usually found in women's magazines that "treat women as passive, dependent, conformist, incapable of critical thought" and confine them "to their traditional role of girlfriend, housewife and mother."[18] For many women *Spare Rib* provided their first exposure to the politics of women's liberation.

Unlike existing women's magazines, feminist publications of the 1970s and '80s did not distract, titillate, and pass the time of day—they created alternative images of women, actively engaged in political struggles or cultural projects. *Outwrite*, for example, was a British-based internationalist feminist newspaper started in 1982 founded by women of color; it aimed to support "the development of feminism worldwide" and placed women's lives "in the context of imperialism, racism and class divisions."[19] As interactive communication tools, feminist print media helped spread information and open up new forms of political action.

Women's bookshops

Throughout the 1970s and '80s, chain bookshops and convenience stores with large magazine sections might willingly sell pornographic material yet refuse to carry either *Ms.* or other journals and books of the women's movement. This led to the growth of a women's bookstore network, fostering women's access to feminist materials in spaces that also functioned as community centers for support and activism. Never hugely profitable, women's bookstores were nonetheless a lifeline for individuals emerging from isolation. They offered an alternative to bar culture and an affirmation of authentic women's history and lived experiences.

London-based shops such as Sisterwrite and Silver Moon Women's Bookshop were specifically set up as feminist bookstores. Other radical outlets decided to transform how they were run in order to empower women booksellers and support feminist ideas. In Britain Liverpool's News from Nowhere, Oakleaf Books in Milton Keynes, and Wordgames Community Bookshop in Bethesda, North Wales, became run by women-only collectives.[20] Other projects, such as the Women's

Opposite: Women's liberation magazines proliferated throughout the 1960s to the 1980s, with some of the most influential being *Off Our Backs* (US), *Spare Rib* (UK), *Ms.* (US), *Outwrite* (UK), and *Red Rag* (UK).

volume xii, number 6
June 1982
Washington, D.C.

off our backs

$1 a women's news journal

controversy at sexuality conference

children's literature

comparable worth

spare Rib

A WOMEN'S
LIBERATION
MAGAZINE
ISSUE 122
SEPTEMBER 1982
50p ***
$1.50/IR 70p inc. VAT.

stuff this for a lark...
he said he'd help!!

PHEW!

THE MYTH OF THE HELPFUL FATHER

WHERE THE ACTION IS!

AUDRE LORDE: FIGHTING BACK AFTER CANCER • CUBA: WHAT'S HAPPENING NOW

inside:
LABOUR & LOVE

WOMEN and the ECONOMY
INTERNATIONAL STRUGGLES
  spain
  portugal
  namibia

SEXUALITY and FILM

BERLIN

RED RAG

20p

A MAGAZINE OF WOMENS LIBERATION No 10

Outwrite 20p.
women's newspaper

THE NEW WOMEN'S NEWSPAPER! OUT NOW!

Distributed by: Full Time Distribution, Building K.
Albion Yard, Balfe St. London N.W.1.
Subscription from: Outwrite, Oxford House,
Derbyshire St. London E.2. Telephone 01 7294575.

GLORIA STEINEM
ON HOW
WOMEN VOTE

MONEY FOR
HOUSEWORK

Ms.

NEW FEMINIST:
SIMONE
DE BEAUVOIR

BODY HAIR: THE
LAST FRONTIER

WONDER WOMAN FOR PRESIDENT

PEACE AND JUSTICE '72

Liberation Book Bus, sold books at feminist events in rural settings. The bus also parked outside factories, nurseries, and schools, hoping to expose uninitiated women to the politics of women's liberation. In the US women-only bookstores sprang up in major cities across the country and became beloved institutions, from Women and Children First in Chicago, Sisterhood Books in Los Angeles and Lammas Women's Books & More in Washington, D.C., to New Words Books in Boston and Crazy Ladies in Cincinnati, Ohio.

Women's bookshops were a place where women could find information about the movement, whether that was a political meeting or the address of the nearest Women's Aid shelter. "Sometimes I felt more like a social worker than a bookseller,"[21] reflected Jane Cholmeley from London's Silver Moon Women's Bookshop, on the various times customers asked her to recommend books on traumatic subjects such as incest or sexual abuse.

Women's bookstores were also social spaces that held events, such as talks from touring international authors, poetry readings, and, in the US, the occasional concert—bookstores also promoted the recordings of the women's music movement. Many housed cafés, stocked records and tapes by women musicians, mugs, teddy bears, jewelry, badges, and speculums.[22]

How did such spaces change women's lives? Those escaping abusive marriages or just curious about feminism (and/or their sexuality) might be too shy to enter at first. But bookstores altered the urban landscape by making the feminist revolution a walk-in experience. Carol Seajay, who went on to edit the American journal *Feminist Bookstore News*, recalled, "Some women walked many times around the block before they found the courage to enter."[23] Others found the home they'd been searching for and plunged into the movement of words and ideas.

Women's bookstores certainly made feminism visible in the community, but this also meant staff could suffer abuse, and the properties themselves were at risk from vandalism. Bricks through windows, arson, hate mail, and threatening phone calls sometimes occurred. Stores would occasionally receive stock in damaged boxes, deliberately ruined by postal staff.

There was also a backlash from within the feminist community. Poetry readings, new publications, and bookstore events made some feminist writers into cultural icons, which did not sit well with those who preferred a nonhierarchical and collective model of sisterhood. Other critics lambasted the idea of any feminist businesses that used a capitalistic model rather than remaining strictly nonprofit. Writers Karla Jay, Jan Clausen, Ruth Rosen, Alice Echols, and Jo Freeman all noted the phenomenon of feminist leaders being "trashed" if they were too successful or attracted too much positive media coverage. The combination of economic struggle, ever-shifting political priorities, and mainstream publishing's consolidation into a few large conglomerates, as well as urban gentrification of once-affordable neighborhood storefronts, drove most feminist bookstores out of business by the early twenty-first century; yet many of the books and authors launched by the women's movement are now a mainstay of university reading and freely and widely available online.

By the end of the 1980s, women's lives had entered the printed word. Hélène Cixous's injunction for "woman" to "put herself into the text—as into the world and into history" had borne fruit, as women did so on a historically unprecedented scale. It was the outcome of two decades of creative political fury filled with the sound of typewriters banging and Gestetner machines clunking. Ink was spread across paper and newspaper columns lined up, typeset, and printed. In many cases, the authors were women who had never thought they were entitled to write; the printers were women who never believed they could learn how to print. As feminist books and magazines filled the shelves of libraries and entered mainstream bookstores, it all seemed a far cry from the early days of the women's movement when women struggled to find words and images to describe their experience. This was the outcome of a determined collective effort, "a labour of love,"[24] arising from the actions of publishers, distributors, printers, typesetters, booksellers, book fair organizers, magazine editors, writers, and readers. As writer Audre Lorde reminds us, in her own work, "poetry is not a luxury," but rather will always be an essential expression of struggle and identity.

"I longed for something more than the usual anti-war, male, socialist-type rhetoric. . . . As I entered through the door, it was apparent that this was a place that had never existed before. . . . Poetry, novels, music, art, ideas, questioning, sexuality, politics, relationships, non-monogamy, class, culture, race, age, abilities, gender, spirituality, sadomasochism, magic, desire, parenting, collectives, women's land, separatism, women's studies, women's festivals, women's bodies, women's bars, women's spaces, violence and rape and incest, self-defense, dance, creativity, addictions, radical therapy—all of it was found within the pages of books, on the walls, spoken during readings and events, argued over at meetings."

Wendy Cutler, recalling the opening of Oakland, California's, A Woman's Place Bookstore in January 1972

Top left: Silver Moon Women's Bookshop, London, opened its doors in June 1984 and finally closed in 2001.

Top right: Womanbooks was New York City's feminist bookstore, founded in 1972. Dozens of cities and towns across the US featured women's bookstores in the 1970s, '80s, and '90s. Some of the better-known feminist spaces were Lammas Women's Books & More in Washington, D.C.; New Words Books in Cambridge, Massachusetts; Amazon Books in Minneapolis, Minnesota; Sisterhood Books in Los Angeles; Charis Books in Atlanta, Georgia; Bookwoman in Houston, Texas; and Women and Children First in Chicago, Illinois.

Middle and bottom right: Mary Farmer and Beth Crimi of Lammas Women's Books & More in Washington, D.C. This historically significant image shows the importance of feminist bookstores in marketing women's music albums—then only available on vinyl—as well as books by lesbian and feminist authors. Here Beth Crimi stands with a display of women's music releases, many from Olivia Records artists. The black-bordered album to her right is Woody Simmons's popular *Oregon Mountains*. Lammas was an important space for women in which they could explore feminist arts and culture.

"IF I CAN'T DANCE . . . I DON'T WANT TO BE A PART OF YOUR REVOLUTION"

Music and the arts

Music, performance, and the arts were vital sites of struggle and political transformation for women.

In order to challenge the restrictive images of "woman" constructed by man-made culture, women inhabited, parodied, and exploded stereotypes. New images, stories, sounds, and feelings were also invented, cut from the freshly discovered fabric of women's once private, now public, lives.

Graphic art, writing, music, publishing, magazines, performance, photography, theater, craft, and film were all mobilized to explore a culture in which women were not marginalized or derided. The sounds, images, feelings, questions, and cultural practices generated were diverse and multidimensional. They ranged from agitprop (politically provocative shows) to avant-garde experimentation, and from skill-sharing workshops to collective art making. Rarely was this culture "just entertainment." It was a political tool and a force for social change.

Women soon discovered they also had a right to claim a history of their own and began to ask how the legacies of previous women artists informed and inspired new works. Who *were* the female sculptors, composers, painters, poets, choreographers, and performers whose works had been lost, scorned, or written out of history as somehow less worthy? Why were their contributions not taught as part of the artistic canon in schools and studios? What had enabled these women to produce life-sustaining art and material even in conditions of slavery, imprisonment, poverty, and sexual assault? Feminist art and music historians devoted themselves to the academic detective work of finding their foremothers in the arts, demanding that they be known as equals to men. Thus, both rediscovery and invention drove the artistic wing of the women's movement.

As feminist scholars rushed to bring buried information on women's lives into the classroom, new artists and instigators staged events of woman-identified imagery and sound.

> "It would not be an exaggeration to say that during [the 1970s] we have developed an alternative feminist culture."
>
> **Feminist Anthology Collective**, *No Turning Back: Writings from the Women's Liberation Movement 1975–1980*, 1981

Page 164: This drawing is taken from a poster advertising the stage show *Out of Bounds* by London-based theater group Scarlet Harlets. The identity of the artist is unknown, although it is signed Julia and dated 1983.

Far left: Sistershow was an anarchic theater cabaret group based in Bristol, UK, between 1973 and 1975. Performer and poet Pat VT West (left) and graphic artist Jackie Thrupp (right) sit under the giant hat.

Left: Women-only discos and music benefits not only formed an important part of women-defined culture, but also were a good way to raise funds for activist causes and collectives. This "benefit bop" featured the now-famous duo of Dawn French and Jennifer Saunders.

Above: Feminist Improvising Group (FIG) (left to right: Corinne Liensol, Georgina Born, Maggie Nicols, Lindsay Cooper, and Angèle Veltmeijer) performing at Battersea Arts Centre, London, March 1978. FIG pioneered women's engagements with free improvisation and pushed the boundaries of creative expression.

Spectacular strategies for defining a culture

Creativity is an important resource when protesting injustice, and activists in the women's movement understood this well. They asked the important question: if male-defined culture offered a limited view of women's lives, would the culture look different if women had created it? How would it feel or sound?

Early responses to this question often mocked feminine stereotypes. In Britain, the Women's Street Theatre Group paraded giant sanitary towels and deodorant cans in their play *Sugar and Spice*, performed after the first national Women's Liberation march in 1971; the Feminist Improvising Group (FIG) experimented with new forms of music and theater. Active between 1977 and 1983, FIG's performances interwove mundane scenes from daily life with avant-garde creativity, fusing the unpredictability of improvisation with an ethos of women's empowerment. The first FIG performance, which took place on October 31, 1977, featured a "hoover, softly whirring in endless vacuity, and the Kenwood mixer, grinding and circling." These domestic objects "were shown for what they are— not liberators, but enslaving accoutrements, women's assigned instruments that allow precious little room to improvise."[1] FIG toured Europe several times, playing in

Paris, Berlin, Rome, Copenhagen, Stockholm, and Reykjavík. In 1983, FIG members Irène Schweizer, Maggie Nicols, Lindsay Cooper, and Annemarie Roelofs established the European Women's Improvising Group (EWIG) with Joëlle Léandre and Annick Nozati, and a thriving network of European female improvisers collaborated in festivals, recordings, and performances throughout the decade.

British activist Pat VT West found that performance made activism fun and unpredictable. In the early 1970s, she was becoming tired of the seriousness of the movement, claiming, "It was getting amendment like. I had got so fed up with sitting in meetings and passing motions and not getting anywhere, so I thought it was time to move into theatre."[2] Alongside others Pat set up Sistershow, an anarchic feminist cabaret active in Bristol between 1973 and 1975. Sistershow used irreverent humor that encouraged audiences to look at women's liberation differently. Pieces such as "Impregnated Duster" and "Holy Padlock" poked fun at marriage and the role of the housewife. Other sketches—such as "Rape Dance," "Female Bisexual Song," and "Secretary and Tits"— tackled taboos about sexuality, identity, and power. Sistershow, like many other theater groups in the 1970s, was influenced by agitprop. As well as performing in venues, actors claimed the street as their stage. Through confrontational street "happenings," Sistershow interrupted the business-as-usual patterns of daily life.

Dance, as a medium of feminist performance, also found new expression in companies staging thematic liberation pieces, such as American groups the Wallflower Order Collective and the Dance Brigade. These performance groups were noteworthy for including sign language interpretation onstage, making the spoken-word portion of staged pieces accessible to deaf audiences. Viewers would be challenged by breakthrough dance performances featuring large-sized and disabled bodies. And perhaps most significantly in response to those who claimed that the women's movement had no sense of humor, a slew of emerging American feminist comedians broke new ground in the 1970s and '80s, delighting audiences at clubs and festivals with the refreshing routines of Kate Clinton, Lea DeLaria, Marga Gomez, Paula Poundstone, Lily Tomlin, Suzanne Westenhoefer, Karen Williams, and others paving the way for Ellen DeGeneres, Wanda Sykes, and Samantha Bee.

Meanwhile, British feminist music makers took to the streets alongside their agitprop sisters. The York Street Band and Nottingham's Fabulous Dirt Sisters were regular street performers and reveled in the freedom of claiming public space for women. Sometimes passers-by would spontaneously dance with the band, transforming a watching audience into active participants.

In the US, women also claimed public spaces on a never-before-seen scale with centers of feminist solidarity and creativity in the arts found on both coasts: in New York's Greenwich Village (where lesbian dance critic Jill Johnson and feminist rock critic Ellen Willis both wrote reviews for the Village Voice), and in Los Angeles, at the Woman's Building founded in 1973 by artist Judy Chicago, art historian Arlene Raven, and designer Sheila Levrant de Bretteville. Location and networking between women's institutions supported an economy of feminist art and politics. Artist Terry Wolverton recalls of those years, "When it opened in 1973, the Woman's Building was home to three galleries dedicated to women's art—Womanspace, Grandview, and 707. Sisterhood Bookstore sublet space and sold feminist and nonsexist literature and music. Three women's theater groups—the LA Feminist Theater, the Women's Improvisational Theater, and the Women's Performance Project—staged productions in the auditorium. Other tenants included an office of the National Organization for Women (NOW), a coffeehouse, and Womantours, a feminist travel agency."[3] Though not as extensive in scope and size, women's spaces in other cities offered similar intersections of art, music, classes, and hanging out; in the nation's capital, the Washington Area Women's Center housed the Sophie's Parlor radio program featuring female jazz artists broadcast on the WPFW station and a women's music coffeehouse where the first artists from the Olivia Records label performed.

Similar activity in Europe saw German artist Marianne Pitzen found the first women's museum—the Frauenmuseum in Bonn—in 1981 as a major public cultural space dedicated to showcasing women's cultural and artistic work on an international scale.

Skill-sharing workshops were also a crucial part of the women's liberation project to seize the means of cultural production. Workshops enabled women to gain confidence and practical knowledge within supportive, women-only environments. Sometimes these were aimed at young women and girls, but often they were for adult women who had not, like their male counterparts, been actively socialized to make, play, and construct.

Skill-sharing events could be vital for building networks and community. Over one hundred and fifty women of color attended the Black Women and the Media Conference that took place in London in 1984. The weekend was filled with practical workshops on radio, music, photography, theater, silkscreen printing, video, TV, writing, poetry, and newsletter-making. Attendees also discussed racist and sexist stereotypes of black women in the mainstream media, and how "the feminist media / black media could be made more accountable to black women's needs and issues."[4]

Producing culture was one side of the equation, but the other was distribution. Several distributors were set up during the 1970s to ensure the growing body of work made by women artists was seen and heard. US-based Women's Independent Label Distribution and UK-based Women's Revolution Per Minute distributed women's music; New Day Films and Cinema of Women specialized in feminist documentary work, issue-based shorts, and feature films; Circles focused on experimental artist film and video. While, in the early 1980s, Feminist Audio Books (FAB) was set up to increase access to feminist books for visually impaired people.

Through such strategies and networks, women began to redefine film, theater, music, and art in spectacular ways.

A SHOCKING PINK & SPARE RIB BENEFIT BOP
Sisterhood of Spit
Contradictions
Sister Culture
(black women's reggae sound system)

The Drill Hall (Arts Cap)
Chenies Street, London
Tel. 01-631-1353

JULY 25th
8pm
£2.50 waged
£1.50 unwaged
or low wage

Bring your own booze
Creche by men against sexism
Cafe open. Raffle

Women Only

the fabulous dirt sisters

five strong swimmers

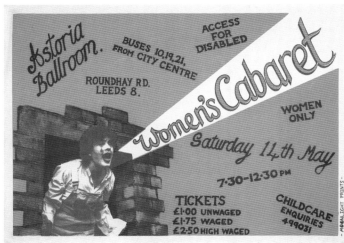

Astoria Ballroom.
BUSES 10,19,21, FROM CITY CENTRE
ROUNDHAY RD. LEEDS 8.
ACCESS FOR DISABLED
Women's Cabaret
WOMEN ONLY
Saturday 14th May
7·30-12·30 PM
TICKETS
£1·00 UNWAGED
£1·75 WAGED
£2·50 HIGH WAGED
CHILDCARE ENQUIRIES 499031

Internationale Vrouwenfestival, Amsterdam

D-M Withers

The transformative power of feminist culture was celebrated in five international women's festivals that took place in Amsterdam between 1977 and 1985.

Internationale Vrouwenfestivals created a platform for the transnational exchange of "women's culture." Theater, music, literature, film, dance, lectures, exhibitions, workshops, and discussions were part of an ambitious one-week jamboree of feminist culture and politics. Feminists from all over the world traveled to perform and attend these immensely popular events.

The founder of the Internationale Vrouwenfestival was Suzanne Dechert, an artist with a feminist attitude. Although the Netherlands had a vibrant women's movement, Dechert was never directly involved; instead she used her role as cofounder of the Melkweg—an internationally celebrated cultural center located in a former milk factory in old Amsterdam—to make the Vrouwenfestivals happen.

Dechert regularly visited London during the 1970s in search of talented performers. Here she was exposed to and wowed by the city's alternative theater scene, especially plays such as Sidewalk's *The Son of a Gun* and Monstrous Regiment's *Scum: Death, Destruction and Dirty Washing*. In 1977 she became determined to create an event that would enable other women to come into contact with the groundbreaking feminist culture she had witnessed in London. With the Melkweg at her disposal,

the first Internationale Vrouwenfestival happened over the course of a week in September 1977.

The event constructed a fantastical atmosphere, designed to shift the perspectives and feelings of those who moved into it:

> On entering [the festival], the hall itself has been decorated with care and attention to detail which [is also evident] throughout the building—everyone has lent extra time to make it just that little bit nicer, what with beautiful arrangements of flowers, decoration of the main theatre room and corridors, the erection of a bamboo and hessian geodesic dome for privacy in discussions—and the atmosphere in the entrance is more anticipatory than usual, with a sense of 'what we will find around this corner,' [and] almost bated breath among visitors.[5]

As women-only spaces, staged within a "feverish night full of entertainment, excitement and expectations of mysterious pleasures and unknown adventures," Vrouwenfestivals created new dimensions of erotic and social freedom.[6] "In the first festival, on the third night or something, some women would walk around bare-breasted.

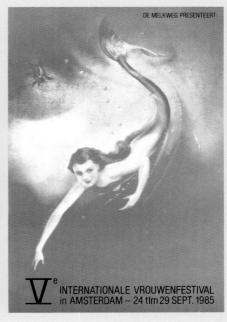

Far left: Rosa King performs for a Vrouwenfestival audience in 1985.

Left: Poster for the 1985 Vrouwenfestival.

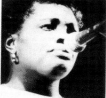

Far right: Women informally gather at the Vrouwencafe during the 1985 festival.

Right: Program of events for the 1985 Vrouwenfestival.

In the second festival, maybe a hundred women would walk around bare-breasted. At the third festival nearly all the women would walk around with naked [breasts], and I loved it, it was wonderful," remembered Dechert.[7]

Women flocked to Vrouwenfestivals to be entertained, restored, inspired, empowered, titillated, and turned on.

> "When the program was over, women would dance with each other and have a good time, and everyone was happy, then I thought: that was a good day. I could mirror myself in the feelings, it was something like electricity going through everybody, and that also went through me."
>
> Suzanne Dechert, interview with D-M Withers, February 13, 2017

Day and night, the program was packed with activity. Women might unwind in women-only saunas or meet with friends in the "Vrouwencafe," which offered a unique opportunity to be "together with other women in a pleasant way, just to talk or to do whatever you like."[8] For the more daring, boat trips and motorcycle tours showcased Amsterdam's hot spots.

For serious types, there were workshops on a range of topics: sexuality in theater, women's music in theater and collective playwriting, self-examination, women and herbs, African dance, yoga, silkscreen printing, and the herstory of matriarchal civilization. During the 1985 festival, Pat Califia held a workshop titled "Women Write (About) Sex" that advised participants, "If you don't feel that you can keep an open mind about other women's sexuality and work, please do NOT sign up for this workshop."[9] The same program included a panel discussion about sex featuring Kathy Acker and Candida Royale and, later that day, the authors of *Lesbian Nuns: Breaking Silence* shared their stories.

In the evening audiences were always treated to an adventurous assault of feminist performance, whether it was the theater of Beryl & the Perils, Theatre of Black Women and Spiderwoman, or solo performances from Amsterdam's World Champion body builder Ellen Van Maris. Music was always integral to the entertainment. Amsterdam-based saxophonist Rosa King, post-punk band the Au Pairs, US trio Unknown Gender, British jazz aficionados The Guest Stars, German lesbian folk-duo Monika and Barbara, and Women's Music poster-girls Alix Dobkin and Holly Near all graced the Vrouwenfestival stage.

Vrouwenfestivals were multidimensional and provocative. The program was designed to incite change in consciousness and feeling, and embraced contradiction and controversy. "My rule was there are no rules," reflected Dechert, "and we see what happens."[10]

Feminist film, theater, and satire

Throughout the 1960s and '70s, a diverse network of groups defended free speech and called for an end to what they perceived to be institutional bias surrounding gender, class, and race in the media. Such groups included men and women who produced and distributed commercial and underground pornography. Primarily directed at male consumers, the pornography of the times frequently featured violent exploitation of women's bodies, new exposure of female nudity in film and theater, and themes of rape in both R- and X-rated films such as the Franco-Italian movie *Last Tango in Paris*—but audiences were rarely offered women's viewpoints on sexuality and erotica or feminist perspectives behind the camera. The US genre known as "blaxploitation" made Pam Grier an action heroine in a series of films that nonetheless relied on the sexualization of black women. Hollywood remained an old boys' club for the most part, with directors, producers, and studio executives almost entirely male (and white). Feminist filmmakers and cartoonists who told a story from a woman's angle fought for a place at the table, often producing work that was primarily marketed to other women through the underground press; their efforts and the shifting sex roles of mainstream film were critiqued in the US by new feminist film historians Molly Haskell and Kathi Maio. One remarkable American director, Barbara Hammer, contributed the first lesbian lovemaking film actually directed by a lesbian with her 1974 classic *Dyketactics*. Movies such as *Snuff* and *Laura X* (which exposed the violent world of male pornography) and documentaries including Washington-born Connie Field's *Life and Times of Rosie the Riveter* and New York–born Barbara Kopple's *Harlan County, USA* introduced audiences to the real women on America's union battlefronts. These feminist films became a staple of women's studies classes and part of the growing catalog of distribution company Women Make Movies. Eventually, within mainstream Hollywood culture several actresses became notable for outspoken advocacy of feminism and gay rights, and comedian Lily Tomlin proudly appeared on the cover of *Ms.* with an unshaven armpit aimed at the viewer, visualizing a different kind of "celebrity cover girl."

Meanwhile, *Wimmin's Comix*, *Sylvia*, and other feminist comic book series showcased the wit and daring of American cartoonists such as Roberta Gregory, Nicole Hollander, Trina Robbins, Lee Marrs, and (eventually) a very young Alison Bechdel, whose *Dykes to Watch Out For* comic series debuted in 1983.

In Europe, there was a strong tradition of avant-garde filmmaking that feminist directors could draw upon and some truly remarkable movies were released during the 1970s and '80s that may not have reached the wider viewing public, but certainly attracted acclaim and controversy, and spoke powerfully to their feminist audiences. Belgian-born Agnès Varda has been cited as critical to the development of the French New Wave film movement and works such as *Vagabond* (1985) showcase her ability to subvert the traditional female role to pose key questions about the perception and place of women in French society. Similarly, Margarethe von Trotta, who embarked on her career during the rise of New German Cinema in the 1970s, explores in films such as her 1981 *Marianne and Juliane* (also known as *The German Sisters*) the female experience of the tumultuous postwar period in West Germany. Italian feminist film *Io sono mia* (*I Am Mine*, 1978), with an almost all-female cast and directed by feminist director Sofia Scandurra, is considered a sort of feminist manifesto.

International film festivals also helped to distribute the work of women filmmakers and feminist narratives. Films de femmes / International Film Festival of Creteil was founded in 1979, and the Feminale, Germany's oldest film festival, was established by students of film theory from the University of Cologne in 1984. The Rocky Mountain Women's Film Festival and Canadian St. John's International Women's Film Festival were founded in 1988 and 1989 respectively, with the latter proudly bearing the slogan "Made by Women, for Everyone." Italian artist and philosopher Lina Mangiacapre set up one of the first women's international film festivals in Europe, called Rassegna del cinema femminista di Sorrento, in 1976.

Mangiacapre also established the Neopolitan performance collective Le Nemesiache in the same year. The group used mythology and performance to express new ways of being a woman and female independence.[11]

Meanwhile in Britain, a vibrant theater scene developed in and around the women's movement. Monstrous Regiment, Cunning Stunts, Sadista Sisters, Siren, and Hormone Imbalance were just some of the companies that made hard-hitting feminist theater.

Theatre of Black Women's plays were an experimental "mixture of dramatic poetry, visual symbolism, fragmentation, movement and music; a theatrical collage, if you like, a kind of poetry-theatre." The group's name was "an act of self-determination and self-affirmation: a naming of ourselves in a theatre culture that was predominantly white and male."[12]

Jamaica's Sistren Theatre Company, which visited Britain in the 1980s, influenced activists in the Black Women's Movement. "Having sisters come over from Jamaica

Opposite, clockwise from top left:
Theatre of Black Women used theater to promote positive and inspiring images of black women; their plays employed a poetic aesthetic that allowed a deeper exploration of black female identity.

International feminist film festivals from Paris to Sydney became an important platform for female directors and screenwriters to showcase new work.

Sadista Sisters were part of the groundbreaking feminist theater movement that developed in Britain during the 1970s and '80s.

Monstrous Regiment's *Scum* was set in nineteenth-century Paris, during the time of the Commune. The play, which depicted women's roles in the radical socialist and revolutionary government that ruled Paris for two months in 1871, galvanized audiences into action.

THEATRE OF BLACK WOMEN

presents

'SILHOUETTE'

written and performed by
BERNARDINE EVARISTO
and
PATRICIA HILAIRE

DATE: ....
TIME: ....
VENUE: ....
TICKETS: ....

For more
information contact P.O.Box 6
136 Kingsland high street E.8. 2N5.

249·7742   249·1045

Sponsored by Marks & Spencer and
Greater London Arts Association

Designed and printed by
Springboard Hackney
at Harambee II

FESTIVAL INTERNATIONAL DE FILMS DE FEMMES

13-21 MARS 82

LES GEMEAUX
Centre d'Action Culturelle 49 av. clemenceau 92330 sceaux tel 6600564

FEMINIST FILM WORKERS
present

A forum on the image of women in Australian feature films

a presentation of film clips followed by discussion and speakers

I WAITED FOR YOU WOMEN TO GET HERE ALL MY LIFE

ONLY THE CHAINS HAVE CHANGED

SYDNEY FILM FESTIVAL
STATE THEATRE
MONDAY, 25th JUNE, 1979
1pm—4pm

FEMINIST FILM WORKERS
212 5074

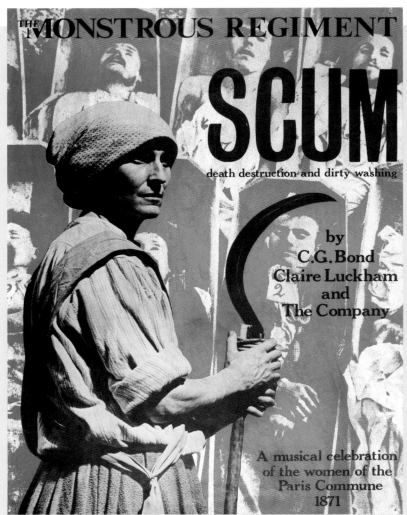

THE MONSTROUS REGIMENT

SCUM

death destruction and dirty washing

by
C.G. Bond
Claire Luckham
and
The Company

A musical celebration
of the women of the
Paris Commune
1871

THE BOULEVARD THEATRE
Walkers Court, Brewer Street, London, W.1. Tel. 01 437 2661

Special student Rate!
at £2·50

SADISTA SISTERS

Photography by DAVID SIBLEY

SA/2034

The Michigan Womyn's Music Festival

Bonnie J. Morris

For the forty summers from 1976 to 2015, woman-identified art, music, dance, theater, workshops, and goddess rituals could all be found at the largest women-only gathering on the planet: the Michigan Womyn's Music Festival.

America's first women's music festivals appeared in the early 1970s, starting with day festivals at the Sacramento State and San Diego State University campuses, a Midwest Women's Festival held in Missouri, the Boston Women's Music Festival, and the National Women's Music Festival at the University of Illinois in Champaign-Urbana. These regional events exposed audiences to feminist (and openly lesbian) artists, most of whom toured independently of the mainstream recording industry. In addition to staging new artists, offering workshops, training women in construction and sound production, and pledging commitment to anti-racist practices, festivals of the 1970s and '80s provided fans of women's music with a temporary haven where performances, politics, and spirituality affirmed a woman-loving sensibility. The exclusion of men became a radical hallmark of those festivals able to use privately owned spaces. The longest-running festival, the National Women's Music Festival (NWMF), met on Midwestern university campuses, with the advantages of dormitory beds and concert halls—but in a public setting where men remained part of audiences or worked as union techies at concerts. Sisterfire, in Washington, D.C., met at a public school site and included men. Other festivals, such as the Michigan Womyn's Music Festival (MWMF), Campfest, the Northeast Women's Music Retreat (NEWMR), and the West Coast Music and Comedy Festival, were committed to producing women-only events where female workers filled all roles from drumming to plumbing.

As a private, women-only, and clothing-optional camping event, the Michigan festival was started by nineteen-year-old Lisa Vogel, her sister Kristie Vogel, and friend Mary Kindig, and first met on one hundred and twenty acres near Mt. Pleasant. A larger site in Hesperia, Michigan was leased from 1977 through to 1981 (now affectionately referred to as "the Old Land" by longtime festival workers). The festival operated as a collective called WWTMC (We Want The Music Collective), later becoming a cooperative, then a company. Small salaries or honoraria went to longtime "coordinators" who led crews such as security, garbage, childcare, kitchen, land maintenance, and stage production.

While the early years were marked by much trial and error in terms of weather, building without damaging the natural environment, and food preparation, the festival continually increased its attention to diversity and care. Adamant that all women should have access to feminist events, the festival initiated ASL interpreting for deaf campers, a "DART" area (Differently Abled Resource Tent), childcare, sober support, and a women of color tent and sanctuary. Diversity workshops were led by experienced facilitators, including Papusa Molina, Amoja Three Rivers, Penny Rosenwasser, and Margaret Sloan-Hunter.

By 1978, the festival's logo of an oak tree and a piano, designed by artist "Sally Piano" (also known as Sirani Avedis), began appearing on brochures and sale items. Some longtime workers and "festiegoers" sported a "treeano" tattoo. With an identifiable logo and a returning fan base, the festival initiated sales of "festiewear" (T-shirts, caps, and tank tops), and "festievirgins" arrived from as far away as Japan, New Zealand, and Australia. Artists in the first five years included the stars of the burgeoning women's music movement, such as Holly Near, Margie Adam, Sweet Honey in the Rock, Linda Tillery, the Dance Brigade, Mary Watkins, Alive!, Edwina Lee Tyler, Teresa Trull, Woody Simmons, Alix Dobkin, Maxine Feldman, Cris Williamson, Meg Christian, Ferron, and Casselberry & Dupree.

By the festival's fourth year, the expansion of performance space included a popular Day Stage. Artists including Kay Gardner, Z Budapest, and Ruth Barrett brought a focus on women's spirituality and goddess heritage; comedy expanded with talented performers such as Kate Clinton, Marga Gomez, Karen Williams, and Suzanne Westenhoefer. Festival artists mixed with fans and offered workshops; such easy access to performers was another contrast to mainstream rock festivals in the same era.

"We used 37,200 feet of twine this year."

"We ordered 4,416 rolls of toilet paper."

"The massage crew gave over 890 massages."

"The interpreters worked with forty-five deaf women from five different countries."

"Childcare had sixty toddlers under age four; our youngest camper was three months old."

Quotes from the workcrew wrap-up meetings

Margie Adam
Maxine Feldman
Ova

Alix Dobkin
Mary Watkins Trio
Witch One

Teresa Trull & Julie Homi
The Harp Band

Linda Tillery Band
Breakwater

Deuce
Robin Flower & Nancy Vogl
Therese Edell

Chévere
Sirani Avedis
Terry Garthwaite

THE 5th MICHIGAN WOMYN'S MUSIC FESTIVAL – AUGUST 14th–17th, 1980
A GATHERING OF MOTHERS & DAUGHTERS IN HESPERIA · FOR ALL WOMYN OF ALL AGES
FOR INFO SEND SASE TO THE WE WANT THE MUSIC COLLECTIVE · 1501 LYONS AVENUE · MOUNT PLEASANT, MICHIGAN 48858

Above: Poster for the 1980 Fifth Michigan Womyn's Music Festival, designed by Sirani Avedis.

In 1982, the festival, in its seventh year, moved to six hundred and fifty acres near Hart, Michigan, attracting the largest audience to date (upwards of eight thousand campers) and soon adding an Acoustic Stage and an August Night open-mic stage. Some paved walkways were added to make life easier for women with mobility challenges and baby strollers. Barbara "Boo" Price became Lisa Vogel's business partner after the 1985 festival and was increasingly involved with production until the two parted ways in 1994, during a decade which saw many challenges—including the production of a tenth anniversary double album in 1985; the growth of the festival to five days (with new Intensive Workshops) by 1986; and ongoing debates over racism and inclusion of trans women.

Recognizing its global community, the festival added an international welcome greeting in many languages as part of the opening ceremonies, and featured more award-winning international artists, such as New Zealand's Topp Twins and Canada's Sawagi Taiko drum ensemble. A film festival, showcasing women's independent documentaries and feature-length films, drew enthusiastic crowds, as did the popular "traditions" during festival week, such as the redhead parade, Drumsong Orchestra, barter market, traditional sweat lodge, dance lessons, children's procession, and a 5k "Lois Lane" run. The coy phrase "I see August in you" appeared on festival bumper stickers as a means of women signifying their Michigan allegiance.

Most festival goers concluded that even a few days in a women-only space was a life-changing experience that was not available anywhere else. One song served as the essence of the festival experience, an anthem of sorts—the late Maxine Feldman's composition "Amazon," later adapted into an upbeat version by longtime performer and opening ceremonies director Judith Casselberry. Hearing the first notes of "Amazon Womyn Rise" from the Night Stage on opening night, with thousands of women singing along, set the mood for the festival week itself.

authorised our work, and educated us too. They were doing similar things to what we were doing, but were showing us even more what could be done," remembered activist Gail Lewis. "With the Brixton Black Women's Group they did workshops about our lives. We began to know more about each other as a whole group."[13]

For American actresses and directors, feminist theater companies such as Earth Onion and One Foot on the Mountain offered the possibility of training and production with women's lived experiences at the center. Writer Clare Boothe Luce contributed a one-act play, *Slam the Door Softly*, a feminist version of Ibsen's *A Doll's House*, to *Life* magazine in 1970, where it reached millions of readers, starting with this opening line from a pompous husband: "God, these Liberation gals! Still at it."

Women's music and dance

During the youth-driven 1960s, the music industry accelerated and capitalized on protest music. Throughout the US radio and record stores delivered the sound of authority being questioned, and that included new feminist narratives, from Aretha Franklin's "R-E-S-P-E-C-T," to Buffy Sainte-Marie's tributes to Native American culture, to Helen Reddy's hit "I Am Woman." However, despite these commercially successful artists, a number of acclaimed female singer-songwriters, and the all-woman rock band Fanny making the Top 40, women were often more visible in front of male bands or in girl groups singing pop tunes of boy-girl love than they were as independent artists defining their own sound.

Some women's liberationists wanted to create a culture that was separate from men and independent from capitalism. They viewed popular music as a cultural battlefield with "the mighty male wielding his instrument like a weapon."[14] Citing songs such as the Rolling Stones' "Under My Thumb," which they interpreted as celebrating men's power over women, they urged that new music be invented that was relevant to liberated women's lives. Many American women artists who had been a powerful force in the folk and civil rights movements of freedom songs and anti-war performance now shifted their energy to a new genre called "women's music," which took root in the early 1970s.

Appalled by themes of violence against women in male rock music, the Chicago Women's Liberation Rock Band and the New Haven Women's Liberation Rock Band released a 1972 album titled *Mountain Moving Day*,

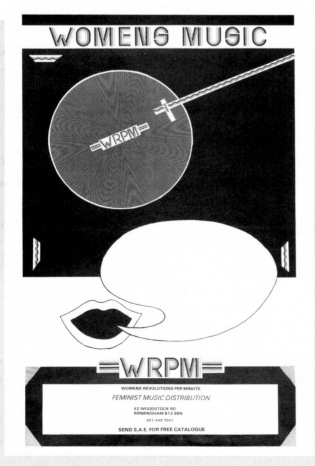

Far left: Women's Revolution Per Minute (WRPM) distributed women's music within Britain. WRPM was set up in 1977 and remained active until 2004, and helped circulate the large corpus of women's music from the US and, in the 1980s, music that was recorded in Britain.

Left: WRPM also sometimes produced concerts for touring artists, such as American women's music star Meg Christian. Note that tickets were sold through Sisterwrite, the London-based women's bookstore.

tackling issues of rape, abortion, equal pay, and patriarchy. These bands would influence the burgeoning women's music scene in Britain, with groups such as the London Women's Liberation Rock Band, the Stepney Sisters, and the Northern Women's Liberation Rock Band taking the stage at conferences, organizing workshops, and writing manifestos. Music daring to address love between women soon followed, including Maxine Feldman's anthem "Angry Atthis," Alix Dobkin's 1973 album *Lavender Jane Loves Women*, and the artists of Olivia Records.

Women's music outside of the US differed as widely in genre, style, and concept as "mainstream" music, ranging from German and Italian punk bands Die Ätztussis and Clito respectively to Toronto's The Curse and Japanese five-piece Girls—women were participating in music making in groundbreaking and diverse ways.

Between 1974 and 1975, the growing popularity of women's music in the US spawned new institutions, expanding fans' access to the music while keeping control of production in women's hands. There were women's music festivals, women-only sound corporations, and female album distribution companies.

In the US, to promote these artists, the first full-blown women's music festival met on the campus of the University of Illinois in 1974. It was produced by Kristin Lems, who originally invited Roberta Flack and Yoko Ono to perform, and instead ended up presenting Cris Williamson, Woody Simmons, and Margie Adam as the new stars of women's music. By 1975, Boden Sandstrom's WomanSound company and the Goldenrod music distribution network were in place (later joined by Ladyslipper), able to deliver the sound and product of feminist music to any venue: stage, park, campground, bookstore, church basement, or private living room. Nor was this movement limited to adult listeners: albums intended to raise the feminist consciousness of children also proliferated, most famously the release *Free to Be . . . You and Me*, produced by feminist actress Marlo Thomas. These works reached new audiences through the creative programming of America's independent radio stations, many located on college campuses and others part of the progressive Pacifica network. With names like Radio Free Women, Sophie's Parlor, Face the Music, Amazon Country, and Something about the

Women, feminist shows brought art and argument to the airwaves. From these origins in clubs and college campuses, the women's music movement also created jobs and opportunities for female artists in the male-dominated recording industry. In the same way that rock 'n' roll changed the American landscape forever and launched a youth revolution with a recognizable set of values, fashions, and products, radical feminist culture contributed a musical genre that went well beyond marketing concert tickets and albums, particularly when openly lesbian artists both shaped and reflected the values of their audiences. And the performers, producers, album distributors, and fans supporting this underground-yet-visible subculture forged a network of accessible lesbian celebrities, at a time when almost no other performers or politicians were out.[15]

Women-centered music would be the backdrop at women's discos, independent social spaces "free of the usual sexual competition and cattle-market/wall-flower syndrome."[16] For lesbians, women's discos provided a safe space within a homophobic culture. "I remember on the inside of the disco it was absolutely fantastic. The bonding of women together, they were dancing and throwing their tops off. It wasn't like an average disco. There was real self-discovery and recognition. But the energy on the outside was very threatening."[17]

Troubling the image

Radical art defined the aesthetics of the 1960s and '70s, giving the countercultural movements their signature historic backdrops of psychedelic swirls, poster graphics, protest music, and themes demanding inclusion. The red or black raised fist image appearing on posters for student strikes and black solidarity in the late 1960s soon became a mark of "woman power" as well. A raised fist, inside the now-recognizable woman's symbol (originally indicative of the goddess Venus), became a movement image and a demand for equality—one easily laminated onto pins or spray-painted on walls.

Meanwhile, other artists celebrated women's spirituality or experimented with images of female anatomy and goddess culture. When Swedish painter Monica Sjöö's "God Giving Birth" was exhibited in 1970 at Swiss Cottage Library, London, the police seized it due to its alleged blasphemous content. The painting depicted a black woman giving birth; for Sjöö this image embodied the spirit of the Great Cosmic Mother giving birth to humanity.

"We are sick and tired!" Feminist songs in Italy

Andrea Hajek

"We went to demonstrations and we sang and played the guitar, we sang feminist songs, we always did very creative things. . . . For us creativity was a way of doing politics in a very different manner, precisely because we understood that if you do masculine politics you always get the usual masculine discourse. You should also invent, reinvent forms of communication, ways of being with others, including with men."[18]

This is how feminist singer and songwriter Antonietta Laterza recalls her experience of the women's movement in 1970s Italy, which found expression in many different ways. One of these was music: singing and playing instruments offered women a way of doing politics differently and more creatively. Most importantly, it allowed women to (literally) give voice to more personal matters and experiences that usually remained outside of traditional politics, but which were of particular relevance to women. For example, in the famous collection *Alle sorelle ritrovate*,[19] the song "Cara madre" ("Dear mother") casts light on the difficult mother-daughter relationship that many feminists were confronted with, at a time of generational conflict and changing sexual norms. As we can read from the opening lines, the sexual liberation brought along by the 1968 student movement was not necessarily a liberation for women:

Dear mother
so fat and defeated
I have rejected your image
I have emancipated
free love, equality
'68, the factory, the demonstration
but I have aborted like a witch
class struggle fooled me too

Abortion was another key theme in feminist songs. Although Laterza herself declined to have an abortion when she got pregnant at a young age, eventually giving birth to a baby girl, the intimate song "Aborto sacrificio" ("Abortion sacrifice") narrates the difficult choice of abortion that affected many women:

I remember
throwing up
and without making a sound
a life without eyes and without hands
had hidden itself in my womb.
Rejected by my consciousness
by the shudder of lifeless dolls
maternity
has pursued me
with its jovial smile
in an absurd embrace
I have locked it
into a copper saucepan
and the wind
has dispersed its existence . . .

Antonietta Laterza recorded many of her songs and performed in public, but singing was also a very common feature of feminist gatherings and demonstrations. This often led women to create feminist singing groups; one of the most successful of these groups was the Canzoniere femminista (Feminist Songbook), which was part of the Wages for Housework committee in the northern city of Padua. Here music served as a political means of communicating women's struggle: "Siamo tante siamo belle" ("We are many, we are beautiful") from the 1977 album *Amore e potere* (*Love and power*) perhaps best expresses the demands put forward by the Wages for Housework campaign:

We are many we are beautiful
we throw the frying pans at you
We are women we are fed up
we are fed up with struggling!
Let's reclaim our lives
reclaim love,
We are many we are strong
all the world we want to change!

Power to the women!

Enough with children to exploit
and live only to get old,
enough with misery and slavery
no longer will we work for free!
We don't want more work
but time and money also for us
we are the most exploited of all
now it's time for you to pay up!

Another well-known musical group came from within the Roman feminist movement. It authored what is perhaps the most famous feminist song to have come out of this decade, "Noi siamo stufe" ("We are sick and tired"). It was an adaptation of the 1950s American song "Sixteen Tons," about the hardships of a coal miner. This version focused on the double burden and other social injustices suffered by women:

We are sick and tired of giving birth
washing dishes ironing nappies
having a man for master
who prohibits our contraception

We are sick and tired of making ends meet
every month we tally the family balance sheet
we wash, sew, clean, cook
for those who claim that they maintain us

. . .

We are sick and tired of abortions
every time the risk of dying
our body belongs to us
for all this we fight together

They always tell us to endure
but from today on we want to fight
for our liberation
come on women let's make the revolution!

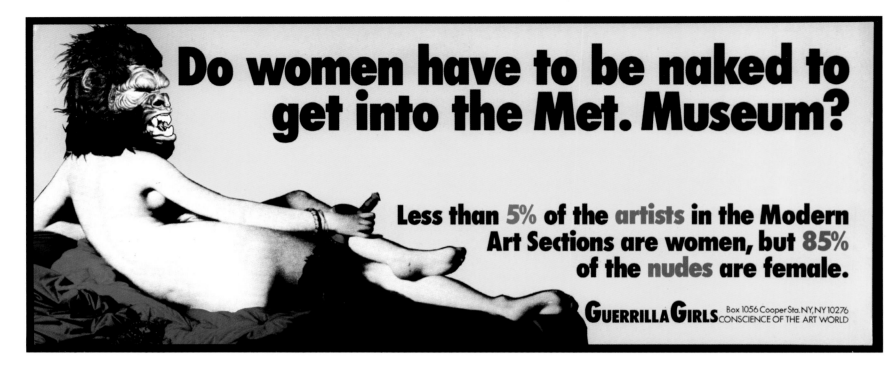

Do women have to be naked to get into the Met. Museum?

Less than 5% of the artists in the Modern Art Sections are women, but 85% of the nudes are female.

GUERRILLA GIRLS Box 1056 Cooper Sta. NY, NY 10276
CONSCIENCE OF THE ART WORLD

Artists such as the Egyptian-born Nil Yalter, based in Paris, used new mediums of performance art on film to explore female objectification in *Headless Woman (Belly Dance)* (1974), while Austrian artist VALIE EXPORT shocked audiences with her defiant *Genital Panic* (1968) performance piece.

American artists, like Betsy Damon, created live street actions or, like Carolee Schneemann, sought to present authentic perspectives of the female body, unwilling to let male-generated pornography define the female nude. Others magnified the realities of their own ethnic communities: Faith Ringgold's *Slave Rape Series* and *Women's Liberation Talking Mask* situated the question of African American legacies in feminist art; and Yolanda M. Lopez's *Portrait of the Artist as the Virgin of Guadalupe* series showcased working-class Chicana role models in contrast to the traditional visions of saintliness depicted by the Church. Other powerful artists included Miriam Schapiro, Ana Mendieta, Marina Abramovic, photographers Hannah Wilke and Cindy Sherman, and sculptor Carolyn Whitehorn, who exhibited her works at women's music festivals.

In the US, national attention to feminist art burgeoned when Judy Chicago unveiled her great signature installation, *The Dinner Party*, a triangular setting with vulva-themed plates of homage to powerful women in Western heritage. In Britain, American artist Mary Kelly displayed her work *Post-Partum Document*, a durational study of the mother-child relationship, at the ICA in 1976. Among a range of different items, the work displayed stained nappies, an inclusion that caused outrage in the tabloid press.[20] Despite

these high-profile exhibitions, women, on the whole, remained marginalized within the art world. By the late 1980s, a group of female artists and agents formed a masked group called the Guerrilla Girls: Conscience of the Art World—activists who disrupted New York's gallery and museum culture with feminist broadsides questioning why the works of women artists were so seldom on display.

In Britain, there were moves on a local scale to rectify this imbalance with exhibitions and collectives devoted to women's art. The Pavilion Women's Photography Centre opened in Leeds in 1983. This cooperatively run project had a gallery space, darkroom facilities, and meeting rooms. Pavilion's mission was to challenge the elitism of traditional art galleries, and focused on photography due to its accessibility and presence in everyday life. The center held exhibitions about feminist issues of the day, such as Greenham Common, and featured touring exhibitions by Jo Spence and and the Hackney Flashers, though the latter did not see their work as art but as the use of documentary photography and photomontage, along with other visual material, for political purposes. The first exhibition, *Collective Works*, explored the process of setting up a feminist photography center, and the politics of working collaboratively. Other exhibitions included *Our Day Will Come: An Exhibition of Photos About Irish Women* by Quinn, *Risky Exposure*, and *Testimony: Three Black Women Photographers*.

"Another vital priority for the Pavilion—we prefer not to be called a 'gallery'—is to break down the elitist image art galleries have and to create a friendly atmosphere where people won't feel alienated by what's on the walls."

Liz Heron, "What's on at the Pavilion?"

Opposite: The Guerrilla Girls art collective stages agitprop and creates activist art highlighting sexist imbalances in the art world. This 1989 poster was originally displayed on advertising spaces on buses and caused a sensation when it first appeared, sparking much-needed debate about the lack of prominence given to female artists in major museums and galleries.

Below: The Pavilion in Leeds, UK, showcased women's photography and created an empowering environment in which amateurs could learn the rudiments of photography. The poster on the left advertises one of their key exhibitions, *Testimony: Three Black Women Photographers*, held during the summer of 1986, and the flier on the right celebrates the opening of the center.

The Women's Postal Art Event began in 1975 when a group of women, most of them housewives, sent each other small artworks through the post. Imagined as a long-distance consciousness-raising session, "their art was very flexible, could be knitted, sewn, collage, painted and largely made out of things lying around the house. A knitted egg and bacon on a plate was strikingly grotesque—showed the gory work that goes into feeding a family . . . they stressed their art was disposable—if something got lost or destroyed they just made it again."[21] The Women's Postal Art Event reclaimed creativity of domestic space while simultaneously critiquing the drudgery and potential violence of women's confinement in the home. Art generated by the project was exhibited in Manchester, Liverpool, Birmingham, Edinburgh, London, Melbourne, and Berlin and in 1977 was presented at ICA London in the installation *Portrait of the Artist as a Housewife*.

Artists from all over the art world engaged in the discourse; Japanese artist Yayoi Kusama also reflected on "woman's work" in *Oven Pan*, as did Martha Rosler in *Semiotics of the Kitchen* (1975), while Paris-born Louise Borgeouis explored the nature of patriarchy in her *Destruction of the Father* (1974) installation piece.

Feminist art flourished from the 1960s through to the 1980s, creating an entirely new genre, of which the works referenced above are only a brief snapshot.

Artists came together during the period at the International Festival of Women Artists, first held at the Carlsberg Glyptotek Museum in Copenhagen, Denmark, from July 14 to 30, 1980, with a second festival held in Nairobi in 1985. Both festivals were organized to coincide with the United Nations World Conferences on Women. The festivals featured work by artists from over thirty different countries and were a celebration of the rich diversity of feminist art during the 1980s. These artists evolved a new visual language for women that not only challenged perceptions but also redefined the image of womanhood in the public consciousness.

Undoubtedly, the women's liberation movements created many opportunities for women to participate in culture, a sphere from which they had historically been excluded. They provided the social context where women could develop confidence to make art and show it to another woman, start independent record labels, organize a women's disco, take a photograph, learn how to make a video, or perform on stage. Many of these cultural endeavors were partially recorded and their legacy is ephemeral, much like the art from the Women's Postal Art Event that fell apart because it was too fragile or simply got lost in the mail. Many of the works have survived in archives but are rarely part of mainstream culture. They all are marked by the power of women's collective and individual voices at a time when they inventively claimed cultural space and transformed society.

war
is
not
healthy
for
children
and
other
living
things

THE PEACEMAKERS

The anti-war and anti-nuclear debates

Are women biologically predisposed to be less aggressive and violent than men? Are women by nature more cooperative, more likely to resolve conflict through dialogue and peaceful means?

These are some of the questions that women peace campaigners have explored through their activism.

At a time when most mothers of draft-age sons still could not vote, a variety of American feminist organizations opposed the US's entry into World War I, including the Women's Peace Party and the Women's International League for Peace and Freedom (WILPF). The first woman elected to Congress, Jeanette Rankin from Montana, cast the sole vote against the United States going to war: "I want to stand by my country—but I cannot vote for war. (I vote NO.)" However, some suffragists firmly believed that throwing support behind an Allied war effort would convince both America and Britain to award women the vote after victory. In both cases, this proved true eventually.

During most of the twentieth century, as the US shifted its foreign policy alliances, official efforts to contain Communism limited women's networking as pacifist feminists—both in the 1920s (which saw women like the Russian anarchist political activist Emma Goldman deported), and again in the 1950s (as Senator Joseph McCarthy investigated any form of "radical" activity). Between 1919 and 1963, feminists daring to forge bonds across borders with like-minded peace groups in Russia were dismissed as naïve or investigated as Communist fronts. Then, in 1961, frustrated by the health hazards of nuclear weapons testing which resulted in the radioactive byproduct Strontium 90 being found in milk bottled for children, the new group Women Strike for Peace (WSP) instigated demonstrations across America.

WSP's leaders made it clear that they were appalled by male justifications for nuclear war, yet they carefully emphasized that their group was no radical cell, "just mothers and housewives." Still, a framework for feminist theory quickly emerged. In 1963 a cartoon in the *Los Angeles Times* depicted an older woman telling the WSP picket line, "You'll never abolish war as long as men are running the world. Now, if you want to do something about that, I'll march with you!"

Similarly, in Britain, growing fear of nuclear war led to the founding in 1957 of the Campaign for Nuclear Disarmament (CND) within which "women often formed the majority of local activists."[1] In 1958 philosopher, educator, and writer Dora Russell traveled to Europe in a journey now known as the "Women's Peace Caravan." At the height of the Cold War, Russell intended to make connections with female peace campaigners in Eastern Europe. On her way, she collected artifacts and signatures, and created a visible record of women's resistance, friendship, and solidarity across borders.

After the assassination of President John F. Kennedy in 1963, the 1960s were dominated by student protests against the Vietnam War, hippies flashing the peace sign at rallies, and male draft resisters willing to go to jail (or to Canada) rather than kill. Music, clothing, and the use of the peace symbol to communicate an anti-war stance defined a generation. Once the US withdrew troops from Southeast Asia, the 1970s saw ambivalence toward Vietnam veterans plus new efforts to build an all-volunteer military by integrating female recruits. Meanwhile the Reagan administration that dominated the 1980s, with its nuclear arms buildup and Cold War hostilities toward the Soviet Union, reintroduced fear of a World War III.

Through each decade, women played important roles in every aspect of peacemaking or military action. But women's roles differed significantly from men's in both anti-war organizations and in the military itself. Moreover, within radical feminism there was certainly no one united viewpoint on pacifism or the necessary participation of women in violent action. Women calling themselves feminists committed to liberation could be found across the spectrum, from anti-militarism to pro-armed conflict, each believing hers was the true stance. Radical women could and did continue to use violence as members of armed groups such as the Weather Underground and the Black Panthers in the US, and Rote Zora in West Germany; some feminists who protested both war and domestic violence against women were nonetheless willing to participate in public defacement or destruction of property in anti-pornography actions. Other women acted on feminist politics by demanding women's access to promotion and top security roles in the military and intelligence work. In their relationships to men, as mothers, wives, and girlfriends of soldiers, many women were forced into relationships with a government that drafted their sons and husbands. Women choosing to serve in the military themselves, seeing that role as an equal right and responsibility, faced off against pacifist

Page 182: This poster features the sunflower logo designed by Los Angeles artist Lorraine Schneider for the Another Mother for Peace (AMP) association. AMP was founded in 1967 as a grassroots campaign "dedicated to eliminating the use of war as a means of solving disputes among nations, people, and ideologies. To accomplish this, they seek to educate citizens to take an active role in opposing war and building peace."

Above: This button was proudly worn by protesters, who had been incarcerated for causing civil unrest or civil disobedience in the name of the anti-war movement.

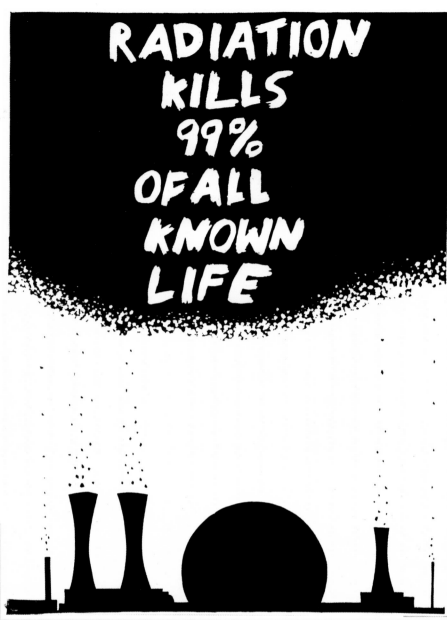

Above left: American woodcut poster, designed by Yolanda Fundora during the 1980s, demanding an end to the draft and citing it as a feminist issue. While women were not required to register for the draft (or, later, for Selective Service registration in the US), pacifist feminism and radical opposition to warfare imperialism led to a variety of female-led groups embracing coalitions with men who also opposed the draft.

Below left: The Women Strike for Peace button was a common sight at Vietnam War demonstrations and other anti-war protests during the 1970s and '80s.

Above right: British poster, c. 1980s, highlighting the potentially harmful effects of radiation from nuclear power plants.

Below right: The international women's movement Stop the Arms Race met in Brussels in 1983.

Below far right: This rather disturbing image was intended to galvanize women to take up the fight against nuclear armament.

feminists who opposed the military-industrial complex: a debate that had raged since the suffragette era. Terrified by the prospect of a nuclear strike, which had loomed over society since the end of World War II, feminists on both sides of the Atlantic took creative, nonviolent action by constructing peace camps at the three sites where NATO's nuclear missiles were built, stored, and deployed. And as the gay and lesbian rights movement gained momentum after the Stonewall Riots, lesbian activists challenged the American military's hurtful campaigns against gays and lesbians in uniform. Could feminists support that struggle, too? Whose position was the radical feminist one? Who was a sister?

During the draft years of the Vietnam conflict, American women who marched for peace and supported male draft resistance found their own issues ignored, trivialized, or put on the back burner by their supposed allies. Rape, as a war crime or as a product of male violence, was a particularly challenging concern. Women began to see their own bodies as sites that could be

invaded, and drew attention to the casual sexism of military language—as when commanders reported, "We penetrated deep into enemy territory, but were forced to make a strategic withdrawal." However, some female peace activists employed sexual imagery to support male draft resisters. American folk icon Joan Baez and her sisters posed for a suggestive poster that affirmed, "GIRLS SAY YES to boys who say NO."

By 1967, a different US poster and slogan had become emblematic: "War Is Not Healthy for Children and Other Living Things." Designed by Los Angeles artist Lorraine Schneider, this golden sunflower image was the logo for the US organization Another Mother for Peace (AMP), but was soon adopted by peace work offices and newsletters around the US. But the authority women claimed as informed, active critics of war was tested by tension between feminism and the male Left. Although some high-profile American activists like Holly Near and Jane Fonda traveled to Vietnam to show solidarity with Vietnamese women and to encourage an anti-military

Above: The first class of women was admitted to West Point Military Academy in July 1976. The legislation requiring federally funded service academies to admit women was signed into law by President Gerald Ford; both critics and supporters of military women watched the few female cadets struggle through their first year. Today the integration of the academies is a non-issue, with many women achieving top honors and leadership at West Point, the Naval Academy at Annapolis, and the Air Force Academy. However, sexual harassment and assault remain a huge problem, as recently depicted in the film *The Invisible War.*

Below: These c.1980s peace buttons display international symbols of peace. The Women's International League for Peace and Freedom was founded in 1915 and continues to work with global organizations, such as the United Nations, to this day.

stance among American GIs, other anti-war feminists were dismayed to hear male leaders of anti-imperialist, anti-military groups reducing women to sex objects. Breaking ranks with men to perform their own actions, radical feminists spent the 1970s and early '80s developing new theories of the intersections between war and sexual violence.

Critics of women's war resistance countered with charges that feminists were hardly pacifists at all, but instead were karate-chopping, man-hating threats to society. Pro-life opponents of the abortion rights movement charged that any expectant mother who terminated her pregnancy was committing child murder: the ultimate act of violence. These divisions separated men from women (and women from women) in the peace movement. Meanwhile, tests of female equality and toughness emerged unexpectedly at America's service academies—West Point, the Naval Academy at Annapolis, and the Air Force Academy—which grudgingly enrolled their first classes of women after being ordered to do so by President Ford. However, women in the regular military continued to be investigated for homosexual activity at a ratio wildly disproportionate to their actual numbers; those seeking

a long-term military career with rank and promotion were in fact forbidden to marry while serving, making it difficult to confirm their heterosexuality. Not surprisingly, rape and sexual harassment of servicewomen by male officers became an ongoing problem.

Like their male counterparts in the 1960s, women in the feminist revolution were, as revolutionaries, abandoning old codes of behavior in pursuit of social change. This meant disruption, but with limits—trying to make sure that during nonviolent sit-ins or civil disobedience, one might refuse to cooperate with police but not resort to taunting them. For both military security police and media onlookers, the unladylike behavior of women protesters was somehow more shocking than the possibility of planetary annihilation—a possibility which had moved so many ordinary women to such dramatic action.

The Greenham spirit

A group of women huddle around a fire that has not gone out for six months. Surrounded by makeshift tents known as "benders," made from branches and thick plastic sheets that act as shelter against volatile weather, women share fears about the future of the planet, a planet they have come together to save.

Far right: Ring Around Congress, Washington, D.C., June 1972. In this photograph by Dorothy Swarthmore, a young mother with her baby in a backpack demonstrates against war funding, her poster making clear the devastating impact of war on mothers and children.

Right: This famous poster featured Joan Baez and her sisters Pauline and Mimi, their folksong instruments subtly on display, in a bid to encourage male draft resisters. The implication that peace-activist "chicks" would agree to sex with radical men frustrated many feminist critics of the exploitative sexual liberation movement. Baez, who was strongly identified with the anti-war movement and married to a man jailed for draft resistance, later declared, "I'm not a feminist."

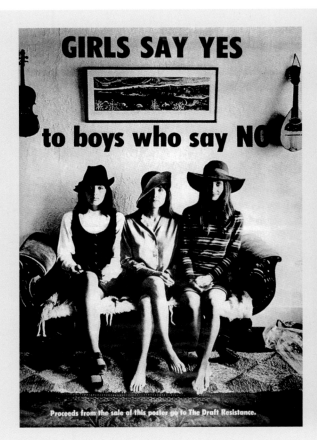

Women for Life on Earth

D-M Withers

In August 1981, a small band of women set off from Cardiff, Wales, and went on to found one of the most significant protests in the history of the anti-nuclear movement.

"How far would people like us, people like me, have to go to stop a war happening, to really get disarmament? What do people have to do to get through to these leaders that they mean it?"[2] wrote Ann Pettitt, cofounder of Women for Life on Earth, the group that organized a 120-mile women-led walk from Cardiff to RAF Greenham Common from August 27 to September 5, 1981.

Like many people in the early 1980s, Pettitt was deeply disturbed by the news that cruise missiles would be stationed in Britain. Nuclear war was not some abstract idea; it could happen at any point.

How to protest against the military might of superpowers and their deadly weapons? Old campaign methods, whether petitions, marches, or meetings, seemed unattractive and ineffective. The Campaign for Nuclear Disarmament was male-dominated and slow to take action; the feminist movement ideologically splintered.

As Pettitt casually browsed a copy of *Peace News* in March 1981, a news report caught her eye.[3] It told the story of a women-led peace walk from Copenhagen to Paris to protest against nuclear war. The idea to organize a similar event in Britain began to stir in her imagination, and she set to work.

Pettitt gathered a small group of organizers to help make the dream a reality. They called themselves Women for Life on Earth. In their homes in rural West Wales, maps were laid on tables and routes planned. The walk began in Cardiff and proceeded through Bristol, Bath, Melksham, Devizes, Marlborough, Hungerford, and Newbury, before they reached the army base at RAF Greenham Common. The group made contact with peace and women's groups to ask if they could organize accommodation, food, and, in some cases, entertainment for the walkers.

The Women for Life on Earth Peace Walk appealed to women who had never been involved in protest before. Many were mothers or grandmothers, "nearly all said they came because they could see it was organised by someone who was just an individual woman, like themselves, from some weird home address in the middle of nowhere. They also came in response to the universality of the theme—Women for Life on Earth—and because allegiance was not demanded for any particular 'line' or attitude beyond the simple focus on disarmament."[4]

As the thirty-six women, four men, and three children walked from town to town, laughing together under the late August and early September sunshine, they began to fuse as a group. "We all felt like one family by the end of the ten days and were very sad to separate and return to our various lives,"[5] said Effie Leah, who was

> "We knew what we were doing was significant, we could see the effect we were having on the people we met."
> **Ann Pettitt**, "Women for Life on Earth," 1981

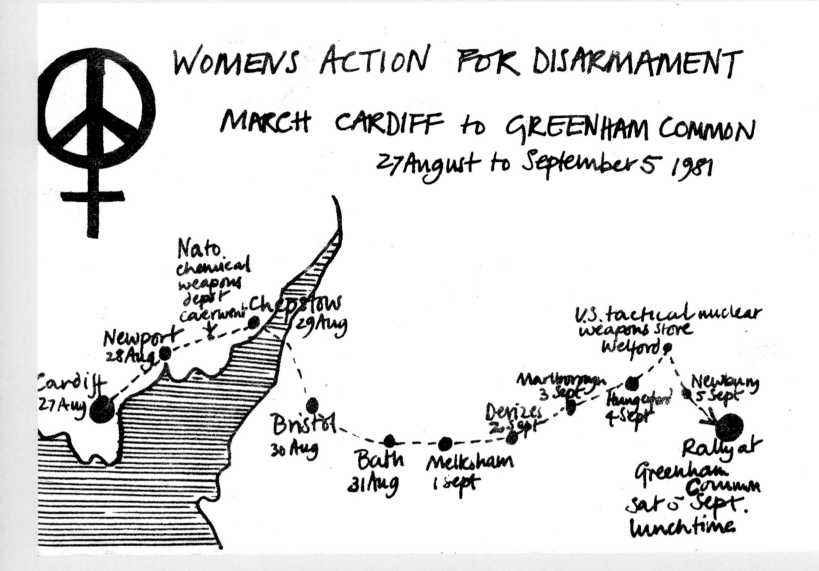

WOMENS ACTION FOR DISARMAMENT

MARCH CARDIFF to GREENHAM COMMON
27 August to September 5 1981

Cardiff
27 Aug

Newport
28 Aug

Nato.
chemical
weapons
dept
caerwent Chepstow
29 Aug

Bristol
30 Aug

Bath
31 Aug

Melksham
1 Sept

Devizes
2 Sept

Marlborough
3 Sept

Hungerford
4 Sept

U.S. tactical nuclear
weapons store
Welford

Newbury
5 Sept

Rally at
Greenham
Common
Sat 5 Sept.
lunchtime

Opposite top: This rainbow button features what has become commonly known as the peace symbol, but was originally designed by Gerald Holtom for the British Campaign for Nuclear Disarmament (CND) in 1958. The rainbow coloration evokes the international peace flag, which was first used on a peace march in Italy in 1961.

Opposite, bottom left: Women for Life on Earth walk over the Severn Bridge from Wales to England in August 1981.

Opposite, bottom right: The Fallout Marching Band help raise the spirits of the walkers.

Above: The route the marchers took from Cardiff to Greenham.

fifty-nine at the time of the walk. The walkers were connected by a shared purpose, spurred on by supporters in towns and villages who echoed their concerns; even when spirits were low, the sudden appearance of street musicians—the Fallout Marching Band—helped raise them again. "Take the toys away from the boys," they sang and walked in unison, and the army base was in their sights.

The group may have felt what they were doing was important, but the media did not see it as a "newsworthy" story. Perhaps if the media had not overlooked this humble group of "ordinary" women, four of its members would never have chained themselves to the fence near the main gate of the army base; an action that kick-started a women's peace encampment that lasted until the new millennium.

In its early months, the original group of walkers and local supporters maintained the camp. Others went home

and spoke of their experiences, or helped to raise funds and generate publicity. Momentum behind Greenham Common Women's Peace Camp continued to build, despite attempts by the police and media to trivialize its significance.

"Please tell all your friends, local organisations etc., to support the camp, and women especially but men too, offer actual time when you can go on the rota for a couple of days, or more," wrote Annie Tunnicliffe, a member of CND who welcomed the walkers when they first arrived at Greenham. "It will be a long, hard winter, and if it's left to too few, we won't make it. People are inspired by the place and what it symbolises. It is magnetic to demoralised members of the peace and disarmament movements as a place to gather strength."[6]

The camp survived the first winter, and then went on and on, to survive many more.

The group feasts on a supper of vegetable stew, followed by foraged blackberries from the common. As the kettle boils for tea, smoke rises from the fire and three women begin to sing, "You can't kill the spirit, she's like a mountain, old and strong she goes on and on and on . . ." Sung as a round, the song continues without interruption into the early hours of the morning. Voices drop in and out, as the night watch moves from gate to gate, keeping an eye out for bailiffs, who may attempt to remove women from their campsite before the dawn.

This is a picture of Greenham Common Women's Peace Camp in England, an activist movement that ignited the political imagination of several thousands of women in the early 1980s, who left home for peace in much the same way that men left home for war. Many women at Greenham had never been involved in political activism before. Their actions reverberated globally and became a symbol of resistance against the madness of the nuclear war that threatened to eradicate "the future."

Greenham was the emblem of the international feminist peace movement that burgeoned in the 1980s. The construction of silos for cruise missiles at the USAF Greenham Common base was part of a military agreement between the Thatcher and Reagan governments to deploy 464 land-based missiles in Europe, as a NATO line of defense against possible Soviet attack.

In February 1982, Greenham became women-only and the camp developed political resistance that sought to express women's values, traditions, and strategies. Activists keened to mourn past and future victims of nuclear war; women cut fences that protected weapons of mass destruction or decorated them with images from "real life"— photographs of family members, dolls, and children's clothes—as well as tampons dipped in red liquid, as symbols of menstruation. On December 12, 1982, thirty thousand women from around the UK traveled to Greenham to "Embrace the Base." Those present had received a chain letter, which they then passed on to ten friends, creating "a spring, who together with others becomes a stream, a river, an ocean," ready to engulf the military base.[7] The action created one of the most potent images of protest in history, as more than thirty thousand women held hands around the nine-mile stretch of the perimeter fence. As night fell candles were lit, creating a spiral of peaceful, yet formidable, resistance.

The spider's web was a common symbol in Greenham activism. Webs evoked the unique forms of collective strength created by women at Greenham: as individual strands they were fragile, yet woven together they became powerful. Webs conjured how the Greenham spirit spread throughout Britain and beyond, as activists who visited the camp "carried Greenham home," and became active in their own communities.

Webs also described the organizational structure of the camp that gave all residents the authority to act, rather

> "I felt compelled to take this action for future generations."
>
> **Nelly Logan**, Greenham activist, 1983, quoted in Paul Brown, "Court Gaols 36 Greenham Women," 2017

Far left: Across the UK women are invited to "embrace the base" on Sunday, December 12, 1982.

Left: Banner of Women for Life on Earth.

Below: Women against Nukes was an offshoot of the Valley Women's Union (1973–77), which was founded in Northampton, Massachusetts. This button combines the nuclear warning colors with the feminist fist symbol.

Above: Photographer Raissa Paige took this iconic image of the women of Greenham dancing on the silos at dawn on New Year's Day, January 1, 1983, at USAF air base, Berkshire, UK.

than be told what to do by a leader. Web making was integrated into protest, too. Large woolen web-meshes were constructed as a protective barrier between protesters and the police, and sometimes women wove themselves into the tangle. Fiddly and complex to unravel, the webs created frustration for the police, and made it harder for women to be aggressively removed from the protest site.

Breaking the law was a common part of protest at Greenham. Women were arrested for obstruction when they lay down in front of the gates, for criminal damage when they cut parts of the fence, and for trespass when they entered the base.

These arrests would sometimes lead to a prison sentence. In a spectacular moment, captured by photographer Raissa Page, women broke into the military base on New Year's Day, 1983, held hands and danced in a circle on the silos. From among the group, forty-four of them were arrested, while thirty-six were sent to prison for fourteen days for "breaching the peace." The eldest protester was Nelly Logan, who was seventy-three and had six grandchildren.

Her reason for protesting resonated with many other women: as a witness to two world wars, she wasn't going to sit back while the government made plans for a third.

Carole Harwood was one of the thirty-six women imprisoned. Her personal accounts, written from inside Holloway prison, describe how a group of women climbed onto the roof of Holloway, as an act of solidarity with the women inside:[8]

The world is turned upside down! Here we are begging for bread and water instead of tea and cakes while our brave sisters break into prison! I can hear the women outside—wow what a noise. The authorities are very grumpy—police, in groups of four! . . . I had a letter from the camp saying patriarchy was dying—it dies hard all the same. . . . Nell's singing 'Take the Toys from the Boys' out the window—the whole of Islington seems to be alive with music—massed chorus outside the gates. Now all the prisoners, not just the Greenham women, are singing. We are on our way, hand in hand with women everywhere.[9]

Puget Sound and Seneca camps

Bonnie J. Morris

Inspired by the actions of their sisters in England, American feminists built peace camps in two key locations of the military pipeline: the city of Kent in Puget Sound, Washington state, where Boeing employees built air-launched cruise missiles, and the Seneca Army Depot in Romulus, New York, where the assembled missiles were stored before being shipped to Greenham.

Each peace camp maintained a similar subculture and structure to the Greenham model: nonviolent protest, civil disobedience, and willingness to submit to arrest. Like Greenham, they also featured education workshops and dialogue with local residents, and a feminist politics of engagement with anti-patriarchal ideals. In response, townspeople who relied on employment at Boeing or at the Seneca Depot viewed the peace camp women as an unwholesome incursion of outsiders, calling them lesbians, witches, traitors, and Communists. At the upstate New York camp, hundreds were arrested during a march for peace in the summer of 1983; when the local jail overflowed, many women had to be warehoused in a nearby school.

Participants came to the peace encampments from all walks of life: as Buddhist nuns, Hiroshima survivors, grandmothers, and students. Mothers' Day actions stressed the maternal concern for life, with some women tying baby shoes to barbed wire as a symbol of nuclear war's threat to future generations. At Seneca, a candlelit march billed as "Four Minutes to Midnight" drew large numbers of feminists on July 4, 1985, in response to a jokey remark by President Reagan, who had tested a (live) press conference microphone with the announcement, "My fellow Americans, we begin bombing in four minutes." In the Seneca Army Depot jail cells where protesters were taken in handcuffs to be booked for illegal trespass at a military site, women whom security guards perceived (accurately or not) to be lesbians were sometimes subject to rougher treatment. Slogans, writings, and songs connecting militarism and male dominance alarmed military authorities and townspeople, who saw peace camp activists as anti-male in their ideology.

In the 1980s, several recordings of peace camp songs presented the music and theory of Greenham and Seneca activists. Serving as a peace camp fundraiser, *One World Peace Songs* featured Peggy Seeger's "Carry

Greenham Home," Holly Near's "No More Genocide," and Naomi Littlebear Morena's "Like a Mountain" and "Four Minutes to Midnight." The Seneca peace camp produced a cassette including "Circle the Boundaries," "Circle for Survival," "The Neutron Bomb," and a song from the Puget Sound women's camp, "Reagan, Can You Hear?" While the peace camps eventually dismantled, they left a remarkable legacy of art and literature, including a range of books such as *We Are Ordinary Women*, *Greenham Common: Women at the Wire*, *Greenham Women Everywhere*, *Prisons That Could Not Hold*, *Reweaving the Web of Life*, and *The Women's Encampment for a Future of Peace and Justice: Images and Writings*. A lasting impact of the peace camp subculture would be women's ongoing participation in the Green movement, fighting climate change and militarism with actions informed by ideals of ecofeminism.

Top: These c. 1983–84 buttons from the Seneca peace camp were worn by women as a show of solidarity, whether they had been to the camp itself or not.

July 6th Action Plans 1985 "SIX MINUTES TO MIDNIGHT"

THURSDAY 7/4	FRIDAY 7/5	SATURDAY 7/6	SUNDAY 7/7
BREAKFAST (HEARTLAND)	BREAKFAST	BREAKFAST	BREAKFAST
WORK+INFO MEETING	WORK+INFO MEETING	WORK+INFO MEETING	WORK+INFO MEETING
ORIENTATION 1hr. (Kitchen) ♥ ♀'s RELATIONSHIPS W/ OTHER ♀: FEELINGS ABOUT OUR SIMS+DIFS. (PAV.)	ORIENTATION 1hr. ● NON-VIOLENCE TRAINING + CD PREPARATION (10-4) (PAV.) ● FACILITATION WORKSHOP (BARN)	ORIENTATION 1hr. ♥ NON-VIOLENCE +CD PREP (10-4)(PAV.) ♥ SELF-DEFENSE (Backyard) ♥ "UPSTATE NY-A NUKE SACRIFICE AREA" (Barn-up) ♥ "SELF-EMPOWERING THRU FIREWALKING" (BARN-DOWN)	ORIENTATION 1hr. REST
LUNCH (KITCHEN: "HEARTLAND")	LUNCH	LUNCH	LUNCH
"STRONGER THAN BEFORE" video in barn (1983 ♀☆♂)	"STRONGER THAN BEFORE" video in barn	"STRONGER THAN BEFORE" video in Barn	"STRONGER THAN BEFORE" video in barn
♥ NON-VIOLENCE +CD PREP (11-6 Y PAV.) ♥ "DEALING WITH AUTHORITIES" (BARN)	♥ DESPAIR + EMPOWERMENT WORKSHOP (BARN)(2-6PM) ♥ HERBAL MEDICINE (BACKYARD) ♥ ♀'s REL. W/ OTHER ♀: FEELINGS ABOUT OUR DIFFERENCES (BARN + SIMILARITIES UP)	♥ NONVIOLENCE TRAINING + CD PREP (BARN) (1-6PM) ● BRIEFING +UPDATE FOR EXPERIENCED CD'ers (WOMB) ● REARING PEACEFUL KIDS IN VIOLENT SOCIETY (UP BARN) ● ♀'s RAGE + NONVIOLENCE (BY.)	♥ PROCESSING + FEELINGS ABOUT ACTION (PAV.) 3PM ACUPRESSURE WORKSHOP BACKYARD 4PM CONFRONTING FACISM: A DISCUSSION among white ♀♀♀ BACKYARD
♥ BRIEFING + UPDATE FOR EXPERIENCED CD'ers (PAV) moved to 7PM	♥ SCENARIO EVOLUTION- GENERAL GATHERING (B.V.) ● CONFRONTING RACISM: A DISC. AMONG WHITE ♀♀♀ (BARN-TOP) ● DIET-US-RADIATION (5-6) (WOMB)	♥ PEACEKEEPER TRAINING (W) ● NICARAGUA SLIDESHOW (B) TIME FOR AFFINITY GROUP DISCUSSIONS + PLANNING!! ♥ 4PM GATHERING FOR INFO ABOUT TONIGHTS ACTION (BACKYARD)	♥ ACUPRESSURE WORKSHOP (BARN-UPSTAIRS) ♥ FIREWALK ... (MAGIC CIRCLE) ♥ VIDEO'S + SLIDESHOWS ABOUT NUCLEAR ISSUES (BARN)
DINNER (HEARTLAND)	DINNER	DINNER	DINNER
7PM JOAN BOKAER - U.S. FIRST-STRIKE NUCLEAR POLICY # THE MYTH OF THE SOVIET THREAT 9:45 video "FINAL EPIDEMIC" (both in BARN)	♥ 7:00-8:00 PEACEKEEPER TRNG. (BARN) MUSIC (Mary Gemini Aro + Avg. Dyke Band)	♥ 7:00 BONFIRE 9:00 PROCESSION TO BASE 11:54 — ACTION + VIGILS AT BASE TILL	♥ 8:00 DISC. ON FUTURE OF WEFPJ!! (PAV.)

Ongoing Events

- "TAKING PEACE CAMP HOME"- WORKSHOP every HOUR IN WOMB. (SATURDAY)
- CHILDREN'S PROGRAM (10-6)
- SALE'S TENT
- NON-REGISTRATION (PLACE TO GET INFO - A PLACE TO GIVE MONEY, RESOURCE MATERIALS, ANN., + NETWORKING INFORMATION ETC)
- OVERNIGHT SECURITY - 9 pm-11 pm 11- 2 am 2 to 5 am

VIDEOS!! We have several really good video tapes on the nuclear issue that you can play any time Just ask Andrea or Julie or Robin

Above and opposite, bottom left and right: The "Six Minutes to Midnight" action of July 1985 brought hundreds of women to a pre-midnight peace march from the Seneca peace camp to the gates of the military base, singing "camp songs" along the way. After the candlelight march, close to seventy-five women elected to scale the barbed wire fence in protest of nuclear war, leading to their arrest and overnight detention in the base jail; once there, some participants were treated roughly based on their perceived lesbian identity. Those choosing to carry out civil disobedience first underwent training in small "affinity groups."

"You are afraid that our struggle is *not* a nonviolent struggle. Afraid that we are willing to destroy the patriarchs as individuals. . . . Do I really have to assure you that we don't contemplate trying to kill off men? . . . We don't hate men, we hate the clearly hateful things that men have done to us, are still doing to us: hate it that they rape us, batter us, exploit us, impoverish us, silence us. . . . When we come together in our women-only circles it is not to try to deny our bond with men; it is to *affirm* our bond with one another. . . . Our gathering together as we do now amounts to civil disobedience— whether or not we decide, while together, to climb some military fence, block some entrance, commit some act for which we can be sent to jail."

Barbara Deming, *Prisons That Could Not Hold*, 1985

Greenham was no ordinary protest camp, and it transformed the lives of those who lived there or visited. For some, this involved exploring lesbian sexuality and relationships. A popular song at the camp describes this transition:

Went to Greenham, cut some fence
Hugged some woman and it all made sense
Well I used to be a Tory,
Now I am a radical, feminist, anarchist, vegan dyke.[10]

Greenham was, for one resident, "the most vigorous force for lesbian liberation in the world that I know of."[11] Lesbianism became so normal at Greenham that "women almost had to opt-out of lesbianism; they had to 'come out' as heterosexual."[12] For the homophobic tabloid press, the presence of lesbians was one way to discredit the protest in the eyes of the public. As one journalist wrote in *The Sun* about the camp residents, "four in every five are lesbians—all are united in their hatred of men."[13]

Some women responded to the question of whether Greenham was intrinsically a feminist act with the argument that the fight against nuclear power was a fight for their, and for everyone's lives.

Yet this attitude made some radical feminists furious. In their eyes Greenham, and the wider women's peace movement, was a distraction—a way to absorb the revolutionary politics of women's liberation into a wishy-washy campaign for peace. "Is there a danger that, in dancing around the symbols of male, militaristic technology, we are diffusing the energy we may need to recognise and deal with a more physical manifestation of male supremacy and violence: the man next door?" they asked.[14] There was also criticism of how Greenham mobilized stereotypical ideas about women's maternal and caring nature, ideas that reinforced attitudes about women's "natural" role that the women's liberation movements fought so hard to destroy. Greenham Common made women's protest acceptable. It transformed feminists from "'shrill, aggressive, short-haired, man-haters' into 'peace-loving, idealistic givers of life.'"[15]

Concerns about the politics of Greenham came from activists in the British Black Women's Movement, too. Activists Pratibha Parmar and Valerie Amos criticized the women's peace movement for its hypocrisy and parochialism. "Internationally, while black and Third World women are fighting daily battles for survival, for food, land

> "I'm not a feminist and I'm not radical. I'm just a woman who's fighting for her life. It's that simple for me. I have nothing to lose and everything to gain."
>
> **Simone**, *The Greenham Factor*, undated

and water, Western white women's cries of anguish for concern about preserving the standards of life for their children and preserving the planet for future generations sound hollow. Whose standards of life are they fighting to preserve? White, middle-class standards undoubtedly."[16]

As Greenham Common gained visibility in the international peace movement, it nevertheless became a symbol in wider struggles against militarism, imperialism, and environmental destruction. Women Working for a Nuclear Free and Independent Pacific met at Greenham Common in 1984 and campaigned to place women's peace activism in an international context. The group highlighted the damaging impact of American imperialist activity in Micronesia, a group of islands that effectively became a test bed for the US's nuclear arsenal after World War II. The group promoted the message of indigenous people across the Pacific region in their struggle to become nuclear free and independent. They hosted visiting speakers, such as the Māori activist Titewhai Harawira from Aotearoa, and the Chamorro activist Chailang Palacios from Micronesia, whose speaking tour of Britain presented "personal evidence of the destruction caused by colonialism, racism and sexism in the Pacific over the centuries."[17] Their message echoed the concerns raised by Amos and Parmar: "while the Western world is preparing for the possibility of nuclear war . . . people in the Pacific are already dying from it."[18]

Greenham also inspired solidarity camps across the world, such as Pine Gap, Australia, which stationed themselves outside other US military bases. Pine Gap was established in December 1983, the same day that cruise missiles arrived at Greenham.[19] Camps also sprang up in America, at the city of Kent in Puget Sound, Washington state, and the Seneca Army Depot in Romulus, New York. Large-scale events in the US such as the Women's Pentagon Actions in 1980, 1981, and 1985 drew thousands of participants to stage "die-ins" on the threshold of Washington military structures. Feminist writers Grace Paley, Barbara Deming, and Professor Cynthia Enloe (who critiqued the camp towns adjacent to US military bases overseas) emerged as key theorists of peace activism in the 1980s. Another important voice was Australian Dr. Helen Caldicott, head of Physicians for Social Responsibility, who responded to a pattern of "nuclear nightmares" she saw in young children consumed by anxiety that nuclear war was imminent. At the heart of all of this stood Greenham Common.

Greenham Common Women's Peace Camp was more than a social movement. It invented new ways of life, networks, and forms of resistance whose desire to protect life on earth resonated internationally. The final protesters left in 2000, when it was clear that they had reclaimed the common land. For nearly twenty years, and with great intensity during the 1980s, the women-centered politics created at Greenham showed that when women's lives are woven together they create potent webs of power and resistance.

Australian peacemakers

Alison Bartlett

The anti-nuclear movement in Australia was a powerful rallying cause for women across the country.

In response to escalating fears of a nuclear war and inspired by the women of Greenham Common, two women-only peace camps were organized in Australia: in 1983 at Pine Gap in central Australia, and in 1984 on the western seaboard of Fremantle at Cockburn Sound. These were partly a response to a particular event— the installation of cruise missiles in NATO signatory countries—and also foregrounded specifically Australian concerns about the 1951 ANZUS pact, which bound Australia, New Zealand, and the United States to cooperate on military matters in the Pacific region.

The 1983 camp in the desert of central Australia was held for two weeks at the gates of a joint US-Australian defense facility, which is still pivotal to the operation of satellite tracking, triangulating signals from the northern hemisphere and implicating Australia as a potential target in the event of nuclear hostilities. The 1984 camp was at the entrance to a military harbor in Cockburn Sound where US naval ships with nuclear missile capacity were docked for rest and recreation, which included the organization of sexual activities with local women during their stay. The particularity of place is evident in the extensive consultation and coordination with indigenous women, especially at Pine Gap where women came from their remote homelands to join the protest, and for whom British nuclear testing at Maralinga in the 1950s was still within living memory. Hundreds of women traveled for days to reach the camps from across the country, generating a spectacle for the media and drawing attention to the little-known military sites and questioning Australia's alliance with the US arms race.

The peace camps were intense events that became part of a tradition of women's peace campaigns. For example, the Save Our Sons movement contested conscription and the Vietnam War more broadly from 1965 onward. During the late 1970s, and continuing for almost a decade, Women against Rape (WAR) used the national commemoration of ANZAC Day to mourn women raped in war: they caused much scandal by joining the returned servicemen's parades in various cities and laying wreaths at war memorials, drawing attention to one of the ways in which women are affected by war. Organizationally, women were rejecting male-dominated peace and anti-nuclear movements to proliferate their own, like WANG (Women's Anti-Nuclear Group), WAND (Women's Action for Nuclear Disarmament), and FANG (Feminist Anti-Nuclear Group). For the peace camps a coalition was formed called Women for Survival to network these organizations.

Peace and anti-nuclear activity manifested alongside other women's movement activism, and were ideologically supported by the progressive Australian Whitlam Labor government elected in 1972, ending conscription and appointing the first women's advisor to the prime minister. Government funding distributed for the 1975 United Nations International Women's Year enabled financial stability for women's shelters and health centers, as well as conferences and public debate around women's lives. Key legislation was passed, such as the Family Law Act of 1975 which legalized no-fault divorce, the establishment of the Family Court, the single mother's benefit, equal pay for women, and the removal of restrictions on access to the Pill. Australia's women liberationists became known for infiltrating politics and policy-making through strategically placed "femocrats," or feminist bureaucrats. This reformist agenda effectively split the women's movement between liberal and radical agendas, although arguably both were necessary.

The Labor government's championing of the arts and education contributed to a proliferating women's culture in Australia: women's presses, writers, artists, and performers flourished, as entry to training institutions such as the Australian Television Film and Radio School in 1973 and the abolition of university fees in 1974 meant women could access education and pursue professions. The impact of this was particularly felt in the lead-up to the bicentenary of the British landing and claiming of Australia in 1988. The country's perceived benign history was fundamentally challenged by women, migrants, and indigenous Australians who were absent from the official (his)tories of great men and victorious moments. Historical reassessments were evident in Burgmann and Lee's

Above: This button commemorates November 11, 1983, when Aboriginal women guided approximately seven hundred activists to the gates at Pine Gap and led an eleven-minute silence to remember those who had died in war and the arrival of the cruise missiles at Greenham Common.

Above left: The Australian campaign for nuclear disarmament produced this poster during the 1980s.

Above right: The Feminist Anti-Nuclear Group's (FANG) poster, undated, for a fundraiser with the slogan "bread not bombs."

Staining the Wattle: A People's History of Australia since 1788 (1988) and Grimshaw et al.'s *Creating a Nation* (1994), which begins with a birth scene of an indigenous woman and traces the historical conditions of social relations intersecting race and gender. Grenville's novel *Joan Makes History* (1988) was commissioned by the Bicentennial Authority, imaginatively rendering the life of Joan during major and mundane events over two centuries, critiquing existing histories using fiction.

The fundamental violence of colonization has been a particularly enduring legacy of these contestations, arguably emerging from the broad critique of the continuum of male violence through the use of the military industrial complex in dispossession, diaspora, and domestic abuse. These concerns were integral to the women's peace movement, and the peace camps at Australian military sites that drew attention to social structures that actively manufacture war and dispossession.

LIBERATION WITHOUT LIMITATION

Radicalization, fragmentation,
and educating the next generation

The twenty-first century has seen women all over the world reclaim and redefine the "F-word" in myriad ways for future generations.

The 1980s ended with a profound act of violence against feminist social change. On December 9, 1989, gunman Marc Lepine burst into a classroom of Montreal's École polytechnique, first separating the male from the female engineering students and then killing fourteen women while shouting, "You're all a bunch of feminists."

This tragedy was but one highly visible act of backlash against greater female higher education, sexual freedom, and public power—the trifecta of cultural shifts in the 1966–88 feminist revolutions. Violent attacks on abortion clinics and the rise of hate-filled talk radio in America (with host Rush Limbaugh's introduction of the term "feminazis") stunned those who believed that the women's liberation movements would foster permanent social change. The 1990s introduced both high and low points for women's rights and political visibility, as feminist organizing moved to the global stage.

Indeed, as the 1980s passed into the '90s, the media was filled with triumphant stories about the death of feminism. Articles declared that women's liberation was now redundant in post-feminist times. And women were, indeed, empowered to make choices about their lives, wear power suits, and intrude upon the corridors of male power like never before. There was a feeling, perpetuated by the media, that collective politics were tiresome and old hat (what's there to complain about anymore, anyway?). Capitalism had won, the end of history occurred—a new world order had emerged where the old rules of inequality, protest, and resistance no longer meant anything. Or so the somewhat fantastical story went.

The women's liberation and black women's movements underwent profound changes in the 1980s, certainly.

In Britain, the independent organizations set up by activists in the 1970s evolved alongside the wider cultural, historical, and economic change of the late twentieth century. Some groups became reliant on state funds, which placed them in a precarious position when the political climate shifted further to the Right. For many progressive initiatives—including those which received generous grants from the Greater London Council— funding cuts meant that they were simply forced to close.

Some women from the movement became active in local government and pioneered gender equality work, integrating feminist ideas into mainstream, public life.[1]

In the US in 1992, women watched tensely as Equal Employment Opportunity Commission lawyer Anita Hill

ACTION FOR EQUALITY, DEVELOPMENT AND PEACE
4-15 SEPTEMBER 1995 · BEIJING, CHINA

Page 198: Original drawing by artist/illustrator Nina, showing the vibrant voice of modern feminism.

Far left: Law professor Anita Hill waves to her audience after speaking at a conference called Women Tell the Truth. Hill became a symbol of the government's refusal to believe women's reports of workplace misconduct.

Left: The UN Fourth World Conference on Women was an important landmark in the modern feminist movement.

Above: Hillary Clinton speaks at the UN Fourth World Conference on Women in 1995.

testified before a critical Senate panel of white males, detailing her experience of sexual harassment by then Supreme Court nominee Clarence Thomas. Hill's treatment—including being asked "Are you a scorned woman?"—enraged viewers, who renewed their political commitment to the women's movement. In the next midterm election, feminist voters sent a fresh slate of female candidates to the Senate, forcing the first-ever construction of a women's bathroom near the Senate floor.

However, the same year saw Mattel's Barbie doll complaining "Math class is tough!", drawing a formal rebuke from the American Association of University Women (AAUW).

But, as in Britain, the 1990s saw mounting tension between conservatives and liberals in the US, with right-wing women's groups such as Concerned Women for America and the pro-life movement joining with Focus on the Family, the Traditional Values Coalition, the Christian Coalition, and other religious lobbies to disavow feminism and LGBT rights. It took a 1994 Supreme Court decision to rule that obstructing access to an abortion services clinic was illegal.

The US media coverage of the rise of the Taliban in Afghanistan and Pakistan and the resulting closure of schools for girls and the crushing new repression of female work, education, and personal freedoms ignited global debate. The use of gender violence in ethnic conflicts shocked the world, as evidence of rape camps emerged during Serbian aggressions against Bosnian Muslim villagers throughout Yugoslavia. In Italy this led to the birth of the Italian version of the anti-war Women in Black movement in 1991, the Donne in Nero. Israeli women in Jerusalem had founded Women in Black at the end of the 1980s to protest human rights violations against Palestinians. Their actions inspired solidarity groups throughout Israel and, later, the world, whose members similarly dressed in black to mourn the victims of all war and conflict.

Against this contradictory background, the Fourth UN World Conference on Women meeting in Beijing released a platform for women's rights in the fall of 1995 that set out some important goalposts on progress:

1. We, the Governments participating in the Fourth World Conference on Women,

2. Gathered here in Beijing in September 1995, the year of the fiftieth anniversary of the founding of the United Nations,

3. Determined to advance the goals of equality, development, and peace for all women everywhere in the interest of all humanity . . .

5. Recognize that the status of women has advanced in some important respects in the past decade but that progress has been uneven, inequalities between women and men have persisted and major obstacles remain, with serious consequences . . .

WE ARE CONVINCED THAT:

14. Women's rights are human rights.[2]

The memory of resistance: cutbacks, fightbacks, and liberation

D-M Withers

Remembering the history of the women's liberation movements is playing a central role in redefining feminism for the twenty-first century.

Like activists in the women's liberation movements who sought to connect with women "hidden from history," those who came to feminism in the early twenty-first century often felt displaced from their activist roots.[3] In the US, activists have similarly rooted their activism in the work of preceding generations. Visionary educator and poet Alexis Pauline Gumbs established the Eternal Summer of the Black Feminist Mind, a multimedia intergenerational black feminist community education project based in Durham, North Carolina, but active in 143 countries around the world. The Eternal Summer of the Black Feminist Mind draws on the "insights, literatures, and practices of black feminism" to sustain and inspire contemporary struggles.[4] The School of Our Lorde is based on the poetics, pedagogy, politics, and publishing of Audre Lorde, and the Juneteenth Freedom Academy honors the black feminist educator, poet, parent, and political activist June Jordan. Central to the Eternal Summer of the Black Feminist Mind is a belief in the transformative and healing powers of education grounded in the transmission of black feminist traditions.

In Britain, the Do You Remember Olive Morris? project mobilized the memory of Olive Morris, discussed in chapter three, to revive the legacy of the 1970s British Black Women's Movement. The group took advantage of the new digital technologies to publish forgotten histories, as well as collecting oral testimonies and curating exhibitions.[5] Around the same time, the Black Cultural Archives ran their important Heart of the Race project which recorded the memories of black women who were politically active in the 1970s and '80s.[6]

The Remembering Olive Collective met at Lambeth Women's Project (LWP) in Brixton, South London. Established in 1979,[7] LWP was one of the last remaining radical spaces in London and a vital home for feminist activism in the 2000s. Local groups such as Lambeth Women's Aid and the Black Deaf Sistahs Group made LWP their home, as well as national networks, such as the Feminist Activist Forum. Between 2007 and 2012, LWP hosted Girls Rock Camp! UK, weekend intensives where women and girls had the opportunity to learn how to play instruments—often from scratch—form bands, and write songs. These activities were combined with workshops on the history of women in music, rudiments of music technology, and self-defense. The camps culminated with a final day showcase where bands performed songs in a unique atmosphere of personal-political transformation.

Despite the importance of LWP to the local and wider feminist community, it had been in a precarious position since 1997, when the local council withdrew its funding.[8] The project was given an eviction notice in June 2012 and, despite a hard-fought campaign, LWP was forced to close its doors five months later. The fate of LWP is a common one in the history of women-centered community activism since the late 1970s. Projects that provide a lifeline to marginalized and often vulnerable communities are forced to shut down, simply because their value is not recognized by the state. The financial crisis of 2008 gave further ideological justification for a new wave of cuts to women's services in Britain, under the guise of austerity. Amid this crisis, activists are fighting back.

"You Cut We Bleed" is the rallying cry of British-based Sisters Uncut, a direct-action collective opposing the savage cuts that have forced the closure of thirty-four domestic violence services since 2010. Sisters Uncut are intersectional[9] feminists who educate, inspire, and agitate. They combine disruptive interventions, such as dyeing the fountains of Trafalgar Square red in memory of women who die at the hands of abusive partners, with occupations of empty social housing, and shaming local councils for their lack of support and provisions to women experiencing domestic violence. They fight back with the facts—two women are murdered each week in the UK by a partner or ex-partner—and make clear

> "Safety is not a privilege. Access to justice cannot become a luxury. Austerity cuts are ideological but cuts to domestic violence services are fatal."
>
> **Sisters Uncut**, "Feministo," 2017

Above left: Lambeth Women's Project provided a home to many different feminist projects from the late 1970s onwards, but was forced to close its doors due to funding cuts in 2012.

Above right: Sisters Uncut are part of a new generation of feminists resisting austerity and the erasure of feminist knowledge. They are pictured here at their suffragette parliament action on June 6, 2016.

Right: The Remembering Olive Collective mobilized the memory of community activist Olive Morris, and helped connect contemporary activists to the history of the British Black Women's Movement from the 1970s.

demands to the government, namely that they must restore and protect long-term funding for domestic violence services.

In the twenty-first century, feminists often struggle to keep alive the practical wisdom created by activists in the past fifty years. The legacy of the feminist revolution—from the transformative power of black feminist traditions to knowing how to set up shelters and support services—cannot be forgotten. Since the 1970s there have been many attempts by the state and media to appropriate and trivialize feminism. Despite this, feminism continues to offer a myriad of different frameworks for liberation and remains for many a source of hope and a vital tool in the struggle to resist oppression.

Despite claims to the contrary, the 1990s remained a time of vibrant and inventive feminist activism in Britain, even if the effects were often on a smaller scale. 1993 was a big year. As the embers from the many fires at Greenham Common Women's Peace Camp began to die out, some women targeted other sites of military power. Menwith Hill Women's Peace Camp was established to protest what is, to this day, the largest American military spy base in the world, stationed at RAF Menwith Hill in Harrogate, Leeds. A permanent camp existed at the base between 1993 and 1998, and occasional camps are still set up at the base to protest its activities.

The year 1993 was also when the US feminist punk movement Riot Grrrl hit Britain, having originated in Washington state with bands such as Bikini Kill at its forefront. Riot Grrrl was an energizing and rebellious force that activated the political creativity of those who encountered it. Riot Grrrl claimed to speak "in a new voice to a 'post-feminist' [sic] world" according to prolific zine writer Karren Ablaze in her Girl Speak manifesto.

Riot Grrrl groups or "chapters" sprang up in towns and cities across the UK including Portsmouth, London, Aberdeen, Newcastle, Manchester, Birmingham, Sheffield, Leeds, and Bradford. Like earlier feminist movements, Riot Grrrl gave women and girls the confidence to "speak." Zines—small-scale independent publications filled with personal stories and impassioned, political writing—were the media of choice. Music was important, too, and Riot Grrrl provided a context for women to form bands and claim cultural space.

Even the End of Patriarchy was declared in 1993. On August 1, 1993, a group of anarcha-feminist witches—among them the Swedish artist Monica Sjöö—gathered on Silbury Hill in Britain, an ancient Neolithic ritual site, to celebrate the event. They hoped the declaration would inspire a new wave of feminist energy, and carry the momentum of women's liberation forward through the 1990s and beyond. Declaring the End of Patriarchy did not, however, reignite the wider feminist movement; in fact the declaration was only recognized by a select number of activists. These events demonstrate the changing complexion of feminism during the 1990s. Older activists remained committed to causes that defined the politics of previous decades, and new generations adapted feminist ideas to the issues they faced.

The backlash against feminism in the popular media was certainly severe, yet such moments in the '90s showed that the feminist movement was by no means dead—it remained vibrant at the grassroots.

Women's studies

Meanwhile, the fight against the erasure of women who had made or were making history during the 1990s prompted new efforts to foreground female achievement, through calendar events such as Women's History Month and in women's studies graduate programs.

As feminism entered universities, many ideas created within the women's liberation and black women's movements became crucial tools through which students analysed and understood the world. Women fought hard for feminist analyses, and for issues that related to women's lives to be seen as valid topics of academic study. As a result of their efforts, the university became the primary site through which the majority of people—including one of the authors of this book—encountered feminist ideas in the 1990s.

This situation was not without its contradictions, however. Academic feminism in the 1980s and '90s sometimes mimicked the rationalism, detachment, and objectivity of its male gatekeepers. It also rested on a caricature of the grassroots knowledge created by activists in the 1970s–80s as less sophisticated and, therefore, irrelevant to feminists engaged in proper, scholarly work. Such attitudes have shifted in recent years as many scholars, activists, and artists have returned to the archives of past women's movements for inspiration and knowledge.

In Britain, the Feminist Archive (1978), the Feminist Library (1975), and the Glasgow Women's Library (1991) were all established by activists in the women's liberation movements to safeguard feminist legacies for later generations.

In the US, archives and gender studies departments have become the "norm" at most universities and colleges across the country, with key collections being held at the Smithsonian Institution; the Library of Congress; the Sallie Bingham Center for Women's History & Culture, Duke University; the Schlesinger Library, Radcliffe College, Harvard University; and the Sophia Smith Collection, Smith College.

Across Europe many rich repositories of each country's feminist heritage have been established during the 1960s–80s, among them are: Bibliothèque Marguerite

> "Feminism looks like a dying corpse on the corrupt claws of media savages; frequently co-opted and diluted . . . but as herstory shows, female strength is never entirely wiped out. We're back, and this time we don't want equality with the death-merchants that crawl the earth in suits—we want everything."
> **Karren Ablaze**, Girl Speak manifesto, 1993

**GLASGOW WOMEN'S LIBRARY
25 YEARS OF CHANGING MINDS**

Top: The Glasgow Women's Library runs many inspiring projects that empower women in the local community.

Above left: Feminist Archives, Feminist Futures is an international project that explores the roles women's archives have had (and still have) in shaping women's lives.

Above middle: Adelaide's Women's Studies Resource Centre is an important repository of Australian feminist history.

Above right: These gender studies students aptly answer why women's studies matters.

Right: Atria, the institute for gender equality and women's history, is based in Amsterdam and holds one of the most significant global collections of women's history.

Slut shaming and misinformation continue

Bonnie J. Morris

Despite the huge advances made by the women's liberation movements, entrenched views on women's sexuality and identity are still at the heart of women's struggle today.

More than fifty years ago, women's consciousness-raising groups helped to reawaken and organize feminist revolution across America. In these small chapters of private dialogue, the personal became political, leading women of all ages to name everyday woman-hating in their own society, and to examine how such misogyny made the female body itself a site of political contention and shame.

Women today may be astronauts, professional athletes, Supreme Court judges, and presidential candidates. However, these economic and political gains have not eliminated social pressure on women to dress, speak and behave modestly, whether in public or private roles. Shame, secrecy, and misinformation campaigns continue to limit women's sexuality in ways that are not applied to men. One example of this double standard is the distinction made between "good" girls and "bad" girls as early as primary school, when simply being the first in the schoolyard to develop breasts can be enough to give a female student a sexual reputation.[10]

Mainstream media sites are now able to report on subject matter once considered too controversial for the evening news: sexual assault, global gender violence, lesbian rights and gender identities, and fair wages for single mothers. In fact, these are no longer feminist issues *per se*, but part of everyday health and human rights concerns. Such gains in free speech and body awareness have not been welcomed by all sectors of society; the feminist revolution remains strongly opposed by many (though not all) conservative religious leaders and fundamentalist sects. When churches, mosques, and synagogues blame women for tempting men, some followers interpret such teachings to imply that women who dress provocatively (or work in public roles) deserve to be shamed. During the rise in religious extremism that may be seen throughout the world at the time of writing, we have seen repeated episodes of violence against women who dare to act independently of male authority, including incidences of honor killings, acid being thrown in women's faces, and other tragic means of keeping female sexuality (and economic power) in check.

Even moderate backlash from religious conservatives has placed limits on female advancement in the US and beyond, often through perpetuating a basic narrative that women belong in the home under the authority of their father or husband. The concept of male headship makes it difficult for some faith groups to accept a female politician or police chief. Although America's founders envisioned a separation of church and state, elected officials raised with strong religious beliefs can and do shape government policies on sex education, rape, birth control, and pregnancy.

In a dramatic reversal of feminists' demands for sexual health information during the 1970s, "abstinence-only education" became the sole choice for many schools receiving government funding in the 1980s and '90s. Millions of dollars went to sex ed classes that silenced student questions, disappeared LGBT adolescents, presented false information on abortion, and spread shame around teen sexuality. The rise of AIDS in the 1980s allowed abstinence-focused educators to make a simplistic link between sexual activity, disease, and death. To avoid such a fate, young people were instructed to embrace chastity until marriage, to celebrate commitment to celibacy with Purity Ball proms or programs like True Love Waits, and to reject altogether the freewheeling sexuality associated with feminism and LGBT rights. Some adolescents caught (or suspected of) expressing a homosexual orientation were sent to unlicensed camps run by religious programs, such as Exodus International. Eventually, in 2008, a US House Committee on Oversight and Government Reform produced expert witnesses to show that abstinence-only sex education programs were both misleading and ineffective.

By the twenty-first century, slut shaming had become a new term for what women of all ages were still experiencing: blame placed on rape survivors or victims of sexual harassment, backlash against girls who wore what others judged to be provocative clothing, and the attitude

"In Central California, a teen just won the right to wear a shirt that says 'Nobody knows I'm a lesbian' to school. According to the lawsuit, an assistant principal said the shirt was 'promoting sex' and 'an invitation to sex.'"

Sonali Kahli, quoted in "The Problem of Slut Shaming in Schools," 2016

Above: SlutWalks around the world. Clockwise from top: Israel on June 2, 2017; Hong Kong, October 30, 2016; and the UK in October 2016.

that unwanted sexual attention was a woman's own fault. Feminist films, including *The Hunting Ground* and *The Invisible War*, have exposed the lack of serious responses to campus sexual violence and rape within the US military. Additionally, young women (and men) are now able to seek feminist resources and personal empowerment through Internet sites. But greater access to correct information online has not prevented myths about the female body from continuing, and too often such inaccuracies came from women's own elected officials. In 2012, one political candidate insisted that women rarely get pregnant from rape, a statement which he swiftly apologized for.[11]

In 2011, the FBI took steps to acknowledge that non-forcible rape is still rape, and may be experienced by a male or a female victim. Revising its definition for the first time since 1927, the FBI's Uniform Crime Reporting system retired its historic understanding of rape as the carnal knowledge of a female forcibly and against her will. The new definition agreed that rape is any form of forced sexual penetration of a man or a woman, including oral penetration. For too many women, however, shame and blame still proliferate in home communities, where the views of family, religious doctrines, and local politicians are encountered more frequently than FBI definitions. Over and over, across fifty, or one hundred, or two hundred years of feminism, rejecting the narrative of body shame is what continues to bring outraged women of all ages into feminist identity, action . . . and revolution.

Durand, France; the Biblioteca italiana delle donne, Italy; the Atria Institute for Women's History, the Netherlands; the KVINFO Danish Center for Information on Gender, Equality and Diversity, Denmark; and the Stiftung Frauen-literatur-forschung, Germany.

By the twenty-first century, questions and images about the legacies of radical feminism began to appear in the prestigious Advanced Placement (AP) US history exam taken by some high school students, and most universities offered courses addressing women in politics, reproductive rights, and/or the fight for wage equality. The gradual mainstreaming of women's history also overlapped with academia's shift toward *gender theory*, beginning in the 1990s with the influence of Michel Foucault, Judith Butler, and the postmodernist/deconstructionist approach to human sexualities. These approaches extended work that began within women's movements, namely to question how "masculinity" and "femininity" were socially constructed and therefore less rigid than previously assumed.

"Twenty-first century feminism"

The dawn of the twenty-first century saw feminism collide with another profound revolution—the arrival of the Internet. The first decade of the twenty-first century was filled with the stirrings of a resurgent, popular feminist movement. Activist connections were powered by the instantaneous speed of digital technologies as new activist networks formed at a lightning pace through email groups, web forums, and discussion boards. The unresolved debates of radical feminism now raged across the screens and keyboards of the Internet, replacing women's bookstores and consciousness-raising groups as sites of networking and action. Within the newly emergent digital culture feminists embraced blogs, LiveJournal, and social media to raise their voices and challenge rape culture and "everyday sexism." New print and web magazines like *gal-dem*[12] publish compelling stories and eye-catching visuals created by an international collective of over seventy women of color while *sister-hood* offers a platform for Muslim women to challenge damaging stereotypes: "Women of Muslim heritage are always in the news—as victims, as 'jihadi brides,' in innumerable pieces on hijab. We are endlessly spoken for, and spoken about. It's time we got to speak for ourselves," writes founder Deeyah Kahn.[13] Feminism—or the F-word—was rediscovered within a world that clearly still needed it.

Against this background of the digital age, old traditions were revived, such as the Reclaim the Night / Take Back the Night marches, and new ideas ignited, like the British-based Million Women Rise (MWR)—an annual

Below left: Riot Grrrl and Bikini Kill spawned the femzine craze of the 1990s, as young feminists embraced their own cultural approaches to women's liberation.

Below right: Ladyfests were regular occurrences in towns and cities across the world in the 2000s, as activists worked together to create spaces for women, queer, and trans folk to perform, share ideas, and build feminist networks.

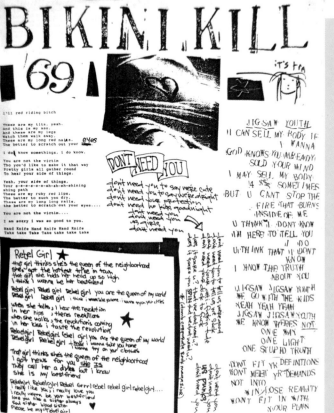

Above: The World Wide Web has seen an incredibly rich cultural feminist landscape open up with websites devoted to feminist and gender issues today or celebrating the women's liberation legacy.

rally and campaign to protest the "global pandemic" of violence against women and children. In Argentina, the Ni una menos (Not One Woman Less) movement began in 2015 to challenge multiple forms of gender sexual violence, and has since spread throughout Latin America. In Spain, Yo decido was formed in response to the Spanish government's proposal to radically restrict abortion legislation in 2013, and led to solidarity demonstrations across Europe.

Riot Grrrl has also continued to inspire new waves of feminist action, from the protest band Pussy Riot, who brought attention to discrimination against women in Russia, to Ladyfest festivals. First held in 2000 in Olympia, Washington, Ladyfests are queer feminist festivals that give women, queers, and trans persons a platform to perform, share ideas, dance, and discuss political issues. In the 2000s, many activists embraced the Ladyfest concept

and organized similar events in towns and cities across the world. Ladyfests continue to happen today, although with less frequency than in their mid-2000s heyday.

Much feminism today is transgender positive, and embraces the struggle for greater gender diversity and difference. Inherited conflicts from feminist debates of the late 1970s continue to generate tension however, most clearly between women who identify as "RadFems" and trans people and their allies.

New concepts, such as cisgenderism, have been embraced by contemporary feminists to express the privileges non-trans people have in a world where transgender persons, and especially trans persons of color, remain subject to disproportionate violence, dehumanization, and intimidation.

International movements such as SlutWalk (2011) and the Women's March (2017) have inspired millions to

The Revolutionary Association of the Women of Afghanistan

The Revolutionary Association of the Women of Afghanistan is a powerful example of the feminist fight in the Middle East.

Founded in 1977, the Revolutionary Association of the Women of Afghanistan (RAWA) is the oldest women's organization in Afghanistan. Over decades it has sought to bring democracy and equality to the women of Afghanistan, as well as lobbying for women's rights on an international scale.

In a country rarely associated with human rights and gender equality, the association has faced many challenges over the years, including the assassination of its leader and founder, Meena, in Quetta, Pakistan, in 1987. It is believed that her assassination was the work of the KHAD (the Afghan branch of the Russian KGB) and their fundamentalist accomplices (who also killed Meena's husband, Faiz Ahmad) in retaliation for Meena's outspoken work within the Afghan resistance movement against the Russian-backed government.[14]

One of RAWA's most powerful acts of activism is the documentation of human rights abuses across Afghanistan. They share publicly through written reports, film footage, and photographs such incidents in order to gain a wider recognition of the struggle that women and Afghan citizens are facing. One such piece of footage

"Today RAWA's mission for women's rights is far from over and we have to work hard for establishment of an independent, free, democratic and secular Afghanistan. We need the solidarity and support of all people around the world."

Revolutionary Association of the Women of Afghanistan website

LES DONES AFGANESES ENS ALIBERAREM SOLES !!!!

OCUPACÓ NI FONAMENTALISTES !

Associació Revolucionària de les do...

Llibertat
Democràcia
Drets de les dones

www.rawa.org

RAWA

مرگ بر بنیادگرایان و متجاوزین

جمعیت انقلابی زنان افغانستان

Opposite and above: RAWA demonstrations raise awareness of the group's mission.

gained worldwide coverage as part of the BBC documentary *Behind the Veil* in 1999, during which RAWA filming was shown of a mother of seven being executed at a football stadium by the Taliban.[15] By bearing witness to such horrors and being determined to speak out, they have exhibited incredible courage at a time when attacks against defenders of women's rights have increased in the country.[16]

They have also continued to protest against successive oppressive regimes within Afghanistan including the Russian invasion during the 1980s, the Mujahideen and the Taliban since the 1990s, and the destabilizing influence of foreign intervention.[17]

Their work reaches beyond protest into practical support for Afghan women and children, with the building of schools, hostels, and hospitals. They have also established training courses in medicine and education for women, as well as craft workshops to bring women together and help combat the trauma of war that so many have experienced.[18]

Their work has attracted criticism both inside and outside Afghanistan, but their exemplary bravery and fearless drive to empower women has nevertheless effected real change for those who they have been able to reach out to.

march on the streets, but such protests have also been criticized for continuing to place white and Western women's liberation at their center.[19] The sensationalist naked activism of FEMEN, originally from Ukraine and now based in France, has been challenged for how it reinforces stereotypes of Muslim women as victims who need to be "liberated" by Western values.

In India, movements such as the Pink Sari, or Gulabi Gang, are fighting against domestic violence and activists, like Nobel Prize Laureate Malala Yousafzai, are highlighting the need to improve educational opportunities for women and girls. In the Netherlands, Women on the Waves blends consciousness-raising campaigns about birth control with providing free, safe abortions in international waters to women who cannot access contraception in their own countries.

The mobilization of feminism in the twenty-first century is not, however, without contradictions, as can be seen in its cooption by conservative rhetoric and legal practices. In the War on Terror, for example, women's and LGBT rights were used by the US and UK governments to symbolize the "civilization" of Western liberal democracies, and became a means to justify military intervention in "uncivilized" countries like Afghanistan and Iraq.

In 1999, the Violence against Women Act (VAWA) was passed in the US—the law introduced increased prison sentences and policing as the preferred solution to reduce violence against women in America. In reality, this "carceral" approach to feminism has occurred alongside the closure of shelters and social programs. It also ignores how "race, class, gender identity, and immigration status leave certain women more vulnerable to violence and that greater criminalization often places these same women at risk of state violence."[20] To counter this, the prison abolition movement has also gained traction, spearheaded by the actions of women, queers, and trans persons of color.[21]

Campaigns that highlight the injustice of racist immigration laws, and their particular impact on women, are a prominent part of contemporary activism. The British Campaign to Shut Down Yarl's Wood, an immigration removal center (IRC) whose inmates are predominantly women and children, has gained momentum in recent years. Many of the women in Yarl's Wood—and in Britain's eleven other IRCs—come to the UK to seek asylum but are locked up and treated like criminals. Many are survivors of sexual violence, rape, or torture. Inside Yarl's Wood, these women are subject to the abusive behavior of guards, who have in recent times been accused of a catalog of harms including

inappropriate sexual contact, racist abuse, and physical assault.[22] Many of these incidents at the prison stretch back to the early years of the twenty-first century. Shut Down Yarl's Wood is now a demand echoed by many. Activists alongside detained women are fighting back against racist immigration laws and institutions that punish women who have already suffered unimaginable violence. In Britain there have also been some victories. After over twenty years of campaigning by Southall Black Sisters and other asylum advocacy groups, the Destitute Domestic Violence (DDV) concession was introduced in April 2012. This policy concession allows abused women who enter the UK on spousal visas a temporary stay of three months to access basic welfare benefits and social housing.[23]

Violence against women remains a widespread, international catastrophe, from honor-based killing and rape as a weapon in war, to domestic violence. However, it must be remembered that many gains have been made since the 1970s. In very many countries in the world, there are at least some laws, policies, and practices that aim to prevent violence against women— it is increasingly viewed as a problem that must be stopped, rather than something unrecognized or even normal. These victories are the direct result of a courageous and determined struggle by grassroots activists, working to ensure that violence against women becomes a historic relic of a bygone society.[24]

What is also clear is that as feminism across the world moves into the future, it will continue to change and be rooted in a range of inspiring and contradictory histories. In an era of rising right-wing nationalism, militarism, capitalist intensification, and border violence, the resources provided by feminist activism and thought are invaluable and more necessary than ever. This book is a snapshot of how women from the 1960s through the 1980s strove for liberation, yet they were part of a longer struggle that stretches across several centuries. Reading these words, you are part of this history; you stand upon its shoulders, within its beating heart. The feminist revolution is unfinished and it is happening now. This is a politics that resists existing injustices and invents new possibilities. You hold this power in your hands; take inspiration, courage, and action.

Opposite, clockwise from top left: The year 2017 saw an explosion of feminist activism around the world: Demonstrations in France; the Pink Sari Gang in India working to empower women; pink "pussy hat" marches in Washington and London; Black Girls Picnic, a global movement in collective self care celebrating the beauty of black womanhood, takes part in the Women's March that took place in towns and cities across the world on January 21, 2017; and mothers protest for welfare in London.

"If you believe in any of the following: reproductive rights; equal pay for equal work; seeing diverse bodies, ethnicities, and gender expressions on screen and in magazines; providing education to 62 million girls who don't have access to it; ending sexual violence; having women in government; having women CEOs—you know, basic gender equality—surprise! You're probably a feminist."

Zeba Blay and Emma Gray, *Huffington Post*, 2017

Endnotes

Chapter 1

1 Jane Arden, *Vagina Rex and the Gas Oven* (London: Calder and Boyars, 1971), 10.

2 Ibid., 11.

3 Sue O'Sullivan "Passionate Beginnings: Ideological Politics 1969–72," *Feminist Review* 11 (July 1982): 70–86, 72.

4 Quoted in Alice Rossi, ed., *The Feminist Papers: From Adams to Beauvoir* (New Hampshire: UNEP, 1988).

5 Jane Lewis, *Women in Britain since 1945* (Oxford: Blackwell, 1992), 65.

6 Helen McCarthy, "Women, Marriage and Paid Work in Post-War Britain," *Women's History Review* 26 (2017): 1, 46–61, 53.

7 Phillida Bunkle, "The 1944 Education Act and Second Wave Feminism," *Women's History Review* 25 (2016): 5, 791–811, 793.

8 Pat Thane, "Women and the 1970s," in *Reassessing 1970s Britain*, eds. Lawrence Black, Hugh Pemberton, and Pat Thane (Manchester: Manchester University Press, 2013), 167–87.

9 With thanks to Andrea Hajek; for more information, see Molly Tambor, *The Lost Wave* (Oxford: Oxford University Press, 2014).

10 Sheila Rowbotham, "The Beginnings of the Women's Liberation Movement in Britain," in *Once a Feminist: Stories of a Generation*, ed. Michelene Wandor (London: Virago, 1990), 22.

11 Ibid

12 Sheila Rowbotham, "Sheila Rowbotham," in *Once a Feminist: Stories of a Generation*, ed. Michelene Wandor (London: Virago, 1990), 36.

13 Janet Hadley, "Janet Hadley," in *Once a Feminist: Stories of a Generation*, ed. Michelene Wandor (London: Virago, 1990), 77.

14 "Interview with Gerlin Bean," held in the Black Cultural Archives, ORAL/1/3; transcribed by D-M Withers.

15 Selma James, "Selma James," in *Once a Feminist: Stories of a Generation*, ed. Michelene Wandor (London: Virago, 1990), 198.

16 Ibid., 195; italics are D-M Withers's.

17 Rowbotham, "Sheila Rowbotham," 36.

18 Val Charlton, "Val Charlton," in *Once a Feminist: Stories of a Generation*, ed. Michelene Wandor (London: Virago, 1990), 163.

19 Martin Pugh, *Women and the Women's Movement in Britain since 1914*, 3rd ed. (London: Palgrave, 2015), 265.

20 Paul Maughan, "Hannah Gavron: A Woman Ahead of Her Time," *New Statesman* (November 12, 2015), http://www.newstatesman.com/culture/observations/2015/11/hannah-gavron-woman-ahead-her-time.

21 Beverly Bryan et al., *Heart of the Race: Black Women's Lives in Britain* (London: Virago, 1986), 24.

22 Ibid., 22–23.

23 For more on images of women in 1960s television, see Susan Douglas, *Where the Girls Are: Growing Up Female with the Mass Media* (New York City: Time Books, 1998).

24 With grateful thanks to Andrea Hajek for her insights into the German and Italian narratives.

25 With grateful thanks to Andrea Hajek for the material on the Italian women's movement.

26 Sheila Rowbotham, "The Beginnings of Women's Liberation in Britain," in *The Body Politic: Women's Liberation in Britain 1969–1972*, ed. Michelene Wandor (London: Stage 1, 1972), 91–103.

27 Sheila Rowbotham, n.d., "Memories of the Revolutionary Festival," http://www.essex68.org.uk/comm4.html.

28 Thane, "Women and the 1970s," 173.

29 Abortion Act 1967, http://www.legislation.gov.uk/ukpga/1967/87/contents.

30 Juliet Mitchell, "Women: The Longest Revolution," https://www.marxists.org/subject/women/authors/mitchell-juliet/longest-revolution.htm.

31 "Asphodel," in *'68, '78, '88: From Women's Liberation to Feminism*, ed. Amanda Sebestyen (Bridport: Prism Press, 1988), 9–10.

32 Pugh, *Women and the Women's Movement in Britain since 1914*, 272.

33 Elizabeth Heineman, "Liebe, lust und last: Die pille als weibliche generationserfahrung in der Bundesrepublik 1960–1980," *Ger Hist* 29, no. 2 (2011): 348–49, doi:10.1093/gerhis/ghq133.

34 E. Ketting, "Contraception and Fertility in the Netherlands," *Fam Plann Perspect* 15, no. 1 (1983): 19–25, https://www.ncbi.nlm.nih.gov/pubmed/6680699.

35 With grateful thanks to Andrea Hajek for her insights into the Italian women's movement.

36 O'Sullivan, "Passionate Beginnings," 80.

37 Simone de Beauvoir, *The Second Sex* (New York: Alfred A. Knopf, 2009 [1949]), xv–xxix.

38 Ibid., 485.

39 Ibid., 518.

40 Simone de Beauvoir, *The Second Sex*, trans. Constance Borde and Sheila Malovany-Chevallier (New York: Vintage Books, 2011), 283.

41 Sue Bruley, "Women's Liberation at the Grass Roots: A View from Some English Towns, c.1968–1990," *Women's History Review* (2016) 25: 5, 723–40.

42 Alison Sinard, "The Birth of the MLF: 'There is still more unknown than the unknown soldier, his wife,'" franceculture (January 20, 2017), https://www.franceculture.fr/societe/la-naissance-du-mlf-il-y-encore-plus-inconnu-que-le-soldat-inconnu-sa-femme.

43 With grateful thanks to Andrea Hajek for her insights into the Italian women's movement.

44 Anon, "Women's National Co-ordinating Committee," *Shrew* (February 8, 1971).

Chapter 2

1 Anon, "A Short History of the Socialist Current in the British Women's Liberation Movement," held in the Feminist Archive North, GC/02/07, University of Leeds Special Collections.

2 Sheila Rowbotham, "Sheila Rowbotham," in *Once a Feminist: Stories of a Generation*, ed. Michelene Wandor (London: Virago, 1990), 37.

3 "Interview with Gerlin Bean," held in the Black Cultural Archives, ORAL/1/3; transcribed by D-M Withers.

4 "OWAAD Draft Constitution," held in the Black Cultural Archives, DADZIE /1/1/4–6; transcribed by D-M Withers.

5 The Milan Women's Bookstore Cooperative, *Sexual Difference: A Theory of Social-Symbolic Practice* (Bloomington: Indiana University Press, 1990), 32. D-M Withers thanks Alex Martinis Roe for sharing this resource.

6 Michelene Wandor, "The Small Group," in *The Body Politic: Writings from the Women's Liberation Movement in Britain 1969–1972*, ed. Michelene Wandor (London: Stage 1, 1972), 107–16.

7 Sue Bruley, "Women Awake: The Experience of Consciousness-Raising" in *No Turning Back: Writings from the Women's Liberation Movement 1975–1980*, ed. Feminist Anthology Collective (London: Women's Press, 1976/81), 60-67, 63. Italics in original.

8 "Consciousness Raising," Edinburgh Women's Liberation Newsletter (n.d.).

9 "Is the Women's Liberation Movement Vanishing Up Our Own Collective Cervix?" WIRES paper 1 (1977), conference folder, held in Feminist Archive South, DM2123-FA-Arch-Box 32, University of Bristol Special Collections.

10 Information for New Groups, WLW, "The Four Demands" in *Papers from the Women's Liberation and Socialism Conference, London 22/23 September 1973* (1971 [1973]), 5.

11 Ruth Wallsgrove, "British Feminist Publications," *Off Our Backs* 13 (1983): 3, 24–25, 24.

12 Amanda Sebesteyen, "Tendencies in the Women's Liberation Movement," *Feminist Practice: Notes from the Tenth Year (Theoretically Speaking!)* (In Theory Press, 1979).

13 Takumba Ria Lawal, interview with D-M Withers, February 18, 2017.

14 Betty Hagglund, "1977 Women's Liberation Song Book—Like Gold!" (2008), http://www.gaybirminghamremembered.co.uk/memories/1977%20Womens%20Liberation%20Songbook%20-%20like%20gold%21.

15 Gillian, "Thoughts on the Conference (Acton Conference)," 1972 conference folder, held in Feminist Archive South, DM2123-FA-Arch-Box 32, University of Bristol Special Collections.

16 Anon, "Contraception and Abortion Campaign," *Shrew* (February 5, 1971).

17 Lesley Hall, "National Abortion Campaign Archives Now Available" (2012), http://blog.wellcomelibrary.org/2012/08/national-abortion-campaign-archives-now-available.

18 London Women's Liberation Campaign for Legal and Financial Independence and Rights of Women, "Disaggregation Now! Another Battle for Women's Independence," *Feminist Review* 2 (1979): 19–31.

19 "National Women's Centre Conference Report," held in Feminist Archive North, FAN/WIRES/02/11, University of Leeds Special Collections.

20 Anon, "How Not to Start a Woman's Centre," *Peace News* (May 24, 1974).

21 Caroline New, "Personal Histories of Second Wave Feminism," vols. 1–2, summarized from interviews by Viv Honeybourne and Iona Singer, Feminist Archive South, Bristol University Special Collections. http://feministarchivesouth.org.uk/wp-content/uploads/2013/02/Personal-Histories-of-the-Second-Wave-of-Feminism.pdf, 30. Quoted in Sue Bruley, "Women's Liberation at the Grass Roots: A View from Some English Towns, c.1968–1990," *Women's History Review* (2016) 25: 5, 723–40.

22 With grateful thanks to Andrea Hajek for her insights into the Italian women's movement.

23 With grateful thanks to Andrea Hajek for her comments and insights on the French and Italian legal reforms.

Chapter 3

1 Hazel Carby, "White Woman Listen! Black Feminism and the Boundaries of Sisterhood!" in *The Empire Strikes Back: Race and Racism in '70s Britain*, ed. Centre for Contemporary Cultural Studies (London: Hutchinson, 1982), 211–34.

2 Max Robson, quoted in D-M Withers, *Sistershow Revisited: Feminism in Bristol 1973–1975* (Bristol: HammerOn Press, 2011), 27.

3 Organisation of Women of Asian and African Descent (OWAAD) Conference (video), held in Black Cultural Archives, Record 1/54.

4 "Editorial," *FOWAAD!* 1 (July 1979): 2.

5 Black Cultural Archives, Record 1/54.

6 Ibid.

7 "Editorial," *FOWAAD!* 1 (July 1979): 2.

8 "Letters," *FOWAAD!* 1 (July 1979): 9.

9 Ibid.

10 Dadzie, "Heart of the Race Oral Histories."

11 Natalie Thomlinson, *Race, Ethnicity and the Women's Movement in England, 1968–1993* (Basingstoke: Palgrave, 2016), 65.

12 Brixton Black Women's Group and Alice Henry, "Black Politics = Black Feminism: Brixton Black Women's Group Talks about Its Part in British Black Feminism . . ." *Off Our Backs* 14 (1984): 11, 14.

13 Roisin Boyd, "Women Speak Out against Zionism," *Spare Rib* (1982), 22–23, 121.

14 Michele Wallace, "To Hell and Back: On the Road with Black Feminism," in *The Feminist Memoir Project*, eds. Rachel Blau DuPlessis and Ann Snitow (New York: Three Rivers Press, 1998), 441.

15 Pat Parker, "For the white person who wants to be my friend," *The Complete Works of Pat Parker*, ed. Julie Enszer (A Midsummer Night's Press, 2016), 76.

16 Fran Beall, quoted in the film *She's Beautiful When She's Angry*, dir. Mary Dore (2014).

17 Audre Lorde's essays appear in *Sister Outsider* (Crossing Press, 1984).

18 Robin Morgan, ed., *Sisterhood Is Powerful* (New York: Random House, 1970), xxvi–xxxv.

19 Combahee River Collective, "A Black Feminist Statement," *Women's Studies Quarterly* (1981): 42.

20 Diana Watt, email communication with D-M Withers, April 11, 2017.

21 See Diana Watt and Adele D. Jones, *Catching Hell and Doing Well: Black Women in the UK—the Abasindi Cooperative* (London: UCL Press, 2015).

22 Black Women's Action Committee, "The Black Woman," 89.

23 Thomlinson, *Race, Ethnicity and the Women's Movement in England*, 71.

24 Emma Allotey, "Biographical Note: Olive Morris," Remembering Olive Morris Collective, https://rememberolivemorris.wordpress.com.

25 *FOWAAD!* 1 (July 1979).

26 Barbara Omolade, "Sisterhood in Black and White," in *The Feminist Memoir Project*, 403.

27 Brixton Black Women's Group, "Black Women Organizing," *Feminist Review* 17 (1984): 84–89, 85.

28 Dr. Anita Patel, "Surveillance and Control," *Edinburgh Women's Liberation Newsletter: Scottish Black Women's Group Issue*, 41 (1986).

29 Watt and Jones, *Catching Hell and Doing Well*, 140.

30 *Outwrite* 21 (January 1984); and *Outwrite* 25 (May 1984).

31 *Outwrite* 25 (1984): 5.

32 Scottish Black Women's Group, "Scottish Black Women's Group," *Edinburgh Women's Liberation Newsletter: Scottish Black Women's Group Issue* 41 (1986).

33 Angela Y. Davis, "History Cannot Be Deleted Like Web Pages: Transcript of Angela Y Davis's Women's March speech" (2017). http://www.elle.com/culture/career-politics/a42337/angela-davis-womens-march-speech-full-transcript/.

Chapter 4

1 Some nursing students were apparently threatened with having their grades withheld if they did not complete the clinical trial; this is discussed in Jonathan Eig, *The Birth of the Pill* (New York: W. W. Norton, 2014).

2 The Campaign against Depo–Provera, "The Ignorance Injection," held in Black Cultural Archives, DADZIE 1/10.

3 Ibid.

4 Kate Kay, "1976–1978," https://www.womensaid.org.uk/about-us/history.

5 Women's Aid Federation, "Aims of Women's Aid," held in Feminist Archive North, GC/01-GC/02.09.

6 Women's Aid Federation, "He's Got to Show Her Who's Boss," in *Spare Rib: 100 Issues of Women's Liberation* (London: Penguin, 1978), 443.

7 Gill Hague, interview with D-M Withers, October 27, 2016.

8 Anon, "Cardiff Women's Aid," *Rhiannon*, held in Feminist Archive South, DM2123/5/5.

9 "The June Greig Campaign," *Speaking Out: The Story of Scottish Women's Aid*. Exhibition text, http://womenslibrary.org.uk/discover-our-projects/speaking-out.

10 Ibid.

11 Asian Women's Network, January 1986 Newsletter, 1.

12 With grateful thanks to Andrea Hajek for her insights into European abortion reform throughout this passage.

13 Choisir de la cause des femmes, http://www.choisirlacausedesfemmes.org/anglais.html.

14 Ibid.

15 With grateful thanks to Andrea Hajek for her insight into Italian rape-marriage laws.

16 Finn Mackay, *Radical Feminism: Feminist Activism in Movement* (Basingstoke: Palgrave, 2015), 72.

17 With grateful thanks to Andrea Hajek for her insights here on the Circeo massacre.

18 Reclaim the Night Group, "We Will Walk Without Fear, November 12th," *Spare Rib* 66 (January 1978): 22–23.

19 Ruth Wallsgrove, A. Phillips, and J. Nicholls, "Immigration Tests in Britain," *Spare Rib* 81 (April 1979): 10.

20 Pratibha Parmar, "Gender, Race and Class: Asian Women in Resistance," in *The Empire Strikes Back: Race and Racism in '70s Britain*, ed. Centre for Contemporary Cultural Studies (London: Routledge, 1982), 245.

21 With grateful thanks to Andrea Hajek for her insights into women's health centers.

22 Kathy Davis, *The Making of Our Bodies, Our Selves: How Feminism Travels across Borders* (Durham: Duke University Press, 2007), 52.

23 Lillian Faderman, *Odd Girls and Twilight Lovers* (London: Penguin, 1991), 64.

24 Boston Women's Health Collective, *Our Bodies, Ourselves*, 2nd ed. (Boston: Boston Women's Health Collective, 1979), 47.

25 Ruth Rosen, *The World Split Open* (New York: Viking, 2000), 177.

26 Sophie Laws, *Down There: An Illustrated Guide to Self-Exam* (London: OnlyWomen, 1981), 5.

27 Ellen Malos, Oral History Interview, Feminist Archive South (2000).

28 Sisters against Disablement, "Open Letter to the Organisers of the Lesbian Sex and Sexual Practice Conference, April 1983," in *Sweeping Statements: Writings from the Women's Liberation Movement 1981–1983*, eds. Hannah Kanter et al. (London: Women's Press, 1984), 303–04.

Chapter 5

1 Beatrix Campbell, "Beatrix Campbell Discusses Consequences of Sexual Pleasure" (2010): https://www.bl.uk/collection-items/beatrix-campbell-consequences-of-sexual-pleasure.

2 Ibid.

3 See documentaries: *Last Call at Maud's*, *Forbidden Love*, and *Before Stonewall*.

4 Radicalesbians, "The Woman-Identified Woman" (Know Inc., 1970).

5 Jo Spence, "**The Picture of Health?**" exhibition poster, held in Feminist Archive North, Pavilion 15/07 (2 of 4).

6 *Yorkshire Evening Post*, September 28, 1981, held in Feminist Archive North, WAVAW, Box 3, Sandra McNeil Collection.

7 Susan Ardrill and Sue O'Sullivan, "Upsetting an Applecart: Difference, Desire and Lesbian Sadomasochism," *Feminist Review* 26 (1986): 31–57.

8 Rebel Dykes, http://www.rebeldykes1980s.com/.

9 Emma Healey, *Lesbian Sex Wars* (London: Virago, 1996), 100.

10 Ardrill and O'Sullivan, "Upsetting an Applecart," 44.

11 SM Debate, London Women's Centre. Courtesy of the Rebel Dykes archive.

12 Ibid.

13 See Howard Malchow, *Special Relations? The Americanization of Britain* (Stanford: Stanford University Press, 2011), for an interesting discussion about ideological splits between Socialism and American-style Radicalesbians within lesbians in the GLF.

14 "First National Lesbian Conference," held in Feminist Archive South, DM2123/8/Archive, Boxes 116, Folder 3.

15 Ibid.

16 Ibid.

17 The debates were passionate and intense and raged throughout the 1980s. Many responses to the paper were published in the collection *Love Your Enemy? The Debate between Heterosexual Feminism and Political Lesbianism* (London: Onlywomen Press, 1981).

18 Leeds Revolutionary Feminist Group, "Political Lesbianism: The Case against Heterosexuality" in *Love Your Enemy? The Debate between Heterosexual Feminism and Political Lesbianism* (London: Only Woman Press, 1981), 5.

19 Leeds Revolutionary Feminist Group, "Political Lesbianism," 5.

20 Siva German, "What Is Male Supremacy?," paper presented at What Is Male Supremacy? Conference, London (1977).

21 With grateful thanks to Andrea Hajek for this insight.

22 Radicalesbians, "The Woman-Identified Woman" (1970).

23 Trisha McCabe, "Gay Birmingham Remembered," http://www.gaybirminghamremembered.co.uk/interview/41.

24 "Becoming Visible," 61.

25 Ibid., 59.

26 Valerie Mason-John, "Herstoric Moments," in *Talking Black: Lesbians of African and Asian Descent Speak Out*, ed. Valerie Mason-John (London: Cassell, 1995), 4–23.

27 Ibid., 10.

28 Black British Lesbian Timeline, http://blackbritishlesbian.typepad.com/blog.

29 Mason-John, "Herstoric Moments," 12.

30 Ibid., 21. Many records are kept in the Lesbian Archive, housed at the Glasgow Women's Library, http://womenslibrary.org.uk/explore-the-library-and-archive/the-archive-collection-the-lesbian-archive.

31 *Nessie—Thi Radical Raddish Frae Scotland* 1 (May 1979), held in Glasgow Women's Library.

32 Jeanne Cordova, *When We Were Outlaws* (New York: Spinsters Ink, 2011), 311.

33 Ibid., 427.

34 Vicki Eaklor, *Queer America: A GLBT History of the 20th Century* (Westport, CT: Greenwood Press, 2008), xxviii.

35 Bonnie Zimmerman, ed., *Encyclopedia of Lesbian Histories and Cultures* (New York: Garland Publishing Inc., 2000), 180

36 Sarah Kershaw, "My Sister's Keeper," *New York Times* (January 30, 2009).

Chapter 6

1 Eileen Boris and Annelise Orleck, "Feminism and the Labor Movement: A Century of Collaboration and Conflict," *New Labor Force* (January 3, 2011).

2 With grateful thanks to Andrea Hajek for her insight into the Italian women's labor movement. For a further exploration, see M. Bracke, "Building a 'Counter-community of Emotions': Feminist Encounters and Socio-cultural Difference in 1970s Turin," *Modern Italy* 17, no. 2 (2012).

3 Pat Thane, "Women and the 1970s," in *Reassessing 1970s Britain*, eds. Lawrence Black, Hugh Pemberton, and Pat Thane (Manchester: Manchester University Press, 2013), 167–87, 178.

4   Jonathan Moss, "'We Didn't Realise How Brave We Were at the Time': The 1968 Ford Sewing Machinists' Strike in Public and Personal Memory," *Oral History* 43, no. 1 (2015): 40–51, 44.

5   Cleaners' Action Group, "Cleaners' Voice" (n.d.), Women's Library, 7SHR-D-3-Box-8.

6   Notice published by N. London IS Women, Women's Library 7SHR/D/1.

7   Geoffrey Sheridan, "Rocking the Bucket," *Guardian* (February 17, 1971). D-M Withers thanks George Stevenson for sharing this resource.

8   Sally Alexander, "The Nightcleaners' Campaign" in *Conditions of Illusion: Papers from the Women's Movement* (Leeds: Feminist Books, 1974), 318.

9   George Stevenson, "The Women's Movement and 'Class Struggle': Gender, Class Formation and Political Identity in Women's Strikes, 1968–78," *Women's History Review* 25, no. 5 (2016): 741–755, 746.

10 Sheila Rowbotham, "Jolting Memory: Nightcleaners Recalled" (2008): www.workandwords.net/uploads/files/S._ROWBOTHAM_NightCleaners_-_ENG_.pdf.

11 Black Women's Action Committee, "The Black Woman" in *The Body Politic: Women's Liberation in Britain 1969–1972*, ed. Michelene Wandor (London: Stage 1, 1972), 84–91, 89.

12 Gloria Steinem, *Outrageous Acts and Everyday Rebellions* (New York: Henry Holt, 1983) 11.

13 Sally Priesand in *Judaism and the New Woman* (New York: Behrman House, 1975), xiii.

14 Catherine Hall, "Catherine Hall Describes Collective Childcare," https://www.bl.uk/sisterhood/articles/families-and-parenting.

15 Sally Fraser and Amanda Sebestyen, "Going Orange" in *'68, '78, '88*, 104–16, 107.

16 Gay Preston, "The Ideal Couple" in See *Feminist Posters 1974–1990*, Red Women's Workshop (London: Four Corners Books, 2016), 70–71.

17 *Shrew*, "More Than Minding" in *The Body Politic: Women's Liberation in Britain 1969–1972*, ed. Michelene Wandor (London: Stage 2, (1972); 133–37, 137.

18 Script copyright 1986 by Jane Wagner.

19 M. Bracke, "Between the Transnational and the Local: Mapping the Trajectories and Contexts of the Wages for Housework Campaign in 1970s Italian Feminism," *Women's History Review* 22, no. 4 (2013): 625–42.

20 T. McNeill, "Women in Postwar France II" in *Communiqué* online (1998): http://eserve.org.uk/tmc.

21 Ruth Eliot, "How Far Have We Come? Women's Organization in the Unions in the United Kingdom," *Feminist Review* 16 (1984), 64–73, 65.

22 T. McNeill, "Women in Postwar France II" in *Communiqué* online (1998): http://eserve.org.uk/tmc.

23 Barnsley Women against Pit Closures (1984): http://www.clririshleftarchive.org/document/view/619.

24 Jill Page, WAPC Miner's Strike—photos and press cuttings, held in the Feminist Archive North, FAN/JP/Box 2.

25 Liz Heron, "Getting on Top of the Job: Women in Manual Trades," *Spare Rib*, 72 (1978), 42.

26 Bristol Women's Workshop, Anne—founder of the workshop interviewed by Fanny Wacklin Nilsson (2013): https://www.youtube.com/watch?v=TgqKjB0cWzk. See also: www.bristolwomensworkshop.org.uk.

Chapter 7

1   Rosen, *The World Split Open*, 225.

2   Eileen Cadman, Gail Chester, and Agnes Pivot, *Rolling Our Own: Women As Printers, Publishers and Distributors* (London: Minority Press Group, 1981), Series 73.

3   Ibid., 42.

4   Ibid., 29.

5   Susan Ardill, "The Feminist Book Fair—How It All Came About," *Spare Rib* 143 (1984): 21.

6   Cathy Loeb, "Report on the First International Feminist Book Fair," *Feminist Collections* 6, no.1 1 (1984): 17–18.

7   "The First International Feminist Book Fair June 1984: Provisional Programme," held in the Women's Library, London, 6/0WP2 2000/10 (box 13 of 19).

8   Pratibha Parmar, Jackie Kay, and Audre Lorde, "Frontiers" in *Charting the Journey: Writings by Black and Third World Women*, ed. Shabnam Grewel et al. (London: Sheba Feminist Publishers, 1988), 121–32, 124.

9   Feminist International Book Fair, "List of Recommended Books," 1, held in the Women's Library, London, 6/0WP2 2000/10 (box 13 of 19).

10 "Feminist Book Fair Group Meeting, April 3, 1984," held in the Women's Library, London, 6/0WP2 2000/10 (box 13 of 19).

11 Jane Cholmeley, interview with author, March 31, 2017.

12 With grateful thanks to Andrea Hajek for her insights into the Italian women's movement.

13 Howard K. Smith, August 25, 1970; cited in Susan Douglas, in *Where the Girls Are* (New York: Times Books, 1995), 179.

14 Gloria Steinem, "Gloria Steinem: The Woman Who Paved the Way," interview by Federica Marchionni, CEO of Land's End, 2016.

15 Harry Reasoner, "I'll Give it Six Months": on *ABC Nightly News*, 1972.

16 Quoted in "How Do you Spell Ms.," by Abigail Pogrebin in *New York Times*, October 30, 2011.

17 Carmen, Gail, Shaila, and Pratibha, "Becoming Visible: Black Lesbian Discussions," *Feminist Review* 17 (1984): 53–72, 58.

18 Marsha Rowe, "Facsimile of *Spare Rib* Manifesto" (1972): https://www.bl.uk/spare-rib/articles/introduction-spare-rib-the-first-nine-years.

19 Anon, "Up against the Wall," *Outwrite*, 70 (November 1988).

20 Lucy Delap, "Feminist Bookshops, Reading Cultures and the Women's Liberation Movement in Great Britain, c. 1974–2000" *History Workshop Journal* 81, no. 1 (2016): 171–196, 180.

21 Maureen Paton, "Eclipse of Silver Moon," *The Guardian* (October 23, 2001): https://www.theguardian.com/world/2001/oct/23/gender.uk2.

22 Delap, "Feminist Bookshops, Reading Cultures and the Women's Liberation Movement in Great Britain," 178.

23 Carol Seajay, in *Women's Culture: Renaissance of the Seventies*, ed. Gayle Kimball (NJ: Scarecrow Press, 1981), 81.

24 *Rolling Our Own*, 71.

Chapter 8

1   Susan Hemmings and Norma Pitfield, *Musics* 15 (December 1977): 20.

2   Pat VT West, interviewed by Viv Honeybourne, Feminist Archive South, Oral Histories (2000).

3   Terry Wolverton, *Insurgent Muse: Life and Art at the Women's Building* (San Francisco: City Lights Books, 2002), xvi.

4   Anon, "Black Women and the Media Conference," *Spare Rib* 143 (1984): 18.

5   Anon, Atria, Archief Vrouwenfestivals Melkweg (n.d.), Folder 1: hdl.handle.net/11653/arch706.

6   5th Internationale Vrouwenfestival in Amsterdam, September 24–29, 1985, festival program, 14.

7   Suzanne Dechert, interview with D-M Withers, February 13, 2017.

8   2nd Internationale Vrouwenfestival in Amsterdam, September 20–24, 1978, festival program, 2.

9   5th Internationale Vrouwenfestival in Amsterdam, September 20–24, 1985, festival program, 12.

10 Suzanne Dechert, interview with D-M Withers, February 13, 2017.

11 With grateful thanks to Andrea Hajek for her insights into the Italian women's movement.

12 Bernadine Evaristo, "Theatre of Black Women" (December 6, 2013): http://www.unfinishedhistories.com/history/companies/theatre-of-black-women/bernardine-evaristo-talk/.

13 Gail Lewis, "Response to Sweet Sugar Rage" (2014): https://soundcloud.com/translation-transmission/gail-lewis-responds-to-sweet.

14 *Women and Music*, 1, held in Feminist Archive South, DM2123.

15 Bonnie J. Morris, *Eden Built by Eves* (Alyson, 1999).

16 Anon, "Black Women Fighting Back," *Spare Rib*, 95 (1980): 49.

17 Jalna Runnalls, interview with D-M Withers, 2012.

18 Antonietta Laterza, interview with Andrea Hajek, September 28, 2011.

19 *The Sisters Found*, published in 1975. The songs can be listened to at the following link: http://sool4jo.tistory.com/1112.

20 Mary Kelly, *Post-Partum Document*: http://www.marykellyartist.com/post_partum_document.html.

21 Women's Festival, Manchester Women's Liberation Newsletter, January/February 4, 1975.

Chapter 9

1   Pugh, *Women and the Women's Movement in Britain since 1914*, 265.

2   Ann Pettitt, "Women for Life on Earth," article submitted and rejected to *New Society* (9. 24. 81), held in Glamorgan Archives, D/D WLE 2/23.

3   Ann Pettitt, *Walking to Greenham: How the Peace Camp Began and the Cold War Ended* (Dinas Powys: Honno, 2006), 26.

4   Ann Pettitt, untitled, held in Glamorgan Archives, D/D WLE B28.

5   "Woman in Cruise Missile Chains Protest," *Cardigan & Tiny-side*, September 11, 1981, 116: 13; held in Glamorgan Archives, D/D WLE 2/18.

6   Letter from Annie Tunnicliffe to Women's Peace Camp, October 9, 1981; held in Glamorgan Archives, D/D WLE 2/25.

7   Anon, "Women for Life on Earth Say 'No Cruise Missiles at Greenham Common / Embrace the Base Chain Letter,'" held in the Glamorgan Archives, DWLE.

8   See Sasha Roseneil, *Common Women, Uncommon Practices: The Queer Feminisms of Greenham* (London and New York: Cassell, 2000), 208–10; Margaretta Jolly, "Censored/Uncensored: Lovers in Dialogue," *Auto/Biography* (2004), 12: 147–66: http://autobiography.edina.clockss.org/aub_2004_12_2/10.1191_0967550704ab011oa.pdf for a wider reading of Harwood's letters.

9   Carole Harwood, Handwritten note on back of a letter (February 24, 1983), held in Feminist Archive South, DM2123/2/54, Carole Harwood Collection.

10 Elsewhere titled "Now I'm a Happy Dyke," "Greenham Song Index," Danish Peace Academy Greenham Collection. Available online at: http://www.fredsakademiet.dk/abase/sange/greenham/song66.htm.

11 Anon, "A Greenham Womon Replies to Breaching the Peace" in *Raging Women: A Reply to Breaching the Peace*, held in the Women's Library, 6/OWP 9/1999 3.2, 7–8.

12 Sasha Roseneil, *Disarming Patriarchy: Feminism and Political Action at Greenham* (Buckingham: Open University Press, 1995), 158.

13 Jean Ritchie, "Meet the Greenham Manhaters," *Sun* (November 7, 1983).

14 Lilian Mohin, "Is Greenham Feminist?" in *Breaching the Peace: A Collection of Radical Feminist Papers*, ed. Trisha Longdon (London: Onlywomen Press, 1983), 18.

15 Trisha Longdon, *Breaching the Peace: A Collection of Radical Feminist Papers* (London: OnlyWomen Press, 1983), 16.

16 Pratibha Parmar and Valerie Amos, "Challenging Imperial Feminism," *Feminist Review* 17 (1984): 1, 3–19, 17.

17 "A Tour for Pacific Peace and Justice," *Birmingham Women's Newspaper*.

18 Ibid.

19 Alison Bartlett, "Researching the International Feminist Peace Movement" (2015): http://feministarchivesouth. org.uk/alison-bartlett-researching-the-international- feminist-peace-movement.

Chapter 10

1 See Freya Johnson Ross, *What State Are We in? Activism, Professional Feminists and Local Government* (2014), PhD Thesis, University of Sussex.

2 Beijing Declaration and Platform for Action, from the Fourth United Nations Conference on Women (1995).

3 D-M Withers, *Feminism, Digital Culture and the Politics of Transmission: Theory, Practice and Cultural Heritage* (London: Rowman & Littlefield International, 2015).

4 Eternal Summer of the Black Feminist Mind: https:// blackfeministmind.wordpress.com.

5 Remembering Olive Morris Collective: https:// rememberolivemorris.wordpress.com.

6 Black Cultural Archives, "Black Women's Movement: Subject Guide," (2017): http://bcaheritage.org.uk/ wp-content/uploads/2016/01/2016_Womens-Movement- updated.pdf.

7 Save Lambeth Women's Project: https://savelambeth womensproject.wordpress.com/about-lwp.

8 Ego Sowinski Ahaiwe, "The Venue: Lambeth Women's Project" (2007): http://girlsrockuk.tumblr.com/ image/47402220058.

9 A term first coined by Law Professor Kimberlé Crenshaw which has its roots in earlier eras of black feminist activism.

10 Peggy Orenstein, *Schoolgirls*; Nancy Jo Sales, *American Girls*; Lora Tannenbaum, *Slut!*

11 Chris Gentilviso, "Todd Akin On Abortion: 'Legitimate Rape' Victims Have 'Ways To Try To Shut That Whole Thing Down.'" *Huffington Post* (August 19, 2012): https:// www.huffingtonpost.com/2012/08/19/todd-akin-abortion- legitimate-rape_n_1807381.html. An apology was issued after the statement.

12 Gal-dem: http://www.gal-dem.com/about.

13 Deeyah Kahn, "Welcome to sister-hood" (2017): http:// sister-hood.com/deeyah-khan/welcome-to-sister-hood.

14 "Meena," RAWA.org: http://www.rawa.org/meena.html.

15 "The Revolutionary Association of the Women of Afghanistan," Moesgaard Museum: http://www. moesmus-afghanistan.dk.

16 Amnesty International, "Their Lives on the Line: Women Human Rights Defenders Under Attack in Afghanistan" (2015): https://www.amnesty.org.uk/files/ asa1112792015english.pdf.

17 "The Revolutionary Association of the Women of Afghanistan," Moesgaard Museum: http://www. moesmus-afghanistan.dk.

18 Revolutionary Association of the Women of Afghanistan: http://www.rawa.org/rawa.html.

19 Million Women Rise: http://www.millionwomenrise.com.

20 Victoria Law, "Against Carceral Feminism," *Jacobin* (2014): https://www.jacobinmag.com/2014/10/against- carceral-feminism.

21 Angela Y. Davis, *Are Prisons Obsolete?* (New York: Seven Stories Press, 2003).

22 "What Will It Take to Shut Down Yarl's Wood": https:// www.opendemocracy.net/transformation/gemma- lousley/what-will-it-take-to-close-down-yarls-wood- detention-centre.

23 Southall Black Sisters, "SBS and Eaves for Women Launch a Report on the DDV Concession" (2013): http:// www.southallblacksisters.org.uk/news/sbs-eaves-women- launch-report-ddv-concession.

24 These sentiments were expressed by Professor Gill Hague during a talk entitled "Fighting Violence against Women" in an international context on April 12, 2017, in Bristol. Hague is the cofounder (alongside Ellen Malos) of the Domestic Violence Research Unit at the University of Bristol, now the Centre for Gender and Violence Research, which for over twenty-five years has conducted high-quality research that informs policy, practice, and action on gender-based violence. See also Nazand Begikhani, Aisha Gill, and Gill Hague, *Honour-based Violence: Experiences and Counter-strategies in Iraqi Kurdistan and the UK Kurdish Diaspora* (Aldershot: Ashgate, 2015).

Picture Credits

We feel incredibly privileged to be able to showcase so many wonderful artworks from the feminist movement in this book. As a great number of these are posters and other items that are often considered ephemeral, the details of their original maker or copyright holder sometimes have been impossible to determine. Therefore, we pay tribute to those unnamed artists and apologize if we have unwittingly overlooked or been unable to credit them. Where the maker or copyright holder is known, they are listed below after the relevant page number(s).

We are also very grateful to all the researchers and archivists who have helped us track down so many rare and often unpublished pieces to include in these pages and we apologize if we have been unable to mention you by name.

As far as is possible, book covers featured here are reproduced with the relevant publishers' knowledge and permission.

Unless otherwise noted below, all buttons and badges shown throughout the text are from the collection of Bonnie J. Morris.

Key to image locations on page: l = left, r = right, m = middle or middle row, t = top, b = bottom. Location indicators are often combined: e.g., (mm) middle of middle row; (tl) top left; (l+r) left and right.

The Advertising Archives: 82(l).

Alamy: 19(br): Everett Collection Inc / Alamy Stock Photo, 20(r): Granger Historical Picture Archive / Alamy Stock Photo, 21: Everett Collection Inc / Alamy Stock Photo, 25: Trinity Mirror / Mirrorpix / Alamy Stock Photo, 30: Keystone Pictures USA / Alamy Stock Photo, 36(l): Keystone Pictures USA / Alamy Stock Photo, 70(bl): Everett Collection Inc / Alamy Stock Photo, 155(t): ZUMA Press Inc / Alamy Stock Photo, 201: Granger Historical Picture Archive / Alamy Stock Photo, 211: Carlos Rios / Alamy Stock Photo

ANP Foto / Fotoverkoop: 84

Associated Press: 23 (bl)

Atria: Grateful thanks to this wonderful repository of international women's history for allowing us to reproduce this photograph: 205(b): photograph by Joris van Kesteren

Joan E. Biren: Grateful thanks to Joan E. Biren for allowing us to reproduce her photographs on: 163(tr); 163(r)

Black Cultural Archives: Reproduced by kind permission: p. 75(r): MORRIS/2 Photographs

Alex Brew: Grateful thanks to Alex Brew for granting permission to reproduce these images: 207(bl); 213(ml)

Bridgeman Art Library: 34: Bibliothèque Nationale, Paris, France / Archives Charmet / Bridgeman Images; 56(l): Photo © PVDE / Bridgeman Images; 88: Photo © AGIP / Bridgeman Images; 93(t): Photo © AGIP / Bridgeman Images; 93(b): Bibliothèque Marguerite Durand, Paris, France / Archives Charmet / Bridgeman Images; 141(br): Photo © AGIP / Bridgeman Images

Carhif-AVG, Brussels: Grateful thanks to Els Flour for her assistance in obtaining reproductions from this collection: 31(l); 38(mr): collection Greta Craeymeersch; 38(bl); 99(tl); 107(t): photograph by © Edgard Alsteens

Chicago Women's Graphic Collective: More information about the collective's extraordinary contribution to feminist poster art in the US can be found at: www.cwluherstory.org.

The following images were provided by them and remain in their copyright, with grateful thanks to Estelle Carol: 10; 12(l); 50; 56(r); 57; 80; 98(l)

Jane Cholmeley: Grateful thanks for allowing us to reproduce the following photograph: 163(tl)

The Danish Peace Academy: 195(l): courtesy of Sigrid Møller

David M. Rubenstein Rare Book and Manuscript Library, Duke University: 23(tl): Alix Kates Shulman papers; 23(r): Robin Morgan papers; 58: Third World Women's Alliance (US) / Atlanta Lesbian Feminist Alliance archives; 67 (all): Third World Women's Alliance (US) / Atlanta Lesbian Feminist Alliance archives; 148(r): courtesy of Margie Sved; 153(m)

Susan Dechert: Grateful thanks for sharing these images of the Internationale Vrouwenfest with us: 170–71 (all)

EMMA **magazine archives:** Grateful thanks to *EMMA* for allowing us to reproduce front covers from the magazine on the following pages: 159 (all)

Feminist Archive North, Special Collections, Brotherton Library, University of Leeds: Grateful thanks to the trustees for allowing us to reproduce the following material held within their wonderful and rich collection. The images held in this collection are not necessarily the copyright of the archive and where the copyright holder is known we have detailed them in brackets: 98(r); 181(l+r): the Pavilion collection

Feminist Archive South, Special Collections, University of Bristol: Grateful thanks to the trustees for allowing us to reproduce the following material held within their wonderful and rich collection. With particular thanks to Hannah Lowery, archivist and special collections manager, for her guidance and her time in facilitating the research and reproduction of these images. All of the archive's images reproduced in this book were photographed by Kathryn Smith from TrafficWorks. Images held in this collection are not necessarily the copyright of the archive: 8: © See Red Women's Workshop (for more information on the collective's amazing material: https://seeredwomensworkshop. wordpress.com and their recent book, *See Red Women's Workshop: Feminist Posters 1974–1990*); 18: © The Estate of Monica Sjöö; 33: with thanks to the Brixton Art Gallery, www. brixton50.co.uk; 37: © See Red Women's Workshop; 43(m); 43(r); 45(l); 45(r); 61: © The Estate of Monica Sjöö; 65(r); 76(l); 76(r); 79(bl); 90(r); 94; 95; 97(l); 104; 106(r): © See Red Women's Workshop; 108(tl); 112(tl); 112(tr); 113(r); 120(bl); 123(r); 124: © See Red Women's Workshop; 126(l); 129(l); 129(m); 132(l); 138(l); 139; 137(r); 142(bl); 146: © See Red Women's Workshop; 147; 161(bm); 164: artist identified only as Julia, 1983; 166(l); 166(r); 167(tl); 169(br); 173(tl); 173(bl); 173(br); 176(l); 176(r)

Yolanda Fundora: Grateful thanks to Yolanda Fundora for allowing us to reproduce her artwork: 185(tl)

Getty Images: 13: Fred W. McDarrah / Getty Images; 19(t): The Frent Collection / Contributor / Corbis Historical; 19(bl): *New York Daily News* / Contributor; 32: Universal Images Group / Photo 12 / Contributor; 38(tl): Gamma-Rapho / Christian RAUSCH / Contributor; 38(tr): Sygma / Christine Spengler / Contributor; 38(ml): Archive Photos / David Fenton / Contributor; 47(l): *New York Daily News* / Contributor; 48: Gamma-Keystone / Keystone-France / Contributor; 51: Bettmann / Contributor; 54(r): Bettmann / Contributor; 60: Archive Photos / David Fenton /

Contributor; 63(l): Gamma-Keystone / Keystone-France / Contributor; 69(l): *The Washington Post* / Contributor; 69(r): Archive Photos / Robert Alexander / Contributor; 72: Bettmann / Contributor; 74: Bettmann / Contributor; 85(l): Gamma-Rapho / Richard FRIEMAN-PHELPS / Contributor; 91: Gamma-Keystone / Keystone-France / Contributor; 117(bl): Bettmann / Contributor; 200(l): The LIFE Images Collection / Robin Platzer / Contributor; 207(t): AFP / GALI TIBBON / Stringer; 207(br): AFP / DALE DE LA REY / Staff; 213(tl): AFP / PIERRE ANDRIEU / Staff; 213(mr): WireImage / Paul Morigi / Contributor; 213(br): *Boston Globe* / Contributor

Glamorgan Archives: Grateful thanks to the Women's Archive Wales for granting us permission to reproduce these images: 188(l+r): Margery Lewis Collection, courtesy of Glamorgan Archives, with permission from Archif Menywod Cymru / Women's Archive Wales; 189 and 190(r): Women for Life of Earth Records, courtesy of Glamorgan Archives, with permission from Archif Menywod Cymru / Women's Archive Wales

Glasgow Women's Aid, Speaking Out Project: 87(bl)

Glasgow Women's Library: Images held in this archive are not necessarily in the archive's copyright: 87(t); 87(br); 99(r); 103: © Firebrand Books, artwork by Alison Bechdel; 117(tr); 118(b); 120(tr); 123(tl); 123(bl); 149; 205(t+l+r)

Sue Greenhill: Grateful thanks for allowing us to reproduce her photograph: 157

Hackney Flashers Archives: Grateful thanks to all the trustees for sharing their groundbreaking work with us: 133(t); 137(tl)

International Institute of Social History Archives: This amazing online repository brings together many fantastic resources from around the world, much of their material is uncredited: 14; 15(l+r); 24(l); 26(l): © 1971 by Celestial Arts, 1345 Howard Street, San Francisco, California 94103, World Rights Reserved Printed in by Orbit in USA; 47(r); 49(l); 49(r); 62: designed by Alexander; 79(tl); 79(r); 89(bl); 89(br): designed by V. Vecchi; 108(tr); 117(br); 117(tl): button; 132(r): designed by Joke Dallinga; 141(tl); 141(tr); 142(tr); 173(tm); 185(tr); 185(bl); 185(br); 187(tl): button; 195(l): button; 205(mm): with thanks to the Adelaide Women's Studies Resource Centre

Jessie Street National Women's Library, Sydney: Grateful thanks to Sherri Hilario for her assistance in reproducing the following works: 173(tm): courtesy of the Earthworks Poster Collective; 197(r)

Judaica Division, Widener Library, Harvard University: 38(br)

Labadie Collection, University of Michigan: 122: © Leaping Lesbian Archives

LAKA Foundation: Grateful thanks to Dirk Bannink for allowing us to reproduce: 197(l)

Lambeth Archives: 75(l); 203(tl); 203(b): photograph by Alex Molano, with grateful thanks to the Do You Remember Olive Morris? project and especially to Ana Laura Lopez de la Torre for her assistance

Takumba Ria Lawal: Grateful thanks for sharing this image of FIG with us: 167

Index

Morris, Olive 74–75
Morrison, Toni 71
Mouvement de libération des femmes (MLF) 26, 30, 48, 152
Ms. magazine 154–55, 160
Murray, Pauli 19
music and arts, women in 166–81
    agitprop 168
    anti-war performance 176
    blaxploitation 172
    censorship in media 172
    creativity 167
    female nudity, in film and theater 172
    feminist film, theater, and satire 172–76
    feminist songs, in Italy 178–79
    freedom songs 176
    French New Wave film movement 172
    Grier, Pam 172
    Michigan Womyn's Music Festival 174–75
    music and dance 168, 176–77
    music outside of the US 177
    National Women's Music Festival (NWMF) 174
    R- and X-rated films 172
    radical art 177
    sexualization of black women 172
    skill-sharing workshops 168
    strategies for defining a culture 167–68
    themes of violence against women 176
    troubling the image 177–81
    Women's Postal Art Event 180–81
Myth of the Vaginal Orgasm, The 39

National Abortion Campaign (NAC) 45
National Black Feminist Organization 72
National Gay Task Force 120
National Health Service (NHS) healthcare, for black communities 64
National Joint Action Campaign Committee for Women's Equal Rights (NJACCWER) 129
National Joint Action Committee on Women's Equal Rights (NJACWER) 24
National Organization for Women (NOW) 19, 107, 109, 168
National Women's Aid Federation (NWAF) 86
National Women's Music Festival (NWMF) 174
New York Radical Women (NYRW) 22, 31, 39
night cleaners 130–31
Nine to Five (film) 97–98
Nixon, Richard 46, 51
North Paddington Black Women's Group 65
Northeast Women's Music Retreat (NEWMR) 174
Northern Women's Liberation Rock Band 177
Nozati, Annick 167
nuclear arms race 20

Omolade, Barbara 76
Onlywomen Press 153
Oregon Women's Land (OWL) 113
Organisation for Women of Asian and African Descent (OWAAD) 40, 64–65, 74, 78, 116
    Dadzie, Stella 65
    debates about British citizenship 64
    FOWAAD! newsletter 64–65
    main points for defining black women's liberation 66

    objectives of 77
    on rights of residency 64
orgasm, woman's right to 39
"the Other" women, exploration of 18, 28
Our Bodies, Ourselves (1978) 98
Oxford conference (1970) 16–17, 39

Pankhurst, Sylvia 16
Paris student protests of 1968 40
Parker, Pat 68–69
patriarchal ideology 40
patriarchy, system of 20
Paul, Alice 54
Personal Best (1981) 114
personal decisions, legal control over 39
Petites Marguérites 113
Pettitt, Ann 188
Pierobon, Gigliola 90
Pill (oral contraceptives) 18, 24–26, 51, 84–85, 92, 154, 196
Pine Gap, central Australia 195, 196
Pink Sari (Gulabi Gang) 212
Pitzen, Marianne 168
Police and Criminal Evidence Act (1984), UK 78
political lesbianism 113–23
    definition of 113
    in Europe 113
    Identità lesbica 113
Porn Is Violence against Women (PIVAW) 97
porn shops, violence against 110
"porNO" campaign, against pornography 158
pornography 84, 97
    Angry Women fight against 110
    anti-female propaganda 96
    anti-porn and SM feminism 111
    campaigns against 96
    female sexuality and 110
    magazines depicting 97
    male-generated 180
    obscene and sadistic portrayals of women 110
    "porNO" campaign against 158
    violence against porn shops 110
    as violence against women 110
    Women against Pornography 97
postnatal depression, effects of 102
Powell, Enoch 21
    "Rivers of Blood" speech 21
power feminist 138
Pride, Anne 96
privacy, right to 51
property rights, of women 13
prostitution 84
public defacement 97
Public Law 93-392, US 54
public space at night, reclamation of 95
Publishers Association of Great Britain 150
publishing and media sector, women in 146–62
    best-selling feature of US feminism 160
    career girls 154
    EMMA magazine 158–59, 160
    feminist book week 150
    International Feminist Book Fair 150–51
    male-bias journalism and 154
    Ms. magazine 154–55, 160
    newsletters and low-cost pamphlets 148
    ownership of media 157–60

    women's bookshops 160–62
    women's presses 148–57
Puget Sound, Washington state 192–93
Pussy Riot 209

racial discrimination 19
racial injustice 78
RadFems 209
radical feminism 20, 22, 184
    Italian 31
Rankin, Jeanette 184
rape 82
    Circeo massacre of 1975 95
    crime of 95
    crisis centers 32
    date rape 98
    definition of 207
    marital 36, 91
    non-forcible 207
    protocols for assisting victims of 98
    rape camps 201
    rape culture 208
    Rape in Marriage Campaign 91
    Rocco Penal Code (1931) 91
    themes in film and theater 172
    Vancouver Rape Relief 96
    as a weapon in war 212
Reagan, Ronald 55, 192
Reasoner, Harry 154
Rebel Dykes (London-based sex radicals) 110
Reclaim the Night campaign 91, 94–98, 208
Redstockings 31, 39
religion and spirituality, feminist 134–35
reparatory marriage 91, 95
reproductive revolution of 1960s 26
reproductive rights, of women 25, 91
residency, rights of 64
Revolutionary Association of the Women of Afghanistan (RAWA) 210–11
    mission for women's rights 210
    movement against the Russian-backed government 210
Riggs, Bobby 46
Riot Grrrl (US feminist punk movement) 204, 208, 209
Rivolta femminile 31, 148
Roberson, Pat 55
Rocco Penal Code (1931) 91
Rochefort, Christiane 92
Rodney Riots 21
Rodney, Walter 21
Roe v. Wade decision (1973) 32
Roman feminist movement 179
Rosen, Ruth 146
Rostand, Jean 92
Rote Zora 184
Rothman, Lorraine 101
Rowbotham, Sheila 16
Russell, Dora 184

sado-masochist (SM) 110–11
SAGE: A Scholarly Journal for Black Women (1983) 68
Sari Squad (South Asian female activists) 78
    anti-deportation campaigns 78
Sartre, Jean-Paul 28
Save Our Sons movement 196
"Save the Children" campaign 119
Schlafly, Phyllis 55, 126

Schwarzer, Alice 158
Scritti di Rivolta Femminile 148, 152
Seajay, Carol 162
Second Congress to Unite Women (1970) 107
Second Sex, The (1949) 18, 28
"second-wave" feminism 20, 28, 68, 97
self-actualized woman, notion of 28
self-care, right to 101
self-consciousness, notion of 40
self-defense 96
self-defined sexuality, right to 110–11
self-determination, concept of 20
self-esteem, ideals of 82
Seneca Army Depot in Romulus, New York 192–93, 195
sex bias, in school and colleges 46
sex discrimination, *See* gender discrimination
sex role, stereotypes of 136
sex toy 101
sex wars 84, 110–11
    lesbians 110
sex work 84
sexes, equality of, *See* gender equality
sexism
    everyday 208
    as social problem 19
    in toys, games, and language 127–29
sexist attitudes 24
sexual attention, unwanted 207
sexual freedom, ideals of 82
Sexual Liberation movement 187
sexual pleasure, women's right to 106
sexual revolution 22, 28
sexual slave 66
sexual violence 36
    causes of intimate 97
    feminist mobilization against 95
    feminist sensibility on 97
    marches raising awareness of 96
    protection against 97
    rape, *See* rape
Sheba Feminist Publishers 153
Silver Moon Women's Bookshop 162
Sisterhood Is Powerful (1970) 32, 39, 71
Sisters against Disablement (SAD) 102
    Lesbian Sex and Sexual Practice Conference (1983) 103
    SAD Access Code 103
Sisters Uncut 202
Sistren Theatre Company, Jamaica 172
Sjöö, Monica 204
Skegness conference (1971) 39
skill-sharing workshops 168
slavery, abolition of 13
slut shaming and misinformation 206–7
SlutWalk (2011) 209
Smith, Barbara 153
Smith, Howard K. 154
social isolation, experiences of 40
social segregation, in America 63
Socialist Student League (SDS) 20
Southall Black Sisters 66, 87, 212
sports, women's 46–47
    femininity tests 46
    gender discrimination in 46
    King, Billie Jean 46
    Olympic events 46
    prize money 46

Acknowledgments & sources

The authors would like to thank editor Jo de Vries for her encouragement and receptiveness to ideas, and her hugely impressive, committed, and skillful handling of this project; the team at Elephant Book Company, Editorial Director Will Steeds and Publishing Director Laura Ward, for their enthusiastic support of this project; and to Virago for this publication; and, lastly, but by no means least, Paul Palmer-Edwards of Grade Design for his punchy and powerful design that reflects the creative and courageous spirit of the women's liberation movements.

Bonnie J. Morris
I am most grateful to the following for their love, support, research skills, feminist vision, and generous hospitality during the many months of this book's preparation: Mary Ellsberg and the staff of the Global Women's Institute of George Washington University; Katherine Ott of the Smithsonian Institution; Kathryn Jacob of the Radcliffe Institute's Schlesinger Library; Kelly Anderson of the Sophia Smith Collection at Smith College; You-Me Park and Leslie Byers of Georgetown University's Women's and Gender Studies Program; fellow members of the D.C. Rainbow History Project; Veronica Calarco and my colleagues at Stiwdio Maelor in Corris, Wales; the National Women's Music Festival; the artists and staff of Olivia and the Michigan festival; Patrick Nero and Tanya Vogel of George Washington University's Department of Athletics; thoughtful colleagues Dr. Cindy Deitch and Dr. Cindy Burack; sharp-minded friends Lillian Faderman, Jen Wisdom, and Jeanette Buck; and my loving and very patient mother, Myra Morris.

For further feminist wisdom I recommend the following sources:
Karen Blumenthal, *Let Me Play! The Story of Title IX*
Barbara Deming, *Prisons That Could Not Hold*
Rachel Blau DuPlessis and Ann Snitow, *The Feminist Memoir Project*
Alice Echols, *Daring to Be Bad*
Susan Faludi, *Backlash*
Judy Grahn, *A Simple Revolution*
Stanlie M. James, Frances Smith Foster and Beverly Guy-Sheftall, *Still Brave: The Evolution of Black Women's Studies*
Karla Jay, *Tales of the Lavender Menace*
Anne Koedt, Ellen Levine, and Anita Rapone, eds. *Radical Feminism*
Audre Lorde, *Sister Outsider*
Cherríe Moraga and Gloria Anzaldúa, eds., *This Bridge Called My Back*
Adrienne Rich, *On Lies, Secrets and Silence*
Ruth Rosen, *The World Split Open*

Films: *Before Stonewall, Radical Harmonies, She's Beautiful When She's Angry*

D-M Withers
Most of what I know about women's liberation movements has come from talking to activists who were involved at the time, and I want to thank those who have shared their memories with me over the years.

Rummaging in and around archives, in both digital and physical forms, is the other way I have learnt about these histories. Don't forget that archives are for everybody! Not just academics or "professionals," and reading in archives is so much fun.

For this book I consulted the British collections of the Feminist Archive, North (based in Leeds) and South (based in Bristol), which holds a significant amount of material relating to feminist social movements in Britain and internationally from the 1960s onward. I visited the Glasgow Women's Library (Scotland), custodian of the Lesbian Archives and many other fantastic collections. The Black Cultural Archives' holdings relating to the Black Women's Movement are an important starting point for anyone keen to research this area. I also visited the Women's Archive Wales collections to learn more about Greenham, and the Women's Library in London remains a key resource for archival material about feminist activism. Although I did not visit the Feminist Library, also in London, it has an excellent collection of pamphlets and ephemera. In the Reuben Library at British Film Institute I was able to watch digitized versions of rare films made in the women's movement like *The Amazing Equal Pay Show*, *Women of the Rhondda*, *About Time*, and *Fakenham Film*, among others. Cinenova's collection of rare feminist experimental films, narrative feature films, artists' film and video, documentary, and educational videos is also well worth exploring. Outside of Britain, I had a very enjoyable afternoon researching in the archives at Atria, in Amsterdam, Netherlands.

For online sources of information, the British Library's *Spare Rib* digitization project has helped make the landmark magazine accessible for a new generation. The oral history project *Sisterhood and After*, also hosted at the British Library, is a brilliant resource which includes themed articles, videos, and audio clips. *Unfinished Histories: Recording the History of Alternative Theatre 1968–1988* is also worth visiting and contains valuable information about the thriving feminist theater scenes of the 1970s and '80s. *Do You Remember Olive Morris?* holds many links to resources about the Black Women's Movement and black liberation in Britain.

A big thank you to those people—professional and community archivists—who help to organize, preserve, and transmit the histories of feminist social movements for future generations.

Alongside archival resources, books such as *Left of Karl Marx: The Political Life of Black Communist Claudia Jones* by Carole Boyce Davies, *Catching Hell and Doing Well: Black Women in the UK—The Abasindi Cooperative* by Diana Watt and Adele D. Jones, *Feminist Posters 1974–1990* by See Red Women's Workshop, and *In Love and Struggle: Letters in Contemporary Feminism* by Margaretta Jolly are some of my favorite books about women's activism of the twentieth century. For those interested in the Wages for Housework campaign, *Sex, Race and Class—The Perspective of Winning: A Selection of Writings 1952–2011* by Selma James should be on your reading list. Ann Pettitt's *Walking to Greenham: How the Peace Camp Began and the Cold War Ended* is an interesting personal account of how Greenham Common started.

Many of the classic texts and pamphlets from women's liberation movements in Britain are now "out of print," which means you can still buy them secondhand or, if you are lucky, find them in a library, but they are not available through publishers today. *The Body Politic*, which features Sheila Rowbotham's scintillating essay "Women's Liberation and the New Politics," *Conditions of Illusion, No Turning Back*, and *Sweeping Statements* are important anthologies, as is the collection *Heart of the Race: Black Women's Lives in Britain*. Other significant pamphlets include *Love Your Enemy?: The Debate between Heterosexual Feminism and Political Lesbianism*; *Breaching the Peace: A Collection of Radical Feminist Papers*, and *Rolling Our Own: Women As Printers, Publishers and Distributors*. The archives of academic journal *Feminist Review* also contain many key articles, including Sue O'Sullivan's "Passionate Beginnings: Ideological Politics 1969–72" and the *Many Voices, One Chant* 1984 special issue on black feminism.